Praise for
The Opposite of Worry

"*The Opposite of Worry* offers a treasure trove of ideas to help children feel confident and secure. Lawrence Cohen has written a book that will help every parent of an anxious child. He describes the causes and symptoms of childhood anxiety and explains how children can overcome even the most tenacious fears in the context of a loving and playful parent/child relationship."

—Aletha Solter, Ph.D., founder of Aware Parenting and author of *Attachment Play*

"Here's the help parents of anxious children have been looking for! Dr. Cohen's genius is in the warm and generous spirit of the strategies he outlines for parents. He grounds his playful approach in a sound explanation of how anxiety affects children, and how they heal. Parents will come away with plenty of ideas to help them develop their children's confidence. While reading, I found myself thinking, 'I'd like to try that for myself!'"

—Patty Wipfler, Founder and Program Director, Hand in Hand Parenting

The Opposite of Worry

The Opposite of

Worry

The Playful Parenting Approach to Childhood Anxieties and Fears

Lawrence J. Cohen, Ph.D.

Ballantine Books Trade Paperbacks
New York

A Ballantine Books Trade Paperback Original

Published in the United States by Ballantine Books,
an imprint of The Random House Publishing Group,
a division of Random House, LLC, New York,
a Penguin Random House Company.

BALLANTINE and the HOUSE colophon are registered trademarks
of Random House, LLC.

Library of Congress Cataloging-in-Publication Data

Cohen, Lawrence J. (Child psychologist)
The opposite of worry : the playful parenting approach to childhood
anxieties and fears / Lawrence J. Cohen, Ph.D.
pages cm
Includes bibliographical references and index.
ISBN 978-0-345-53933-5
eBook ISBN 978-0-345-53932-8
1. Anxiety in children. 2. Fear in children. 3. Parenting. I. Title.
BF723.A5C62 2013
155.4'1246—dc23   2013020479

Printed in the United States of America

www.ballantinebooks.com

2 4 6 8 9 7 5 3

Book design by Donna Sinisgalli

For Liz

Contents

Introduction
Scary, Fun, and Safe

Do something scary, fun, and safe every day.
—A nine-year-old boy

I needed an idea for my eighth-grade science experiment. My mother was the director of a nursery school, and every spring the children hatched chickens as a project. I cared for the eggs and the baby chicks on nights and weekends. My sister Jeanie was studying to be a psychologist at the time (I guess you could say it's the family business). She told me about her professor's research on tonic immobilization, also known as "playing possum." Many animals, including chickens, play dead when they are too scared for fight or flight, or because they know instinctively that hawks won't eat anything that isn't alive. I had my science experiment!

Once the baby chicks were a few days old, I gently held each chick on its side and stared into one little eye, trying to imagine how a hawk would look at a chicken. After I let go, it stayed immobilized for about a minute. Then it popped up and walked around again, demonstrating the cycle of fear and recovery. In the next experiment I immobilized two chicks at once. They both stayed down much longer than either one alone did—about five minutes. Then I let one chick wander around the box while

I immobilized another one—it popped up after only a few seconds.

My conclusion: A frightened chicken looks to *the second chicken* to see if it's safe. When the second chicken is walking around happily, it seems to signal the first chicken that all is well: *That second chicken isn't scared—and hasn't been eaten—so it must be safe for me to get up and walk around.* When the second chicken is immobilized, the first one seems to think, *I don't see a hawk, but that second chicken must see one, since it hasn't gotten up yet. I'd better stay where I am.* My sister's professor, Dr. Gordon Gallup, found that chickens stay immobilized longest when they look in a mirror—they see their mirror image as another scared chicken.

Years later, as I began to work with families, I wondered why some parents have such trouble reassuring their anxious children. My old second-chicken experiments gave me a clue to this mystery. Children who are slightly anxious just need a brief word of reassurance or comfort from Mom or Dad—the parent is the unafraid second chicken. Children who are highly anxious often ignore reassurance, or it makes them even more upset. Sometimes that's because they have anxious parents. When these children look around they see an anxious parent—a scared second chicken who confirms their view that the world is a dangerous place.

Even when parents are not anxious, children with high anxiety may not notice the relaxed person in front of them. That's because anxiety can lead people to see the world through a lens of danger. It's as if they *always* see a scared second chicken, like chickens immobilized in front of a mirror. Whether their parents are anxious or not, children with high anxiety often remain frozen in that feeling.

I started encouraging parents of anxious children to stop their endless attempts at reassurance. After all, the unafraid second chicken does not soothe the immobilized chicken's fear with logic, words, or behavior modification. I developed a technique I call The Second Chicken Question: "Would you look in my eyes and see whether or not I'm scared?" This draws them out of their frozen fear and helps them find security. It works much better than "There's no need to be scared."

In addition to inspirations from the second chicken, this book also contains ideas for resetting the Security System. That's my term for the mind's response to danger—and safety. The Security System can save our lives. Without anxiety's alarm function we wouldn't bother to look both ways before crossing the street. We wouldn't run, hide, or fight back if we were in danger. The Security System is disrupted by excess anxiety. Children who are prone to high anxiety have an alarm signal that is too sensitive. Thoughts set off the alarm even if there is no immediate danger: *What if lightning hits the house? If only I had studied harder. Someone might laugh at me. What if no one talks to me?*

An effective Security System has to have an *all-clear signal*. After a fire alarm rings, how do you know when it is safe to go back inside? Along with an overly sensitive alarm system, anxious children have a poorly developed all-clear signal. They don't seem to notice any signals of safety, even after the second chicken has popped up and is walking around pecking at all the corn. Rumination, obsessive thinking, compulsive urges, and nonstop worries are examples of alarm bells that are never replaced by an all-clear signal.

Since they don't have a comforting second chicken or an effective Security System, anxious children use avoidance. They don't just avoid danger, they avoid anything that reminds them of danger. Anxious children even try to avoid feeling anxious. Unfortunately, avoidance increases anxiety in the long run. So avoiding avoidance is one of the themes of this book.

WHY I WROTE *THE OPPOSITE OF WORRY*

I have been anxious since my own childhood. I still remember the day I realized that some people don't see the world in the same anxious way that I do. I am embarrassed to admit that I was already an adult when I learned this fact. I was driving on the highway when the exhaust pipe fell off the car in front of me. I swerved around it, straightened out the car, and started to panic. For the next ten minutes I kept repeating, "We could have died! What if we had hit that tailpipe?"

Finally, my passenger said to me, quite calmly, "But we didn't." After a stunned silence I had to laugh. That thought had never occurred to me. I tried to argue, but I couldn't think of anything logical to say. Since the second chicken in the passenger seat wasn't anxious, I could pop up from my immobilization and let my anxiety go. Well . . . anxiety doesn't ever just go away in an instant. After all, it takes years to develop.

I came by my anxiety the old-fashioned way—both nature and nurture. I was probably destined by genetics and temperament to be shy, or "slow to warm up," as we shy people like to say. I also had an anxious father, who had a *very* anxious mother. I had some scary things happen when I was young; traumas that were too hard for me to deal with at the time. In other words, I had just about every source of anxiety a child can have. This is the book that I wish my parents had on hand when I was a boy.

Parents often ask me if children will grow out of their anxiety. I'm sorry to say that just growing up is usually not enough, though it can bring new motivations for change. I worked hard to overcome most of my shyness once I wanted to be in a play at school and to ask someone out on a date. You'll be happy to know I achieved both of those goals. And yet, certain situations still bring back the old feelings. Success in dealing with anxiety does not mean never feeling anxious again. It means that the anxiety isn't as frequent, severe, or long lasting. One of the biggest changes for me is that anxiety doesn't limit my life or get in my way anymore. I enjoy public speaking and meeting new people so much that most people don't believe me when I tell them I am shy. When I feel anxious now, I strive to explore what it means and face the feelings underneath the anxiety, instead of becoming immobilized with fear like those poor chickens in my experiment.

It's never too late to make a change. That's lucky, because the best thing anxious parents can do for anxious children is to deal with their own anxiety. My father had always been afraid to swim because of his mother's intense fear that he might drown. When I was about ten, I invited him to jump into a pool with me. He told me he was too scared, and I told him, "Don't worry, Daddy, I'll catch you." He didn't jump in, but years later he told me that my innocent confidence inspired him to take swimming lessons. At his first lesson he started to tell the instructor about all the childhood experiences that caused his fear of swimming. The instructor said, "All that talk is fine, but it's not helping you to swim. It's time to get in the pool." That instructor was my father's second chicken. Dad got in the pool and learned to swim.

I believe that instructor was correct in his advice to "just get in the pool," but I do not advocate throwing children into the deep end to get over their fear of water, or locking them outside to get over their fear of the neighborhood bully. Parents play a significant role in helping children overcome anxiety, but our role is more delicate than forcing them to get over their fears on *our* timetable. We need to push children to face their fears, but we need to push gently and patiently.

The other main reason I wrote this book is that in my office I am seeing more and more children who struggle with anxiety. I also see more anxiety when I visit schools and hear about more childhood anxiety when I talk to parent groups. Parents are more anxious as well. In fact, the term "helicopter parent" entered the lexicon as I was writing this book. Many of my colleagues report the same thing—a large increase in the number of children who come to therapy because of fear, anxiety, worry, or perfectionism. I believe it would be fair to call it an epidemic.

During one conversation with parents at an elementary school, I heard about children who were too afraid of water to swim or even take a bath without huge emotional meltdowns; children too afraid of making a mistake to function well in the classroom; children unwilling to try anything new; children paralyzed by the simplest choices, such as what clothes to wear to school; and children who couldn't bear to be in a different room from their parents, even to go to the bathroom. None of these children or families was in therapy—though I did give out a few business cards!

A longtime kindergarten teacher told me that for decades she has read fairy tales to her classes. But recently, every class has some children who can't bear to listen to those same stories because they are too scary. A middle school teacher told me that a parent insisted that her son's papers not be corrected in red ink, because it made him too anxious. No one really knows why childhood anxiety is on the rise, but some likely possibilities are increased competition in schools, increased stress at home, over-whelmed parents, and the overall pace of life.

Many parents feel helpless when their children are anxious, especially when reassurance doesn't work. It's a difficult struggle. You're frustrated, angry, and worried about your children's future. You see how anxiety, fear, and worry limit their lives and interfere with their happiness. You want to help them. Happily, you *can* help, in ways you may never have imagined.

There will always be a place for mental health professionals, especially in dealing with severe anxiety, but my approach is designed for parents to use with their children. Even if your child is in therapy, you can still use these playful and emotionally expressive techniques at home to supplement what is happening in the office. I'm a big fan of therapy—it's what I do—but therapy lacks the power of the parent-child relationship, which can be a resource for healing and change. Most approaches to childhood anxiety leave parents out, and I think that's a big mistake. The approach in this book puts parenting at the center. I hope that it will nourish your relationship with your children, which can be strained by childhood anxiety. You may also find help for your own anxiety—if by chance you have any.

A PLAYFUL APPROACH TO CHILDHOOD ANXIETY

Connection is the essence of my approach, as I describe in more detail in *Playful Parenting*. Human life is all about connection: pregnancy, nursing or feeding, rocking and cuddling, eye contact, play, sharing, soothing and comforting, listening and talking, friendship and empathy, love and affection. *Connection helps children feel secure, confident, and happy.*

But disconnection is also a part of life. Pregnancy ends with the baby separating from the mother's body. Infancy ends with the child crawling away to explore the world. We separate from our children to go to work and for them to go to school. Disconnection also occurs, more painfully, when we are angry with our children, when they are angry with us, when they are scared, or when they feel alone. *Disconnection is at the heart of many behavior problems.* We often respond to "bad behavior" with isolation, time-outs, humiliation, hitting, slapping, threats, yelling, or withdrawal of love. These responses create even more disconnection, which is why they don't work very well.

Because disconnection happens, *we need to become experts at reconnection.* Play is one of the best ways for a parent to reconnect with a child, because it is joyful, fun, and it requires us to join them in their world. Many disconnections arise when children have to join our world and our schedule (just think about the stress of bedtime, or places where they have to be quiet, or the rush to get ready in the morning). Yes, we have to impose schedules and limits, but when these create disconnection we can reconnect using extra affection and extra play.

My shorthand phrase for joining children in their world is "getting down on the floor." Many problems are prevented or solved just by being eye-to-eye or shoulder-to-shoulder with a child. With older children you might not actually be on the floor. Instead, reconnecting might involve sitting next to children on the couch watching a TV show you hate (because they love it and you want to connect with them), or staying up late (because they are more likely to talk openly with you at midnight than at the dinner table).

Another way to think about connection-disconnection-reconnection is Filling the Empty Cup. Imagine that every child has a cup inside that needs to be filled with affection, love, security, and attention. With a full cup, children are likely to be cooperative, happy, and creative. With an empty cup, children are more likely to be uncooperative, miserable, and stuck in behaviors that get them into trouble. One of our biggest jobs as parents is to give out emotional refills. We do this by giving our children attention, meeting their needs, giving them choices, listening to them, and offering encouragement.

Love, affection, and play can fill children's cups to overflowing. For example, you can help a child recover from a scary trip to the doctor's office by reversing the roles—letting her be the doctor while you are the scared patient pretending to get an examination. You can also use stuffed animals or action figures to get giggles from scenes that make your child nervous. Roughhousing with children is especially helpful for building confidence, so use playful rough-and-tumble contact to help them feel physically and emotionally powerful. Laughter loosens tension, and closeness helps children recover after an upset.

Full cups and close parent-child connections create security in children. That leads them to act cooperatively, confidently, and flexibly. This security can be missing for children who are anxious, timid, fearful, or worried. It doesn't mean they aren't loved, but something has interfered with them having a full cup and a sense of safety.

Playful parenting is not all fun and games. Children have intense emotions, troublesome behaviors, and unmet needs. At these times children need adults who will listen to them and reflect back what they hear. They need adults who will gently guide them without judgment or criticism. They need adults to welcome their emotions, instead of telling them not to cry or not to be angry unless they have "a good reason."

When we dismiss children's feelings we miss out on the possibility of playful solutions, and our children miss out on empathy and understanding. Here's an example from a mother who tried to protect her child from feeling bad. Her attempt to sidestep his feelings actually maintained his high level of anxiety, until play and empathy turned things around: "When my son was two, he developed a fear of the electric hand dryers in public toilets. He didn't like any loud noises, but his fear of hand dryers became extreme. We initially reinforced the fear by helping him avoid those dryers." She told me about the great lengths she went to in order to protect him from ever hearing this sound.

Finally she realized that this avoidance only made her son's fear worse. "I initiated some silly hand-dryer games, where I was the hand dryer blowing onto his hands, or where he was the hand dryer and I was scared. I pretended to be scared in a goofy way when we went into public toilets. I challenged him to stand near the dryer, while calmly telling him that it's okay for him not to like the noise, but it can't hurt him. I moved slowly, first just suggesting the idea that I might turn it on, then actually turning it on, and finally encouraging him to put his own hands underneath. I also made sure to keep up the pretend play."

A shift to play and emotional understanding made all the difference. Because they were no longer avoiding hand dryers, there was some crying, shaking, and screaming at this stage, but his mother understood that this was necessary for him to work through his fear. "Now, at four, I can't say he likes electric hand dryers exactly, but he at least is willing to let me turn one on and sometimes will put his hands under them."

Here's another example from a playful parent that demonstrates creative parent-child collaboration: "With my daughter,

Becca, anytime we can think of a way to bring a pretend character into the situation, it always helps. For example, Becca may be feeling very nervous about the shadow that her ceiling fan is creating in her room, but Coco the Stunt Woman (a character she created) is not nervous about *anything*. So when Becca becomes stuck in a fearful place, sometimes all it takes is to ask her if Coco has learned any new stunts lately. That breaks the hold and lets her think clearly again."

In both of these families, play made room for something brand-new. Without play, the parents felt confused, aggravated, or stuck repeating things that weren't working. For the boy afraid of hand dryers, make-believe games led to a step-by-step approach toward real hand dryers. His mother also accepted the flow of strong emotions that had been blocked by the earlier avoidance. Avoidance can feel good for a brief time, but at some point it gets in a child's way. For the girl who was generally fearful, imaginative play activated her inner confidence.

SCARY, FUN, AND SAFE

The ideas in this book are applicable to children with an occasional worry, as well as those who are chronically fearful or severely anxious. The goal is to restore the joyful flow of life, freed from the bonds of worry and fear. Toddlerhood through age twelve is the period when we are most able to use playful parenting to help children face their fears and ease their anxieties. Older children may not be as open to your playful intervention, but there are still many techniques in this book that they may enjoy. Teenagers and young adults may want to tackle their anxiety on their own or with a therapist instead of with their parents.

I met with a young boy who wanted to overcome his anxiety. Later, his mother told me he wrote a note and put it beside his bed: "Do something scary, fun, and safe every day." That's a great challenge! So welcome to this scary, fun, and safe adventure, exploring *The Opposite of Worry*.

The Opposite of Worry

CHAPTER ONE

Childhood Anxiety:
Alert, Alarm, Assessment, and All Clear

Sometimes we can cajole her into trying something new, but other times she is just a shaking, sobbing mess.
—Mother of a seven-year-old

THE FACES OF ANXIETY

A typical day at a community pool is filled with swimming lessons and diving competitions. Amid the laughter, splashing, and chatter, each group of children probably includes one or two who struggle with some form of anxiety. Perhaps in the youngest class a three-year-old boy sits in his mother's lap, thumb in his mouth, face buried in her shirt, while a teacher patiently tries to coax him into the water. In another class, a six-year-old girl steps happily into the pool, splashes her feet, then bursts into angry tears when a few drops of water land on her face. In the hallway a nine-year-old boy engages in a fierce debate with his mother:

"You know you'll have a good time as soon as your class starts. You enjoyed swimming last week."

"I just want to go home, I hate swimming!"

A twelve-year-old realizes as she begins her dive that one of her competitors is the top-ranked diver in their age group. She feels butterflies in her stomach and hesitates, spoiling her well-practiced dive.

The youngest child at the pool is anxious about separation from his mother, while the six-year-old is scared by the physical sensation of water in her face. The boy in the hall is eager to swim when he imagines it at home, but gets scared and tries to avoid it once he is at the door. Ashamed of his fear, or perhaps unaware of it, he covers it up with anger. The oldest child has performance anxiety marked by worried "what if" thoughts: *What if I mess up?* Each of these children is anxious, yet each is anxious in a different way.

So what is anxiety? That's a tough question, because we use so many different words with overlapping meanings to describe it. *Anxiety* is sometimes regarded as milder or vaguer than *fear,* but an *anxiety attack* is the same as a *panic attack,* and that can be quite severe. Anxiety can be an emotion, a physical state, or troubling thoughts and beliefs. *Stress* usually refers to prolonged anxiety, while *worries* and *obsessions* are anxious thought patterns. *Nervous habits* and *compulsions* are anxious behaviors. *Dread* and *terror* suggest extreme anxiety, but these words are also hard to precisely define. Most children get anxious once in a while; others are anxious most of the time. Some are anxious and don't even know it. It's confusing! We'll have to settle for a rough guide rather than a precise definition.

You may have noticed that my imprecise definition of anxiety is not based on a list of anxiety disorders. That's because I don't think diagnosis is especially useful in childhood anxiety. I'd rather understand the impact of anxiety on children's thoughts, bodies, emotions, relationships, and behaviors. The opposites of worry, anxiety, and fear are also hard to define. The opposite of danger is safety, and the opposite of anxiety is security—or is it confidence? Or relaxation? What's the opposite of fear? Fearlessness, courage, or calmness? The opposite of worry is trust that all is well. Again, it's confusing.

THE POSITIVE SIDE OF ANXIETY

Whatever words we use, we usually focus on the painful side of anxiety, the side that makes children miserable and leaves parents helpless. But anxiety has a positive side as well. A little bit is necessary for our mental health, our success in life, and even our survival. A healthy dose of anxiety drives us to avoid danger, take effective action, and perform at our peak. Complete relaxation isn't very useful for activities that require alertness and muscle control, like taking a test or diving into a pool. Anxiety only becomes unhealthy when there is excessive distress or excessive avoidance, like the anxious children at the pool.

Too much anxiety and you're "worried sick." Too little and you get nothing done, or you fail to take necessary precautions. We need fear when we are in danger, because fear galvanizes us to call for help, run, hide, or fight for our lives. Of course, that only helps us when our lives are really in danger. Fear when a tiger is actually chasing you is crucial for survival. Fear of a tiger in a zoo is excessive. Fear of a story about a tiger is really excessive.

Healthy anxiety also keeps us from acting immorally. Our conscience uses anxiety as a reminder that we will get in trouble or feel guilty if we do something morally wrong. Again, this anxiety can get out of hand, creating guilt or shame when we haven't done anything wrong.

We don't have time to think things through carefully when we are in real danger. We need a fast system, and anxiety is faster than the speed of thought. If that sounds impossible, consider that we often feel uneasy before we know why. We all have a little bit of "Spider-Sense," the superpower of the comic book hero Spider-Man, which warns us when something feels wrong before we have time to process all the information carefully. Spider-Man wouldn't call it anxiety, but that's basically what it is: a signal to look around carefully for danger and prepare for action. Healthy anxiety shows up really fast, does its job, and then steps aside to let slower and more logical thought take over. With excess anxiety, that reasonable side has trouble stepping in.

Too much anxiety doesn't kill us; it just makes us miserable. Well, it doesn't kill us right away. Stress has terrible effects on health, but in a dangerous situation it's safer to have too much anxiety than too little. That may be why so many children have excessive anxiety. As parents it's hard to get the balance just right. We want our children to worry enough about a test that they study for it, but not so much that they refuse to go to school. We want them to check their homework for errors, but not to be such perfectionists that their papers are in tatters from repeated erasing. We want them to wash their hands, but not for five minutes at a time. We want them to know what to do in case of fire, but we don't want them preoccupied with the possibility of a fire every time they enter a building.

Many anxious children worry that they aren't smart, because they know they act irrationally at times. I always remind them that it wouldn't be very smart to have no anxiety. Intelligence doesn't protect a person from troubling emotions. In fact, many anxious children are highly intelligent—it takes a lot of brain-power to think of the things they worry about! Anxious children also need to know that they have emotional strengths. It's common in childhood for vulnerabilities in one area to be balanced by strengths in another.

I met recently with the parents of Constantine, a boy with significant anxiety. They described him as imaginative, creative, joyful, and funny, with a long attention span—when not in his anxious state. This list is quite typical of children with high anxiety. Their parents and teachers often say they are mature for their age, verbally precocious, sensitive, and able to relate well to adults. We often encourage anxious children to take more risks in life, but on the bright side, we don't have to worry that they will be extreme risk-takers and thrill-seekers.

THE SUFFERING CAUSED BY ANXIETY

When anxiety reaches too high a level, the suffering can be intense. Rob, a nine-year-old boy, sent me an email between therapy sessions: "Lately I've been getting very worried about dying and that hurricanes will reach here. I'm having a really hard time dealing with it and I wanted to tell you before Thursday. I'm getting really, really worried. I feel really tense inside. I'm having trouble falling asleep and just enjoying life. I wish that there is a way to solve this. I'm urgent to find a solution quickly. Can you help me find any solution?"

Anxiety causes a range of suffering from mild to moderate to severe, and from occasional to frequent to nearly constant. The distress of childhood anxiety can take many forms:

- Physical sensations, such as pounding heart, shallow breathing, tense muscles, butterflies or churning in the stomach, trembling and sweating, hot or cold skin.

- Frequent urination, gastrointestinal distress, or incontinence.
- Anxious thoughts, pessimistic beliefs, and worries. *What if something bad happens? If only I had done something differently. I know my teacher hates me.*
- Rumination, in which the same thoughts or images are repeated over and over with no resolution.
- Cognitive inflexibility, which involves a fear of risks, avoidance of anything new, or an intense reaction to changed routines.
- Nervous habits such as nail biting, hair pulling, fidgeting, or chewing on clothes.
- An emotional state of alarm, apprehension, panic, dread, or always feeling on guard.
- Fears of specific things—real or imaginary—such as dogs, bugs, or monsters under the bed.
- A tendency to perceive the world as generally threatening or dangerous.
- Avoidance of anything that arouses fear or anxiety, and extreme emotional upset when avoidance is impossible.
- Behavior patterns such as shyness, clinginess, indecisiveness, perfectionism, compulsions, or an attempt to completely control one's environment.
- Escalating demands for reassurance, with increased feelings of desperation. When reassurance is given, however, it is often rejected.

You can see that anxiety can affect children's bodies, thoughts, emotions, behaviors, and relationships. This means that every child's anxiety will look different and feel different.

Consider two children, Mara and Cal, in a movie theater. Mara sits with her parents. Suddenly a picture of a shark fills the screen, along with scary music. Mara feels strong physical sensations in her body; that is anxiety. She thinks, *I have to get out of here* and *What if that shark comes after me?* Those thoughts are anxiety. She runs for the exit; that is anxiety. She has trouble falling asleep that night and when she does she wakes up with nightmares—more anxiety. The next time her family goes to a movie she doesn't want to go, even though she understands there will be no sharks in it. That avoidance is also anxiety, and it may spread to other activities that Mara used to enjoy.

Another child, Cal, with a different pattern of anxiety, sits in the same movie theater with his friends. When the shark appears, he grips his armrest tightly, unaware that his pulse and respiration rates have shot up. Like Mara, Cal refuses to go to the next movie, but he isn't able to explain why. He angrily rejects the idea that he is anxious or afraid. He says instead that he doesn't like movies, which confuses his parents, because they know this isn't true. Cal also becomes more aggressive toward his baby brother, a common manifestation of anxiety, and one that really upsets parents.

The suffering caused by anxiety falls into two major types: misery and missing out. A nightmare is bad, but so is staying home when everyone else is at the movies. We hate to see our children miserable, so we often say, "Don't worry, you don't have to go to the movie" (or in the water, or outside where there are bugs, or to school). But that leaves children stuck in avoidance, where they miss out on important experiences. As they avoid more and more of life, anxious children have narrower and narrower lives.

Families who struggle with anxiety get used to missing out.

A few months after I received that wrenching note from Rob about his extreme suffering, I received this message from his mother: "Rob went to sleepaway camp for three weeks this summer! I am telling you because you will understand what a big deal this is." Indeed I did. I love to see the expansion of children's lives when they break free from the grip of anxiety.

Sometimes childhood anxiety is pretty obvious. But anxiety can affect children in very different ways, and some anxious children don't look anxious at all. They may look aggressive or obnoxious instead. A boy named Ralph was frequently in trouble for recklessly knocking into people as he ran around the schoolyard. After he bumped into someone he refused to say he was sorry, which made his teachers believe he had no empathy or concern for others.

After I met with Ralph a few times it was clear to me that he had plenty of empathy. His problem was anxiety. Worried that no one would play with him, he raced around aimlessly during recess, unable to "read" the social situation or join in organized games. He bumped into people because he avoided eye contact. After he hurt someone and was pressured to apologize, his social anxiety kicked in even more strongly. He looked away, smiled nervously, and couldn't come out with the "right answer" demanded of him. His silence and smile angered his teachers and worried his parents. Children like Ralph don't fit the image we have of an anxious child, who sits in a corner timidly nail biting. Nevertheless, their problems are best understood as manifestations of anxiety. Next time your child misbehaves, ask yourself whether anxiety might be a factor.

THE ANXIOUS BODY

The misery of anxiety is both mental and physical. Many of the physical aspects come from changes in hormone levels and blood flow. When we perceive a threat, we instantly prepare to run for our lives, fight for survival, or freeze in fear. Hormones and neurotransmitters surge to give us alertness and strength, while blood pumps to our hearts, core muscles, and the long muscles in our arms and legs. Muscles tense while heart rate and respiration increase. On the other hand, digestion isn't so important, and neither is spelling or delicate hand movements. So we get less blood flow to our stomachs, hands, skin, and any part of our brain not necessary for immediate survival. That gives us butterflies in the stomach, cold hands, and clammy skin. We may also have difficulty with language, logic, or memory.

This cascade of events in the body isn't much help for most of the threats we face in the modern world, which don't involve immediate physical danger. We're ready for action, but there is no enemy or predator chasing us. As a result, tension builds up in our bodies. That leads to restlessness, jitteriness, irritability, and agitation—part of the misery of anxiety.

Children are relieved to learn that their physical symptoms of anxiety make sense in this way. This knowledge helps them accept their sensations instead of believing they are serious danger signals or a sign that they are "crazy." Learning about the body's anxiety cascade also helps children understand why anxiety can be so exhausting.

Anxious children are often shocked to learn that some people actually *enjoy* these physical sensations. My father learned this when he was an anxious psychiatrist in the U.S. Army. One of his jobs was to interview soldiers who had volunteered to be paratroopers. My father didn't even like talking about jumping out of airplanes, but the men he interviewed found the idea thrilling and exciting. Some said they had never experienced fear or anxiety in their lives. He asked them if they ever felt a churning in their stomachs, sweaty palms, or racing hearts. "Oh, yes," they said, "is that anxiety? I thought that was excitement!" When adrenaline hits the bloodstream, thrill-seekers say, "Get me more of that," while anxious people say, "Get me out of here."

Many anxious people live in a long-term or even a constant state of alarm. Our bodies, however, are designed to experience this intense fear state in quick bursts, not for long periods. Hans Selye, a pioneer in anxiety research, named this prolonged anxious state *the stress response,* and we now recognize a wide range of troubles—emotional and physical—caused by stress.

THE ANXIETY CASCADE CONTINUES

Anxiety eventually interferes with children's schoolwork and social interactions because their attention is preoccupied with worries and fears. Socially anxious children avoid social contact, which means they get less practice with friendship. They fall further and further behind their peers in social skills. When children's anxiety leads them to avoid looking at faces, they misinterpret or miss social cues, resulting in awkwardness and embarrassment.

Unlike loners, who are happy with minimal social contact, socially anxious children can be painfully lonely. Despite their yearning for friendship, they may still be unable to make friends. It doesn't help to tell them to try harder. Most anxious children try extremely hard, and feel ashamed of their lack of confidence and their lack of social success.

Rituals or compulsive actions can take up more and more of a child's life, like one boy I met who had a stressful two-hour bedtime routine every night, which his mother had to follow exactly in order to avoid a huge emotional outburst that could last several more hours.

Nervous habits, like fingernail biting or shirt chewing, can cause shame, embarrassment, and social rejection. Some people engage in their nervous habits because they *feel* anxious and need a way to soothe and calm themselves. Others engage in those same habits in order *not to feel* their anxiety. As long as they occupy themselves with their habits, they don't have to experience their anxiety, though it may be obvious to anyone watching.

Avoidance is a central problem with anxiety, which is the reason for the familiar advice to "face your fears." That doesn't mean that we should force children to confront their fears when they aren't ready. It is cruel to shove children into their fears, for example by throwing a child who is scared of water into the deep end of the pool to sink or swim. This approach often backfires, creating a much deeper fear, because it undermines the child's sense of safety, security, and the trustworthiness of adults. Therefore the challenge to anxious avoidance has to be done gently, with a great deal of loving emotional support.

Children with anxiety can become extremely agitated, usually when they can no longer avoid what scares them. A child with a dog phobia will someday find herself face-to-face with a dog. The first day of school always arrives whether an anxious child is ready or not. Many parents live in dread of these anxiety overloads. In the words of one mother: "Sometimes we can cajole her into trying something new, but other times she is just a shaking, sobbing mess."

THE SECURITY SYSTEM: ALERTS, ALARMS, ASSESSMENTS, AND ALL CLEARS

The Security System explains how anxiety is triggered, experienced, expressed, and completed. When infants sense a threat, danger, or need, they cry in order to get someone to come close to protect them and meet their needs. Parents and caregivers have two responsibilities. The first is to confront the danger or meet the need. The second is to be a comforting presence so the child can reestablish a sense of safety and security. The Security System becomes more complex as children grow up, but it continues to follow that same sequence from threat to security.

To experience your own Security System in operation, try this exercise: Notice your current emotional state. Take a few deep breaths and clear your mind. Now I'm going to ask you to do something that might be a little scary. Take a minute to remember a time when you were afraid. Vividly recall the details. I know it is uncomfortable, but take some time to notice what you experience in your mind and body. Now clear away that image, and focus on a worry for the future. Vividly project yourself into the images and thoughts that represent this "what if" scene.

Wipe those images from your mind. Take a slow deep breath in. A long, slow exhale. Ahhh. Keep breathing. Place your hand below your belly button and breathe so that your hand moves out and in. Look around the room at the here and now. Notice whether all is well at this moment. You survived whatever scary thing you recalled from your past. Right now the scary things you imagined are not happening.

Did you feel some anxiety? Did you feel some degree of relaxation when you slowed down your breathing? If so, you have just experienced every part of the Security System: alert, alarm, assessment, and all clear.

The sequence begins with a relatively calm and relaxed state. The *alert* activates the system at the first hint of danger. That hint can come from a memory or an image; it doesn't have to be a current threat. The *alarm* is the anxious state, with all its thoughts and physical manifestations. The *assessment* is the thoughtful evaluation of danger and safety. The *all clear* is the signal to the alarm system to turn off: *All is well, I'm safe, and I can breathe deeply.*

If this exercise alarmed you, I hope that the sequence ended with a renewed state of calm. It can take some time for the body to calm down from its hyperalert and alarmed state, to move from alert to all clear. People with high anxiety tend to be on heightened alert all the time. They also have a highly sensitive alarm. They do not always assess situations accurately, and they take a longer time to cool down or receive an all-clear signal. If you are still anxious from that exercise, take some more time to cool off. Slowing down is one of the keys to successful transformation of anxiety.

Every part of the Security System is crucial. To protect us from harm, some part of our mind must always be alert to the possibility of danger. Once alerted, our bodies need to react immediately, which is why we can't just get rid of anxiety in the same way we use antibiotics to eliminate an infection. We need the alarm system to kick into high gear to prepare us to fight, run, or call for help—but only if the danger is real.

How do we know? That requires a good assessment system. Anxious children's assessments are biased toward seeing danger, whether it's there or not. As I described in the introduction, they see a scared second chicken no matter where they look. Nonanxious children make more objective assessments. They recognize danger but can also appreciate evidence of safety. If there is no danger, they have a strong all-clear signal to shut off the alarm and reset the system.

Unfortunately, there are many ways this Security System can misfire. Children who constantly search for danger don't enjoy life very much and limit their daily activities. Children whose alarm sensitivity is set too high have extreme reactions to things that aren't really dangerous, such as thoughts, feelings, or a change in plans. Children whose all-clear signal is set too low have a hard time calming down once their anxiety gets going.

Imagine two children, Ruby and George, enjoying a pleasant hike in the woods on a beautiful day. Suddenly they see a stick that looks a lot like a snake. George has a dramatic reaction. Overwhelmed by fear, he runs away. He rejects his father's suggestion to come back and look at the stick in order to see that it isn't really a snake. His father tells him not to be such a baby and threatens never to take him on a hike again.

What happened here? George's alert worked perfectly, signaling potential danger. Then his alarm blared too loudly and for too long. Responding to the alarm, George avoided the "danger." Unfortunately, George's avoidance meant that his assessment system couldn't do its job. He had no new data to form an accurate assessment. Therefore he never gave himself an all-clear signal. His dad tried to give George the all clear, but that didn't count. The anxious brain is reluctant to believe all-clear signals from outside, even from a trusted source. His father, frustrated by his inability to calm George down, became impatient and angry. George's fear lingered. On future hikes he had a fearful reaction to tiny sticks and to the faintest rustle in the leaves. His alert and alarm systems were set way too high, and his assessment system and all-clear signal never had a chance.

Ruby was startled when she saw the stick. Her reaction wasn't as intense as George's terror, however, and she didn't run away. She was able to notice that it was just a stick, but she didn't calm down. She had already begun a cycle of anxious thoughts: *Oh, it's a stick. But it could have been a snake! What if it was a snake?* For the rest of the hike she had trouble relaxing, and for a long time afterward she said, "I hate hikes." Even though she made an accurate assessment, she was stuck in a loop—each new scary thought reactivated her alarm. Like George, she never found the all-clear signal.

The Alert Signal

Alerts are almost instantaneous (actually, they take about two-hundredths of a second). That's faster than we can process a thought. Because fear is a basic survival mechanism, it has to be extremely fast. A fraction of a second can make a big difference. If there really is a poisonous snake, it's good to jump back before we know why we are jumping.

The alert system does not sit passively and wait for threats. Everyone devotes some mental energy to a constant search for danger. In most people, most of the time, this search only uses a tiny portion of brainpower. It takes place in the background, where it doesn't interfere with other activities. Once in a while, in a high-risk situation, the alert increases its vigilance.

Children with low anxiety let their adult caregivers take over most of the lookout duties. *My parents are on guard, so I don't have to be.* This is a good reason to put down your phone or newspaper when you are at the playground with your children—in case you needed a reason—so they don't feel that they alone are in charge of safety. If they trust in you to handle the alerts, they can have more fun while being both safe and adventurous.

On the contrary, alerts take up a great deal of mental space in children who are caught up in anxiety, worry, or fear. They actively seek out reasons to be anxious. At age seven, Abe was so afraid of thunderstorms that he obsessively checked weather forecasts and became anxious at the sight of the smallest cloud. In addition to worry about lightning, his life was filled with many other anxieties, including a dread of making a mistake. He loved to draw, but a tiny pencil speck on his paper made him rip it up and start over. His alert system was set with an acute sensitivity. The tiniest cloud or smudge tripped his alarm and produced the same blaring siren that you would expect from a major disaster. The result was a wide range of anxiety symptoms.

The Alarm

When there is real danger, a healthy alarm activates us to do just what we need to do: fight, plan, hide, run for safety, or call for help. When there is no danger, the alarm doesn't need to ring. If it rings anyway, the result is anxiety: tension, agitation, avoidance, rumination, and distress. The Security System is fully activated but there is nothing to fight and nowhere to run. Whenever Abe's alarm system was activated—as it was frequently because of his oversensitive alert signal—his response was dramatic. His mother reported that if there was the smallest chance of a storm, "He spent most of the time before camp crying, curled up in a ball in his favorite blanket. He said that I don't understand how afraid he is and that I'm torturing him by sending him to camp. This progressed to his saying that he hates life and he wishes he were dead. I could feel his heart pounding in his chest and feel him tremble. I felt so terrible." You can see every aspect of anxi-

ety's overactive alarm system manifested here: physical symptoms, emotional pain, distorted thoughts, and a strain on the
parent-child relationship.

Assessment

Abe liked to do research about his fears to try to reduce them, so
he was an expert on dinosaurs, terrorism, and especially thunderstorms. After one show on the Weather Channel about severe
storms, however, his plan backfired. He became afraid of lightning *even when he was inside the house*. To understand why, let's
turn to the next part of the Security System: assessment. Abe
was right to think that a documentary on storms might lower his
fear. Accurate information is useful for the thoughtful assessment of danger and safety.

Instead, however, the graphic images in the show made his
alarm even more sensitive. The next cloud triggered a replay in
Abe's mind of scary images from the documentary, even though
it was a white fluffy cloud far in the distance. The statistical information in the show—deadly storms are very rare—might have
soothed his fears, but the statistics were overwhelmed by emotionally loaded images. The result was that his assessment system
didn't get a chance to assess, even with all the new information.
Before he watched the show he knew he was safe from lightning
inside with his mother or father. After the show he was so scared
that this comforting logic didn't have a chance.

I believe children's increased exposure to scary movies, video
games, news, and television is partly responsible for the recent
surge in anxiety. These images are simply too intense for children to process. They create a constant state of high alert and
intensify the alarm response.

Abe was stuck in the alarm part of his Security System.

That's a problem because alarms are not able to discriminate between a dangerous bear, a bear in the zoo, the thought of a bear, or a picture of a bear. They are like smoke alarms that can't tell the difference between smoke from a fire and steam from a teakettle. Alarms are part of the emotional brain, which works on the basis of imagery and intensity, not cool logic. A picture of a bear can be a very intense image. The assessment system *can* tell the difference between all these different bears, but Abe wasn't able to switch from alarm to assessment.

Assessment belongs to the thinking brain, along with logic, language, and judgment. Assessment takes the time needed to confirm the danger or decide that all is well. Assessment tells the alarm to either turn up the fear reactions or turn them off: *It's only a thought about a bear, it's not a bear; false alarm.* Children with low anxiety put their alarm signal "on hold" so that they can perform a good assessment. Children with high anxiety get in their own way—the intensity of their alarms interferes with the accuracy of their assessments.

Alerts and alarms react before a person is even aware of a thought or a decision. If you're trying to outrun a tiger, a half-second head start can make a huge difference. It's safer to run first, and *then* think about it. Consider the alternative: "Hmm, I wonder what that sound was. Could have been a tiger. Or maybe not. Yep, it was a tiger. Oh, no!" Too slow. Eventually, however, we need an accurate system, even if it is slower, as the Nobel Prize–winning psychologist Daniel Kahneman describes in his book *Thinking, Fast and Slow.* Otherwise we'd never stop running or hiding when the danger passes (or the snake turns out to be a stick).

Alerts, alarms, and assessments are designed to work together to provide both speed *and* accuracy. This combination is especially useful when we aren't sure about a danger. We need to be prepared to act while we gather as much information as possible. After that new information is processed, the assessment is complete: *Keep up the alert* or *False alarm*. This effective teamwork is absent in the overly anxious Security System.

The slower, more accurate part of the brain should have the last word. If there is danger, the thinking brain formulates a good plan. If there is no danger, the thinking brain tells the emotional brain to cool off. Anxious children give their automatic alarm signal the last word. The anxious brain tells the thinking brain not to bother assessing—*I already know I'm in danger!* Without assessment, fear and anxiety remain activated. That explains why anxious brains expect danger around every corner, and why they actively reject reassurance or evidence of safety.

We take in more information when we're scared than when we're calm, because the assessment system is activated. However, we don't process this extra information very well. The result is an overload that makes it hard to assess accurately. Even with all the information from outside—*it's a stick, not a snake*—anxious children focus instead on the thoughts and images running inside their heads. These are like video clips that repeat on an automatic loop. George and Ruby couldn't see the real stick, only the imagined snake in their minds. Parents are so frustrated when children can't get past these scary replays in order to notice the real world or listen to rational arguments. The assessment system has an amazing ability to evaluate danger, but only if it is open to new information.

Beliefs about the world can also interfere with accurate assessment and lock anxiety in place. I've been afraid of bats for as long as I can remember. Once when I was a teenager I was walking across a field when several bats swooped toward my head.

Terrified, I ran for the nearest building. I later learned that they were swallows. These birds' swooping movements and dusk flights made them seem like bats to me, especially since I was too afraid to look closely. But I didn't stop being afraid of bats and start being afraid of birds. Emotions flow from beliefs, not from reality. Beliefs are hard to shake, especially when they are linked to fears. Children prone to anxiety tend to have many scary beliefs about the world. Luckily, children's beliefs can be more open to updates than adult beliefs.

When the assessment system isn't certain about safety or danger, it looks for clues in our own bodily reactions. If I'm breathing slowly and calmly, then I must be safe—all clear. That's why relaxation exercises calm the mind as well as the body. Relaxation gives our assessment system a gentle push in the right direction and we become our own calm second chicken.

On the other hand, if my heart is pounding, there must be a good reason, right? That seems reasonable, but it isn't always true. Anxious people are often agitated even when there is no real danger. That's why anxiety breeds more anxiety. People with anxiety tend to have frequent false alarms, and then their assessment system uses the alarm as proof that there is real danger. Sneaky! If George knew that his Security System was prone to false alarms, he could think, *I'm scared because there might be a snake, so now I need to see if there really is a snake.* Because we watch ourselves to see how we are reacting, a common treatment for anxiety is to simply tell yourself, *My heart is pounding and my hands are sweating because I'm anxious, not because anything dangerous is happening.* I call this technique Scared and Safe. For anxious children, that combination is revolutionary.

The All-Clear Signal

Fear, anxiety, and worry serve a vital purpose in our lives, but we need a way to shut these alarms off once the danger has passed or has been discovered to be a false alarm. After a smoke alarm rings and we discover there is no fire, we need to *reset* the alarm. An alarm that never stops is no more useful than one that never rings at all. Imagine a fire drill at a school or workplace with no all-clear signal. Everyone would still be outside, wondering when it was safe to go back in.

Reassurance gives children who are only a slight bit anxious a friendly nudge to their all-clear systems. Our words and gentle tone of voice offer evidence of safety. After Mom or Dad says, "Look, honey, it's just a stick," the child's own assessment and all-clear signals do the rest. The body and mind return to relaxation. I call it resetting the Security System.

No such luck for children who are very anxious. Their alarms are too loud and insistent for the Security System to reset. Reassurance falls flat, or is angrily rejected. Parents expect their children's anxiety to stop instantly as soon as they say, "It's just a stick." But we can't leap into children's Security System and send the all-clear signal for them. It doesn't work that way. Only a child's own all-clear signal can deactivate the alarm. We can provide comfort, protection, and good information, but children have to absorb the evidence and take the final step on their own.

Consider a child with separation anxiety who panics when Mom goes away. Her alarm is so intense that she rejects soothing by her babysitter. In addition, she lacks the comforting all-clear thought that a secure child might have: *I'll be safe while Mom's gone and she'll be back soon.* Without that thought she is inconsolable. She can't remember that her mother always comes back or that she loves her babysitter.

Anxious children have a hard time learning from past experiences of safety because they are so tuned in to potential danger. As one mother said, "I don't understand. We've been to that ballet class twelve times, and she always ends up enjoying it. But each week her panic is just like the first time." Each class, this child works through her fear. Her all-clear signal finally kicks in, and she enjoys herself. But the Security System doesn't reset with a new idea: *Ballet class is safe*. Instead, it signals the same high-intensity alert every week shortly before ballet class. Life is easier for children without excess anxiety. They reset their Security System frequently, building a foundation of basic trust and safety. Sometimes a stick is just a stick.

Anxious children live on high alert. Their alarms are more easily triggered, more dramatic, and less easily reset. They avoid whatever scares them, which means they miss opportunities for accurate assessment. Their all-clear signals are absent, or too faint to be heard over the sirens of the alarm system.

When children and parents understand the alert-alarm-assess-all-clear system they have more power over it. This model can also give you and your child a shared language to talk about anxiety without arguments or emotional meltdowns. In one family, the effect of this shared language was transformative. Whenever Carlos displayed any anxiety or fear, his parents scolded him. "You are being a big baby. There is nothing to be scared of." This made Carlos feel ashamed, but didn't lower his anxiety level. Dismissal and humiliation never do. Things turned around after a family discussion where we named and described the various parts of the Security System. I also had a few private words with Carlos's parents to urge them to stop calling him a baby for being frightened.

I received a follow-up note from his mother: "When Carlos gets scared now, we ask him, 'Are you on high alert, or is the alarm ringing super-loud? Where do you feel it in your body?' Carlos actually thinks about it and then tells us! This is a miracle—you remember how we could never talk about it with him, because he would scream at us to stop talking. We also say, 'Let's all look around and check for danger.' You called it assessment, but we call it hunting for clues. Once he starts to calm down, we say, 'I think I hear the all-clear signal, but I'm not sure, do you hear it, Carlos?'" For me, the miracle was the power of the parents' empathy.

THE SOURCES OF EXCESS ANXIETY

Anxiety is not distributed evenly among all the people in the world; some have more and some have less. This arrangement makes sense if we remember that humans are social. Every group needs risk-takers. Every group also needs some cautious members who peek out from their hiding places to see how those risks turn out. Someone needs to discover if those nice-looking berries are edible or poisonous, or whether those visitors are friendly or unfriendly. If things go badly, someone needs to live to tell the tale. Sadly, those of us who are anxious don't get much credit for our contributions to society! Most of the glory goes to the explorers and adventurers. On the other hand, childhood risk-takers are often labeled as hyperactive, impulsive, or oppositional.

The sources of excess anxiety include temperament, trauma, difficult life experiences, anxious parents, and modern society.

Heredity plays a part too. Many anxious children have anxiety in their family history, though the exact form of anxiety may be different.

Temperament is the style of interaction with the world that babies are born with, the biological starting point of a personality. Temperament doesn't determine a life's path, but it does make some paths more likely than others. It's like height and basketball. There are tall people who can't play and short people who can, but there are a lot more tall basketball stars than short ones.

Jerome Kagan, a Harvard psychologist who has studied temperament extensively, found that about 10 to 20 percent of people are born highly reactive to anything unfamiliar. They take longer to feel safe with a new person or place. Kagan followed a group of people with this temperament from infancy to adulthood. They were less likely to be risk-takers and more likely to be anxious. However, they didn't all become anxious.

How does a small difference in infancy escalate over time in some people into shyness, timidity, fearfulness, inhibition, and anxiety disorders? The answer is avoidance. The heightened sensitivity of their alert and alarm systems leads reactive children to avoid new things. Therefore they don't develop the sense of safety that comes with familiarity. Kagan found that children with this temperament are less likely to develop anxiety if their parents help them develop coping skills, and more likely to develop anxiety if their parents "protect" them by letting them avoid anything that scares them. Avoidance blocks the practice and experience required by the assessment and all-clear parts of the system.

Children with an anxious temperament need challenges that are "just right." They need to be allowed to fail—as long as the failure isn't dangerous. Some children become anxious because they face challenges that are way too much for them, such as abuse or neglect. But other children become anxious because they aren't challenged enough. When children learn to walk, they fall and fall and fall until they get it right. If we tried to protect them from every fall, they would never learn to cope in the world. Teachers tell me they have seen an enormous increase in parents doing their children's homework for them, or making excuses for them. I even heard about a young man who brought his mother on a job interview!

Any child—no matter the temperament—can develop excess anxiety after a big trauma or many small ones. Extreme events, like child abuse or serious injury, overwhelm the system. That's why one of the main symptoms of post-traumatic stress disorder (PTSD) is hypervigilance, a constant state of high alert. Traumas lock the alarm in the on position: *The whole world is dangerous.* That belief stops the assessment process before it even starts. No matter what, the conclusion of the assessment will be *danger.* Without accurate assessment, there can't be an all-clear signal. Children who were betrayed by adults have an even stronger belief that the world is dangerous, because trust is the most basic element of security and safety.

A series of less severe events can also cause an oversensitive alarm and a faulty all-clear signal, especially if the child has no chance to heal from one hurt before the next one hits. I have seen many children who are anxious because their parents are sick, depressed, or argue a lot, or because they have had to move frequently or make other major life changes. Children who lose one parent often develop a strong fear for the safety of their remaining parent or caregiver. Children who are exposed to violence in their homes or their neighborhoods also tend to be highly anxious, though they may cover it up with bravado or aggression.

Anxious Parenting

Temperament and trauma play a large part in childhood anxiety, but let's face it: Parents create a great deal of anxiety in children. Anxious children often grow up in an atmosphere of overprotectiveness or nervousness. "Be careful!" "Are you sure you're okay?" Anxiety is a contagious emotion; it can be caused by watching parents approach life with fear. Children learn from parents to be on high alert, to have an overactive alarm, to have assessments biased toward danger, and to withhold their all-clear signal.

I started out as one of those overprotective parents, but I made a conscious effort to change this when my daughter was around three. Emma was happily climbing at the playground. I was unhappily standing below, shouting, "Be careful, be careful!" A friend casually said to me, "You know, Larry, she'll recover better from a broken arm than from being timid and unsure of herself." I tried to come up with a satisfactory argument to this radical idea, but couldn't. *I* was certainly taking a long time to recover from being timid and unsure of myself. So I decided to encourage Emma's risk-taking and trust her abilities, instead of worrying so much. (She'll tell you I continued to worry, but I promise you I cut way back.) I also pushed myself to be more physically adventurous. I wasn't the most relaxed person on the rock-climbing trip, but I did it!

Looking back at my overprotectiveness, I can see that it wasn't keeping Emma safe. It only exaggerated her alarm signal, interfered with her ability to make accurate assessments, and undermined her all-clear signal—not at all what I hoped for as her father.

Since I've tried so hard to stop worrying, I was intrigued by Heather Shumaker's argument against the phrase "be careful" in her provocative book, *It's OK Not to Share*. This kind of parental overcaution, she writes, "adds general anxiety without offering any specific help, [causing] some kids to avoid risks and stop trying new things." Shumaker suggests asking children, "Do you feel safe?" instead of dumping our worries on them. That question "forces children to take stock of the situation [and] helps kids listen to their own internal warning signals." Of course, we have to trust their answer!

Other Sources of Anxiety

Another source of childhood anxiety is having something to say but not being able to say it, or feeling something and not being able to express it. I think anxiety is commonly felt in the stomach, chest, or throat because feelings and words get stuck there, halfway in and halfway out. We try to push the thought or feeling aside, but it always comes back. Unexpressed emotions and unspoken words do not disappear. Think back to when you were a child. Were there important thoughts you never had a chance to say, or feelings that you never had a chance to share?

The modern world certainly seems to be a major factor in our current anxiety epidemic. The nightly news sometimes seems as if it was intentionally designed to create anxiety. I recently saw an online news headline: "5 Toddler Dangers You Might Overlook" with the subheading: "These risks probably never crossed your mind." They are on my mind now! Commercials also create new things to worry about so they can sell us new products to ease our worries. The ones I remember best from my childhood are "ring around the collar" and "iron-poor blood." Our society is fast-paced and high-pressured. Even after all these generations outside of caves, we still have brains that are wired to respond better to lions and tigers and bears than to math tests, imaginary monsters, or the last few seconds of a close game.

Modern society also expects us to be "cool." As the antiperspirant ad says, "Never let them see you sweat." This is an impossible demand that creates anxiety by interfering with the healthy expression of emotion. Most children are still told not to cry, not to be angry, and to "go to your room until you can have a smile on your face." The result is that some children feel extremely anxious when they have perfectly natural emotions such as jealousy of a sibling, anger at parents, or sexual feelings.

Children can also develop anxiety because of sensory processing difficulties. They just don't feel comfortable in the world. Children with tactile oversensitivity, for example, can feel like they are jumping out of their own skin because of the way that certain clothes or textures feel. Auditory oversensitivity can make a classroom feel like a screeching cacophony of noise. Many children on the autism spectrum are very anxious, partly due to the challenges of living in a society designed for more typical brains.

Medical conditions, such as physical disabilities, can easily lead to parental overprotectiveness and children's belief that the world is unsafe. Medical procedures and examinations can be very scary, especially when children are separated from their parents or held down against their will. Certain symptoms, such as asthma, can trigger panic as the child reacts to not being able to take a full breath. That panic can linger as chronic anxiety.

RESETTING THE SECURITY SYSTEM

Children who grow up free from excess anxiety develop an alert that is careful but not overly sensitive, an alarm that is strong but not overpowering, an assessment system that is rational and accurate, and a confident all-clear signal. Children who don't have this delicate balance need help to reset their Security Systems.

Children with high anxiety spend much of their time "on guard," on the lookout for potential dangers. You can use dramatic play to help loosen up this hypervigilance. When I first met Brook, she was a girl who was easily agitated, especially if her routine was disrupted. When that happened, she asked her mother the same questions over and over, and was never satisfied with the answer. Her mother, Brenda, frustrated with this pattern, was often impatient. When I asked Brenda what she had tried to help Brook, she rolled her eyes and said, "I've tried telling her to relax, that there's nothing to worry about. I tried sticker charts. I guess if any of that worked I wouldn't be here."

Brook loved make-believe play, so I encouraged Brenda to play Security Duck. I loaned them a silly-looking stuffed duck that Brook had enjoyed in my office, and suggested that Brenda make it into a security guard who was overenthusiastic about her job, but frightened by everything. Brenda asked me what she should do with the character of the security duck, but I told her that she and Brook would figure it out at home. They did!

Brenda pulled out the duck and made up a funny "guard" voice for it: "I'm going to guard the whole barnyard to make sure everything is safe. I've heard there are some dangerous *puppies* around here." Brook giggled as her mother made the duck strut around the room, acting super-brave until she saw a tiny stuffed puppy. Brenda made the security guard duck run for cover from the "dangerous puppy," screeching in pretend fear, which made Brook laugh more. Brook went to get all her stuffed puppies and delighted in frightening the duck with them. Over time, the game evolved as Brook found more and more ways to scare the duck, who alternated between outrageous bragging ("I'm not scared of anything!") and silly cowering.

Brook added a new element to the game, in which the puppies bravely protected themselves *and* the security guard duck. Previously, she had been afraid to have anything "bad" or scary ever happen in her pretend play. Now she created wild make-believe dangers. The puppies always saved the day, while the duck hid in fright. After a few weeks of playing these games, Brook's hyperalertness decreased and she was better able to handle changes in her routine.

Brenda was surprised that a silly game filled with giggles could make a difference when more serious approaches had failed. But it wasn't *just* silliness. This game had all three key elements of a playful parenting approach: Mom playfully engaged with her daughter and with the problem that was troubling both of them; they shared lots of laughter; and the roles were reversed, so Brook could be strong and brave (or scary).

I Can't Watch is another game I often play with children who are physically timid. I learned this game from Patty Wipfler, founder of Hand in Hand Parenting. At a family roughhousing event, I used this game with a six-year-old boy named Davy. He was hesitant to try any of the moves I demonstrated, though he watched the other children with interest. His father coaxed him to join in, with no success. I walked over before Dad could get too frustrated. "Wait a minute, Davy," I said, "you're not going to *walk,* are you?" He tentatively nodded his head yes, unsure what I meant by this strange question. "Oh, no," I said, "I can't watch. Walking is so *dangerous.* People sometimes *fall over.*" I whispered the last two words in fake horror.

Davy knew just what to do. He started to walk, making sure I was looking. "Oh, no, no, no," I shrieked, "I can't watch." I cov-

ered my eyes with my hand. Davy said, "Look!" and did a somersault on the tumbling mat. I howled in more mock terror. "Not a
somersault! Dad, did you see that?" Davy's father also knew just
what to do. He said proudly, "Davy can do somersaults, flips,
anything he wants! Just watch him!"

I shouted, "No, please, I'm shaking all over just watching
him walk, what if he falls over?" Davy proceeded to "scare me"
with one physically adventurous move after another, including
ones he had been reluctant to try before this silly game. As always with this type of play, I was very careful that Davy didn't
feel teased, because the goal was for him to feel powerful, not
humiliated.

Once I realized the importance of the all-clear signal, I made
up a game called The Coast Is Clear—Or Is It? I start the game
by hiding dramatically behind a piece of furniture or underneath
a blanket. Then I whisper to the child, "Is the coast clear?" I
make up something outrageous that frightens me—something
absurdly nonscary, like tiny puppies, or something extremely unlikely to appear, like pirates. Don't use something your child
really fears; otherwise the game can become really scary instead
of pretend-scary.

In this game I embody an overactive alarm system, while
children get to play the part of a confident all-clear signal. (They
don't think about it this way, of course.) Once they promise me
that the coast is clear, I come out of hiding, only to discover
something new that scares me. It might be a pencil: "Oh, no! The
pirates must have been here making a treasure map with this
pencil!" I race back under the blanket. The children eventually
convince me that all is well, that I am safe. Their repetition of
the all-clear signal in a playful setting has the magical effect
of increasing the power of their own internal all-clear signals. Of

course, some children don't want to reassure me, they want to point out more and more things that will scare me. The results are the same. Play brings laughter, and laughter loosens fear.

ANXIETY ACROSS CHILDHOOD

Very few children grow up with no worries or anxieties. Some common fears of infants and toddlers include separation, being alone, loud noises, strangers, and anything sudden, intense, and unfamiliar.

From age two to four, children have many of the same anxieties as babies and toddlers. They can also start to have fears about animals, the bath, monsters and other imaginary creatures, and death. Toilet training can create anxieties about bodily functions, and harsh or inconsistent discipline can contribute to anxieties about making mistakes or about emotions and impulses.

Around age four to six, children commonly develop anxieties about the bigger world outside of their immediate environment: storms, war, doctors, and dentists. At this stage, children may have difficulty distinguishing between dreams, fantasy, and reality, which can add to anxiety. Cartoon violence or vivid dreams can seem quite real. Social anxiety is more noticeable at this age, because there is a greater expectation to interact with other children. Anxious children at this age will often regress (act younger than they are), wet the bed, or have other toileting accidents.

Moving up in age, children who are six to eleven can have all the same anxieties as younger children, plus new worries related to school: being late, missing homework, test performance, grades, or bullies. They may fear disappointing or angering the teacher. Social anxieties, such as fear of rejection or ridicule, can become quite intense. Children at this age often experience homesickness as they leave home for more extended periods, and they can also develop fears about germs, burglars, kidnappers, or terrorists. This is an age when the conscience develops more fully. If the conscience is excessively strong, children can suffer anxiety from having "bad" thoughts or forbidden feelings. A healthy conscience understands that there is no such thing as a bad thought or unacceptable feeling, but a harsh conscience floods children with anxiety for being normal. Some anxious school-age children are overly nice. They feel they have to be perfectly good; never make a mistake; and never cause their parents or friends any trouble.

Adolescence can be a time of existential anxiety: What is my place in the universe? What is the meaning of life? Where do I belong? Occasionally a younger child will be preoccupied with these types of thoughts, and that can be quite overwhelming to them. Teenagers also have anxieties about the real-life issues they face, such as choices about drug and alcohol use, romance and sexuality, and conflict with parents.

That's a long list! Childhood anxiety is so common that it can actually be considered normal. No matter how universal it is, anxiety is also painful—sometimes extremely painful. Whether a child's anxiety is typical for her stage of development or not, whether it is mild or severe, you can help with an empathic approach and an understanding of the impact of anxiety on bodies, thoughts, emotions, and behaviors.

CHAPTER TWO

The Second Chicken:
Parenting with Empathy, Parenting for Confidence

When we'd go for a walk in our neighborhood, my son was always scared of the barking dog down the street. . . . My first response was to say, "Oh, don't let it worry you. He can't get out. . . ." But that just didn't help . . . so now I . . . say something like, "I know that sometimes you're scared of that dog. I'll just hold your hand."

—A father quoted by Mr. Fred Rogers

The things that have helped us most through this time [of my daughter's extreme anxiety] are the following strategies: listening, listening, listening.

—A mother in England

THE TROUBLE WITH CHICKEN LITTLE

In the folktale of Chicken Little, an acorn falls on a young chicken's head. She believes the sky is falling. Her panic spreads to all the other barnyard and forest animals. Eventually they all visit the Lion, who tells them that it was only an acorn and sends them home.

I hate this story! Chicken Little and her friends are belittled and scorned. Their fear is seen as ridiculous—it was just an acorn. But it isn't silly to take warnings seriously. If our friends are scared, they might know something we don't know. There will be time to think it through later—but only if we are alert to danger.

Okay, maybe the story isn't so bad. It does get a few things right in terms of the Security System described in the last chapter. A child's internal alarm is like Chicken Little. It can't tell real dangers (the sky falling) from imaginary ones (acorns). A mere thought can trigger the same cascade of anxious feelings as if the sky were really falling. Chicken Little and her friends lack the assessment part of the system. This is the part that can slow down and think: *Let's assess the situation; maybe it wasn't anything dangerous.* The story also captures how contagious anxiety can be. Finally, Chicken Little and her friends make many children laugh, and I can't argue with that. I think children laugh because they can see themselves as brave and competent, not like the silly animals that are so frightened by acorns.

The calm "second chicken" that I described in the introduction is a better role model for parents. When a chicken is immobilized—frozen with fear—it will look around for cues about safety or danger. If it sees another chicken that is also scared stiff, then it will stay scared for a very long time. If it sees a second chicken walking around, the immobilized one will hop right up. If the second chicken is scared, there must be danger. If the second chicken isn't scared, it must be safe. The essence of your role as a parent is to be that calm second chicken for your anxious child.

That's not so easy! You may be anxious yourself. Your child's anxiety may leave you feeling helpless and frustrated, maybe even angry. When you are calm, your anxious child may not even notice. You have probably tried endless reassurance to ease your child's anxiety. You may have tried sticker charts, with rewards for doing something scary or trying something new. By the time a parent looks for help from a professional or a book, most have resorted to bribes, threats, coercion, punishments, and exasperated shouting. I understand. It's painful to see your beloved child feeling so stuck. It's annoying to have your family frozen by a child's anxiety.

Don't give up hope! You can't change your child's genes, or your own. You can't choose your child's temperament, or your own. You can't change the parenting you grew up with. You may have already contributed to your child's anxiety. It's okay! You can help your child. You can be a source of calmness, confidence, and coping skills, starting now. You can parent based on your child's temperament and needs. You can tackle your own anxieties, and you can learn effective responses when your child is anxious. You can help reset your child's Security System, and you can reset your own.

PARENTING WITH EMPATHY

The first step is empathy. What is it like to be inside your child's head, feeling so anxious? Without empathy, it's easy to dismiss a child's fears. Of course, we don't intend to be dismissive. We intend to reassure our children, to help them calm down, to ease their suffering. Nevertheless, children can easily feel belittled. Here are some typical examples of comments that dismiss and invalidate children:

- "Don't be silly."
- "There's nothing to be scared of."
- "Why are you afraid of *that*?"

- "Stop being such a baby."
- "You're fine."
- "Nobody *else* is afraid."
- "Just do it and don't make such a big deal out of it."
- "I told you I'm coming right back, stop crying."
- "You see, everything turned out fine, all your worrying was a waste of time."
- "If you're just going to sit in my lap, we might as well go home."

The opposite of dismissal is acknowledgment. Contrast the dismissive comments above with these empathic acknowledgments of a child's emotions:

- "Wow, that was really scary."
- "You look a little frightened, would you like to hold my hand?"
- "If I had that nightmare, I'd be scared too."
- "Everyone gets scared at times, even grown-ups. Yes, even me!"
- "You wish you could stay home with me today."
- "Would you like to try it together the first time?"
- "Even though everything worked out, I know you were really worried."
- "You can sit in my lap as long as you'd like, and join in when you're ready."

Who are we to say that a child's worry is ridiculous? Sure, the monsters under the bed aren't real, but the child's fear is real. Ridicule is a dead end, while empathy is a road to creative solutions.

Wanda's son, Drew, was scared to go to bed at night because of "dinosaurs in his room." After many failed attempts to talk Drew out of this silly fear, Wanda said that she finally stopped talking and started listening. "The thing that scared him was a shadow cast on the wall. I lay in the bed with him and saw what he was looking at—it did look like a dinosaur! I showed him how the dinosaur shape was created by the shadow, and I asked him what he thought we might be able to do to change it. He suggested that we change the position of the light, and he was right, the shadow went away." What a great picture of empathy: Wanda lying on Drew's bed next to him so she can see what he sees.

Another reason to have empathy for unrealistic fears is that children might really be afraid of something more "real" that they can't yet put into words. If we dismiss children's fears because they seem trivial, they are not likely to share their deeper fears with us. No one wants to pour her heart out unless she knows someone is listening.

It's unsettling to have a fear that you don't fully understand. Many childhood fears are like that, too big for words to capture. Children may worry that a parent will die or get sick or that their parents will get divorced; they may have a well-justified fear of violence; or they may fear that they caused bad things to happen because of their wishes or feelings. Unable to voice these deep-felt fears, children may turn their vague sense of uneasiness into something concrete, such as monsters under the bed.

Whenever you see an irrational fear, don't dismiss it. Put yourself in your child's shoes in order to discover whether there is a deeper fear lurking underneath. This deeper fear is why children are still afraid of monsters under the bed even after we shine a flashlight and they see nothing but dust and stray socks.

When we dismiss a child's silly fear, he may feel that we are dismissing his more serious fear, the one too scary to say out loud.

Many children at bedtime experience two of the most common childhood fears: to be alone and to be in the dark. We often dismiss these fears because *we* know that our children are safe. Children in an anxious state cannot hold on to that comforting idea. They need us to accept that they are scared. Comfort and connection are what anxious children need most at bedtime.

How often have you told children that their fears aren't worth worrying about? I urge parents to give up deciding whether their children's fears are legitimate. All fears are valid because they are the feelings that our children are experiencing. Yet it's hard to give up our habit of judgment: *This fear is reasonable, that one is not.*

Here's an example of a mother who dropped her critical judgment: "My four-year-old son developed a worry about tsunamis. Initially I found this cute, and not a legitimate source of anxiety. It was only after he said he didn't want to go on vacation to Hawaii that I realized he was really worried. His logic was, 'Hawaii has active volcanoes, volcanoes could cause an earthquake, that could create a tsunami, and then where would we go? Into the volcano? Better to not go at all.' It didn't work to tell him not to worry, or that the likelihood was very low. What did work was listening to him tell his worries in his own words and then reflecting them back to him. I let him feel his fear/worry/anxiety without ridicule, shame, or belittling. It's generally difficult for me to watch anxiety in my children if I don't think it is legitimate. With the tsunami fear, I had to keep at the forefront of my mind that even though I didn't consider it to be a good reason for anxiety, *those feelings are real to him.*"

Feelings aren't supposed to be rational. If we stop judging fears as invalid, we can find a deeper empathy. "I see you're scared" is true even if the fear doesn't make much sense to us. We don't have to agree with a feeling or share it. We just need to listen. When we say, "Don't be ridiculous," or "There is no reason to be scared," children can't relax because they can't trust us to be vigilant guardians. Instead of insisting to children that they *are* safe when they don't *feel* safe, you might ask, "Would you be willing to let me be in charge of safety?"

Childhood anxiety is very resistant to change. That resistance is aggravating to parents. So patience is crucial to maintaining empathy. I asked a friend how she managed to be so patient with her highly anxious child. I was surprised to learn that it hadn't always been that way:

"It took me some time to reach this stage. Dina couldn't handle anything new. To leave the house took forty-five minutes of discussion, even if we were going someplace fun. I was not patient at all. My impatience made her more anxious. It was a vicious circle. Because she did not take change well, we did not expose her to change very much, so she became even more reluctant. I was also a new mother with my own anxieties. The breakthrough in our relationship came when I learned about temperaments, and I understood that my kid was reactive to new things. I finally understood that I did not have a 'defective' child. I could see the world through her eyes. Of course she won't try new foods on vacation, everything else is too new already, so we purchased her favorite shape of pasta and asked the restaurant to cook it. And I learned that it will take us longer but we will get there, like spending two weeks of playing in advance of getting a vaccination, so that she won't have to be held down screaming. Dina does many things now I would never have imagined she would do. Having a sister helped her a lot, especially a sister with a more adventurous temperament. I remember how amazed I was when she followed her sister down a new slide after just ten minutes of watching."

Empathy can be expressed playfully as well as seriously. A mother told me what happened when she put herself in her child's shoes and then added play to the situation: "We were at a program at the waterfront center, and my two-year-old was looking at the oyster toadfish in a tank. They are kind of scary-looking fish. Murray looked very nervous and started saying they were eating him. So I said, 'They are eating you? Let's bite them!' He liked that a lot. We pretended to bite them and snap at them and we ate them and ate them. He pulled me over a few more times during our visit to play that we were eating them." I don't think it would have been as helpful—or as fun—if this mother had said sternly, "The fish is in a tank and can't get to you."

When we understand how children feel, we give them the message, *All your feelings are welcome here—even uncomfortable ones.* When we dismiss their feelings or tell them what they should be feeling, we give the message, *Your feelings are wrong.* But empathy doesn't mean that we join them in anxiety: "Are you sure, are you okay, what's the matter?" Nervous adult voices can easily drown out children's inner confidence. When that happens, children are filled with second-guesses and self-doubt.

You may run short on empathy for your anxious child. That's completely understandable. It may help to think about people you have known who embody respect and understanding toward children. They don't have to be people you knew personally. They may be authors, fictional characters, or historical figures who are role models for welcoming children just as they are. Some of my empathy heroes are children's television host Fred Rogers, author

Maurice Sendak, Polish pediatrician Janusz Korczak, and—I'm very fortunate to be able to say—my parents and my sisters. Once you have your Empathy Hall of Fame, use them to remind you how you want to interact with your children. Put pictures or quotes from them up on your walls, ask yourself what they might do in a given situation, and feel their presence as "guardian angels," offering you support, admiration, and compassion.

WHICH CHICKEN ARE YOU?

If empathy is the first step, the second step is projecting calm confidence. First we accept children right where they are, then we gently lead them to a stronger feeling of safety and security. In my chicken-immobilization experiments the first chicken remained afraid much longer when it saw another chicken petrified with fear. Everything depended on the signal from the second chicken: The world is safe or the world is dangerous. Which type of second chicken are you? Which type do you want to be? If you are reading this book there is a good chance that you yourself are anxious. Just a wild guess. To be a calm—and calming—second chicken, you might need to tackle your own anxiety.

That means recognize your worries and fears, practice relaxation and stress reduction, and get help if needed. Think about where and how you experience your anxiety. Is it mostly in your body, your thoughts, your emotions, or your relationships? Pick one fear and face it, one nervous habit and break it, or one thing you avoid and approach it. You don't have to change completely and immediately. Children appreciate when adults are willing to do the same hard things we ask of them.

There is one important difference between childhood anxiety and adult anxiety: You will have to be your own "parent,"

gently pushing yourself to face your fears even though it is difficult. You can ask for help from a partner or friend, but be prepared to be angry when they push you. That might help you
understand why your children often get angry at you when you
push them to face their fears.

I know it isn't easy. Most anxious adults have figured out
how to get by. We set up our lives to avoid most of the things that
scare us. But our children need to see us practice what we preach.
I notice this gap when I work with children whose social anxiety
interferes with making friends. I often suggest to their parents
that they invite over another whole family. The idea is that the
children will get bored with the adults and go off to play, but
there will be safety because parents are nearby. Most of these
parents react with horror at my suggestion to invite new people
over: "I can't invite over someone I barely know!" Yet they want
their children to overcome their inhibitions about friendship!

Even if you are not generally an anxious person, you might
still be an anxious parent. Parents worry. Anxious children gen-
erate extra worry—*What if they can't have a successful life?* Anxiety can be highly contagious, so if you find yourself "catching"
your child's anxiety, pause to notice that you are safe. Your alarm
was activated by your child's alarm, not by danger. Can you send
yourself an all-clear signal? Can you be your own calm second
chicken first, then the calm second chicken for your child?

Parents set themselves up for high levels of anxiety when
they can't stand for their children to suffer, even the tiniest bit.
We will never enjoy our children's suffering, but we have to be
able to tolerate it. That doesn't mean we go out of our way to
make children miserable! But children need a series of small
challenges, each one bigger than the last one, and that inevitably
means frustration and pain. If challenges are too big, children

will feel insecure and ashamed, but if they don't have enough challenges, they won't develop competence or confidence.

This need for challenges reminds me of an old joke about a little boy who never talked. His parents took him to experts and therapists for years, everything checked out fine, but still he never said a word. One day, out of the blue, he asked his sister to pass the salt. Everyone was astonished. They asked him why he never talked before, and he replied, "Everything was fine up until now."

This story is a good one to keep in mind if you have a hard time bearing your children's emotional pain as they struggle with a challenge. *Is this really too hard, or am I just unable to bear my child's pain?* Remember that you can offer love and comfort to ease the sting of that suffering without overprotecting or rescuing.

By stepping out of our own anxieties we can be more helpful with our children's anxieties. When children insist they cannot do something you can simply say, "I know you can do it" in a very gentle and loving voice. They may react with tears or a tantrum. That's normal; all you need to do is sit and listen. Their release of feelings restores confidence, as long as you listen with empathy.

What does your child's anxiety stir up in you? Rage, frustration, aggravation? Painful memories from your own childhood? Are you so worn down that you give in to unreasonable demands? Does your life revolve around things your child can't do or must do? Are you worried what this anxiety means for your child's future?

These are all completely normal and common reactions to children's anxiety. Unfortunately, most parents feel guilt when they have these feelings and thoughts, and they try to deny them or ignore them. It may sound strange, but the best way to get rid of these troubling emotional responses is to be open about them. Parent educator Patty Wipfler recommends the Listening Partnership, in which two parents take turns sharing their thoughts and feelings with each other. This can be done with a spouse or partner, but often it works even better if you exchange this listening time with someone who doesn't have the same child as you. They will have a different perspective. Choose someone who will listen to you with admiration and compassion rather than give you judgment, criticism, or advice. Some parents use this technique to listen to each other every day on the phone for five minutes each, while others have longer exchanges in person as often as they can.

As you build trust with your listening partner, you will be able to share even the most "forbidden" and uncomfortable feelings. This unburdening helps us to be more empathic with our children, more compassionate to ourselves, and more creative in finding solutions. When someone listens to us well—especially someone who really understands—we can let go of guilt about not being good enough parents. We all want to improve, but I never saw guilt improve anyone's parenting! As one father said after he spent some time talking about his daughter's anxiety, "I realized that I expected her fears to be rational. It makes me so mad when she is irrational. But after my friend listened to me complain, I realized that my own fears are irrational too. I guess all feelings are irrational, that's what makes them feelings. I have been able to sit and listen to my daughter so much better since then."

ADVANCED TRAINING IN BEING A SECOND CHICKEN

The second chicken in my experiment didn't have to do much to calm the first chicken, just walk around not being scared. Sometimes that's all parents need to do. Other times—as you already know if you have an anxious child—just being calm yourself isn't enough. New information can't reset the Security System if it doesn't sink in. The anxious brain looks for danger signs constantly, but doesn't always accept new information about safety. Anxiety's attitude seems to be, *I've seen enough to be scared, and that's all I need to know.*

When children are anxious, they don't see the whole wide world as it is. They see life through a filter of danger, so everything looks dangerous. Parents can help children see something different—an unafraid second chicken who represents safety and security.

Many parents who try *The Second Chicken Question*—"Can you look in my eyes and see if I am afraid?"—report a significant change in their children's anxiety level. That invitation is so different from telling children not to be afraid. But what if your child looks into your eyes and sees fear? Well, you are probably not anxious about the same exact things as your child. So you can still say, "Look in my eyes and see whether I am scared of monsters under the bed." At the very least you have made eye contact and established a deeper connection, which are often difficult during a period of anxiety.

If your child won't see calm confidence in your eyes, you can say, "I'm anxious too. I am going to try some ways to lower my anxiety. Would you like to do them with me?" And then share your favorite relaxation strategy, discuss your safety plan, or explain how you "talk back" to your anxious thoughts. In other words, you can search together for the calm second chicken. If there is real danger, of course, it isn't appropriate to be the calm second chicken. Yet you can still help contain your child's concerns by being straightforward: "I am aware of the danger and this is what I am going to do about it."

Being the calm second chicken isn't easy, and it's a new approach for most parents, so here are my responses to the most common questions people ask about it.

Why can I easily calm down my older child, but the younger one can't be reassured, no matter what I say?

Some children effortlessly develop a strong all-clear signal—the brain circuitry that shuts off the anxiety alarm and allows a child to relax. These children weren't born with a reactive temperament, and they didn't experience traumas or frights that set them up for high anxiety. When they are frightened or anxious, their parents just need to offer a little comfort and reassurance and the anxious feelings pass quickly. (It's okay to be jealous of those families!)

Children who are prone to high anxiety need more help to develop their all-clear signals. It's similar to the way that some children learn to read effortlessly while others need extra attention. A simple word of reassurance or reminder of safety isn't enough for children who were born with a reactive temperament or who lived through anxiety-arousing events.

My son picks up my anxiety instantly—it's like he has anxiety radar—but he never notices when I'm relaxed. I work so hard to be calm, why doesn't he even see it?

Anxious children are oversensitive to other people's anxiety and undersensitive to other people's calmness. That's because the anxious brain has a strong bias toward avoiding danger. It is always on the lookout. Your anxiety confirms your child's anxiety. Your calmness, however, doesn't fit your child's expectations, so it can't be absorbed. Anxious children receive constant danger signals from their bodies' anxious state, their worried thoughts, and their scary memories. As a result, they ignore competing information from outside, like Mom's reassurance. In other words, they tune out the calm second chicken.

What if I can't be calm enough to be the second chicken?
Welcome to the club! This is a common problem for parents of anxious children. The solution is simple: Get a substitute second chicken to help you. The world is filled with fearless people, or at least people with different fears from your own. A friend, partner, or relative can give your child the "notice I am calm and therefore you are safe" messages that are hard for you to convey convincingly. You can send your child to summer camp or an outdoor program, where nonanxious counselors can encourage adventurous exploration. I recommend psychologist Michael Thompson's book *Homesick and Happy* to all anxious parents who hesitate to let their children step away from the safety of home.

At a weekend play workshop I conducted in Romania, a mother named Adriana used her husband as her "substitute second chicken." I watched Adriana and her toddler daughter, Ileana, as they stood at the bottom of a wide wooden ladder. Some older children had climbed it, with their parents close beside them, and Ileana wanted a turn. Adriana tried to talk her daughter out of climbing the ladder, but Ileana was determined. I stepped away for a few minutes, and when I came back to the ladder, Adriana and Ileana were at the top. Ileana's father was at the bottom cheering them on. I asked Adriana what had happened.

"Ileana started climbing up the wooden ladder and I was right beside her. Honestly, I did not think she was going to climb that high. When I saw she was going up higher than I could handle, I looked around for my husband and asked for his help. I was afraid that she might fall and that I would not be able to catch her, and I knew Stefan had no such worries. So I chose to call him to help rather than make Ileana climb down. I hoped he would take over and climb with her, but instead he encouraged me to do it myself, saying he would catch us both! In the past I would have insisted it was too dangerous, but I have learned that the problem isn't her falling, the problem is my anxiety."

How can I teach my child safety if I always stay calm? Don't I have to show him that some things are scary?
The second chicken isn't *always* calm—only when there is no danger. Children need to see parents express the whole range of human feelings, including fear. But if our fear terrifies them then we've only given them a bundle of tension that will interfere with their safety. Real security requires flexible intelligence, not conditioned fear. Yet it's so common for adults to deliberately scare children, for example about running into the street or kidnappers. Then parents are surprised when their children are afraid to cross the street, or afraid to stay home with a trusted babysitter. Whenever you share a danger with a child, be sure to also share solutions for managing that danger.

We won't always be around to tell children when to be scared, and how much. We have to gradually step back and let them assess on their own what is safe and what is dangerous. The goal is for children to trust their inner guide, to know the difference inside between dangerous and scary-but-safe. As Heather Shumaker writes, "Hold back your urge to protect. Ask yourself: 'What would it hurt?' Let her take a few risks and knocks."

My daughter refuses to go into any room in the house alone, even the bathroom. If I tell her I understand how she feels, how will she ever get over it?

Many parents wonder how to empathize with a child's fear while still being the calm second chicken. Isn't that a mixed message? Yes, but both parts of the message are important: "I understand you are scared *and* I know you are safe. You can tremble and cry in my arms for as long as you need to, *and then* you can take another step toward that room." If you don't push, you are telling your child that everything is dangerous—even bathwater. If you push with no empathy—"Get over it"—then you are telling your child to face life's dangers all alone and unsupported.

Fortunately, humans can offer one another something that chickens can't: security *plus* empathy. We can say, "If I believed that we might get hit by lightning, I would be scared too." Or "I can understand that you hate getting your face wet, and I'm going to help you get over that fear." Empathy can exist side by side with confidence. It's *the empathic second chicken.*

How can I be the second chicken if my child won't listen to me, especially when he's anxious?

In the quote at the beginning of this chapter, the father realized that all the logic and reassurance in the world would not soothe his son's fear of the barking dog. The boy needed something else first: the security and closeness of holding Dad's hand. He also needed Dad to understand his fear and not to judge or criticize him for it. When the anxious brain is activated it doesn't respond to new information. It has to be soothed and comforted first. In other words, children can't listen to us because they are already listening to their own inner alarm signals and their own inaccurate assessments. Gentle touch and soft murmurings of love work much better at these times than arguments or reasons.

I call this Going Primal, because the emotional part of the brain responds better to primal input—like cuddling—than to sophisticated input like language and logic. That is really hard for many anxious children and their parents to believe, because they tend to overemphasize their thinking brains.

A boy called Sammy, for example, was afraid of terrorist attacks. When his mother told him that this was very unlikely and their home was very safe, Sammy argued with her for hours. He responded more quickly to Going Primal: hugs, quiet singing, and other nonverbal comfort. When he demanded reassurance, she told him she wouldn't try to convince him with words, but would show him with her hugs that he was safe. When she did speak, she stayed away from logical arguments, and instead found simple words that validated his feelings: "I'm right here with you. Can you feel my arms around you? It's scary to think about terrorism." Sometimes Sammy cried when she gave this kind of primal comfort instead of arguing with his anxiety. Those tears are normal. They are healing tears because they break the tension of anxiety and allow a child to work through fears on a deeper emotional level. Sammy's mother realized he could "listen" to her reassurance nonverbally in ways that he never could listen to her words.

*What's wrong with reassurance? Don't I need to tell my daughter that
there are no monsters under the bed?*

If simple, short, matter-of-fact information solves the problem,
then reassurance is great. When anxiety is high and children reject our reassurance, we need to try something different. The
first step is talking less and listening more. This is especially true
for "trivial" fears, like monsters under the bed, because listening
is the only way to learn what is really going on inside your child's
head.

For example, Lorin told her mother, Connie, that she was
scared to be alone because monsters would kidnap her. Connie
tried numerous times to explain to Lorin exactly why this
wouldn't happen. Lorin's anxiety continued. Connie decided to
learn more instead of continuing her ineffective explanations.
She asked Lorin, "What would be the worst thing about being
kidnapped by monsters? What would happen next? What do you
feel in your body when you think about it?" (She didn't ask these
questions all at once! That would just have increased Lorin's
anxiety.)

These questions opened up a deeper emotional discussion,
and it emerged that Lorin was afraid that her mother might die.
Lorin had been thinking about death a lot ever since her grandfather died. She had appointed herself her mother's chief protec-
tor, and she came up with the idea of monster kidnappers to
convince Connie not to leave her side. Once Connie understood
the deeper fear, she could be much more empathic and understanding. She was much more effective, too. For months Connie
had been telling Lorin, "You are safe even when you are away
from me." But now Connie knew to say, "I am safe even when I'm
away from you."

GETTING REASSURANCE RIGHT

Reassurance is tricky. Have you ever felt anxiety and then felt reassured by someone close to you? Have you ever felt anxiety and then felt annoyed or agitated by someone's unsuccessful attempt to reassure you? I think most people have experienced both types of reassurance. The effective "second chicken" for an anxious child knows when and how to reassure.

Reassure without dismissal. I recently saw my doctor for a small bump on my finger. I was nervous to go to the clinic for something so minor, but he took me seriously. He explained his thought process in ruling out anything dangerous, conveyed his confidence, showed me a similar bump on his finger, and welcomed me to come back if it got worse or didn't get better. That experience has become my role model for reassurance without dismissal.

Validate first, reassure second. Many parents jump into reassurance too soon. Children hear reassurance best *after* their feelings are validated. When they feel understood they are more likely to value what we say. The best and simplest way to validate a child's feelings is to simply reflect back what they say to you. Don't leap in to disagree, argue, or correct the facts. Imagine that your child has refused to go to a party because "I won't know anyone there." You know this isn't true, but you can still validate first: "I hear you saying you won't know anybody at the birthday party and you won't have any fun. Did I understand you right?"

After validation, children are usually more open to reassurance. "I think I understand what you're saying. Would you like to hear what I think?" If they say no, and you insist on reassuring them against their will, then you're just going to waste your time and prove that you weren't listening! If they are ready to listen, you might say, "I can see how strong your feelings are, because I think they made you forget the people who will be there at the party whom you know. It seems like anxiety is trying to make you believe you will feel lonely and make you forget how much fun a party can be." Everything goes better if we connect with children first. Validation is a powerful tool for connection.

Reassure using the fifteen-second rule. If reassurance has not worked in fifteen seconds, *stop and do something else.* It isn't going to work. When reassurance works, it works almost instantly, because there is an open channel for your comforting words to reach your child's thinking brain. Your child's Security System welcomes your reassurance. Your child makes a more accurate assessment, then sends an all-clear signal that turns off the anxiety. When there *isn't* an open channel, reassurance won't help after fifteen seconds, fifteen minutes, or two hours. If you have a very anxious child, you have probably offered reassurance until you are both agitated and frustrated. So much for your calming influence!

The fifteen-second reassurance rule is based on my similar fifteen-second rule for hand washing. Since the Centers for Disease Control and Prevention recommends washing hands for fifteen seconds, I tell compulsive hand-washers, "The first fifteen seconds is for germs, but anything beyond that is for anxiety. Why would you want to polish up your anxiety?"

Support your child's assessments and all-clear signals; don't try to replace them with your own. You can't be your children's Security System. Of course you want to—their assessments and all-clear signals aren't functioning very well. Unfortunately, it won't work. If you insist on saying, "You're safe!" your child may dismiss everything you say. Your words can't compete with the anxious thought: *It sure doesn't feel safe.* If you say instead, "I'm here, can you notice that I am here with you?" your child has the chance to finish the thought: *She's here, I can notice she's here, aah, I'm safe.* You helped, but the assessment and all-clear signal came from within your child.

PARENTING FOR CONFIDENCE AND COPING SKILLS

Empathy builds a child's sense of security: *Someone gets me and understands how I feel.* That is a wonderful contradiction to anxiety, but it isn't enough. Children also need confidence and good coping skills. We want children to have courage, an "I can do it" attitude, and the resilience to bounce back up after they fall.

Children develop confidence when they have a secure connection with a caregiver, when they are allowed to feel powerful and strong, and when they are encouraged to take risks. Babies and toddlers need to know that we will hold them safely as we fly them around the room playing airplane, and they need to know we will comfort them when they hurt themselves. But they will take some falls.

Young children develop confidence when they playfully push grown-ups over, especially if they fall down in a silly way. Older children increase their confidence when they use their full strength. When you wrestle or pillow fight, match children's strength for a while before letting them win. Physical challenges, such as climbing over rocks and jumping across small streams, provide enormous boosts to a child's confidence.

I avoid urging children to "Be brave," because many children think it means, "Don't be scared," which is simply not possible. On the other hand, I like to say, "That was brave" or "That took courage." When we notice a child's courageous action, we convey that bravery and courage can be practiced and developed. It isn't something you have or don't have. We also need to teach children that courage is not fearlessness. Courage means being scared and doing something anyway. You *have* to be scared to have courage!

Confident children focus their attention on coping rather than misery or victimization. Friendships and peer groups are a great example. In *Mom, They're Teasing Me,* my coauthors and I wrote about three questions that boost children's ability to cope with social problems: *What did you try? How did it work? What would you like to try next?* If a child says, "I didn't try anything," be sure to ask how that worked. After all, doing nothing is a strategy, and often a good one. These three questions are the opposite of *interviewing for pain,* which involves asking children about all the terrible things that happened to them. The result of interviewing for pain is that children focus on failure, victimhood, and blame, not on coping and confidence.

Anxiety can feel like being trapped inside the scary part of a story with no happy ending in sight. Parenting for confidence and coping can help children get unstuck. When children tell you about something bad that happened to them, listen empathically and then ask, "What happened next?" Even the scariest events can have a "next chapter" about rescue, recovery, or successful coping. If a child felt paralyzed during a scary event, you can ask her what she would have liked to do, and also ask how she eventually "unfroze" after it ended. You can ask a similar question after a child relates a nightmare: "Can you make up a powerful ending to the dream?" The confidence-building ending might be, "I woke up and realized it was just a dream," or it might be, "I had superpowers and threw the monsters into outer space."

Laura was four years old when she had a series of painful and frightening medical procedures. Afterward she was generally fearful and unsettled. When she talked about it, she always repeated the same scary details and buried her face in her father's lap. When he asked Laura to make up an alternate ending, however, she immediately jumped up and showed off some fierce karate kicks in the air. Then she shouted at the imaginary doctors and nurses, "Leave me alone!" She had been too frozen with fear to do any of those things while it was happening. Of course I don't want children to kick medical professionals in order to overcome their fear. But these expressions of power are safe and appropriate during play. No one actually gets hurt. Children heal from powerlessness by acting powerfully in their play. Over time their pretend strength will translate into real (and nonviolent) bravery and skill as they handle real-life scary situations.

Some therapists suggest a system of rewards to build coping skills and confidence in children who are anxious. For example, a parent might give a child a sticker every time she does something that she couldn't do before, then the child gets a prize for a certain number of stickers. This kind of reward program often creates power struggles, because children with high anxiety often excel at "logical" debate: "You didn't say how many seconds I had to stay in the bathroom alone!"

Overcoming a fear for a reward can undermine the powerful feeling that comes from doing it on your own. *I only did it for the toy; it doesn't count.* Reward charts also focus so much on success and failure that they can trigger shame. Finally, anxious kids can become obsessive about systems of rewards and punishments, which defeats the whole purpose.

As a playful alternative to complex systems of rewards and punishments you can ask children to draw goofy pictures of their anxiety, or pictures of the superpowers they will use to vanquish their fears. Putting a fear onto paper can ease its grip on the child. Children can also play a game in which they overcome whatever it is that scares them, such as pretending a pile of pillows is their fear and repeatedly knocking it over. That game is even more fun if you pretend to be the fear. Put on a silly voice and scream in fake anguish whenever the pile of pillows is knocked over: "You will never get rid of me, I will make you miss all kinds of fun, ha ha ha. Oh, no, you knocked me over, help!"

ANOTHER LOOK AT CHICKEN LITTLE

Consider how an empathic second chicken might have talked to Chicken Little about the sky falling on her head, in order to lower her anxiety and boost her confidence:

> "Hey, Chicken Little, you look really scared."
>
> "Yes, the sky is falling, the sky is falling!"
>
> "Wow, that does sound scary. I'd be scared too if I thought the sky was falling. What got you so scared?"
>
> "Something fell on my head. It must have been a piece of the sky. The sky is falling!"
>
> "I can see that idea really has you frightened. It looks like your wings and feathers are trembling."
>
> "And my beak is chattering too."
>
> "I can hear that. That's exactly what happens when little chickens get scared. Can you look in my eyes and see whether I'm scared or not?"
>
> "You don't look scared, but that's because you didn't feel the sky fall on your head!"
>
> "You're right, I'm not so scared about that, and you're right that I didn't have anything fall on my head. I can see you're still pretty worried, though. I wonder if we

could take a few deep breaths together and then maybe we can look around to see if we can find what fell onto your head."

"I don't know about any deep breaths, but that's a good idea to find the piece of the sky. I think it was over here. All I see is this acorn. It must have fallen from that oak tree way up there."

"I think if something fell from so high onto my head, I would think it was the sky falling. Because fear can make little things seem really big, can't it?"

"It was just this tiny acorn. I'm so stupid."

"Not at all. I think anyone might have gotten scared by that."

"Really? I can't wait to show Lucy Goosey and Turkey Lurkey this acorn, and tell them that I thought it was the sky falling!"

"Maybe you can all play The Sky Is Falling game! Hey, before you go see your friends, I want to tell you that I admired how even though you were scared, you stopped to think about what was happening, and then you told yourself everything's okay once you saw it was an acorn."

"Yeah, I did! Maybe someone will write a book about me someday."

CHAPTER THREE

Relaxation and Roughhousing:
Anxiety and the Body

When I relax I get a warm feeling in my solar plexus.
—A ten-year-old girl

INTO-BODY EXPERIENCES

Anxiety throws the body off balance. Anxious children may be fidgety, restless, jumpy, hyperactive, clumsy, awkward, physically timid, stiff, or stilted. They may be preoccupied with aches, pains, or physical sensations of panic: "I can't breathe! My stomach hurts." Sometimes people get so anxious that they have the sensation of leaving their bodies. Instead of these out-of-body experiences, the playful parenting approach helps children tune in to their bodies. Into-body experiences are the opposite of anxiety.

The Security System is responsible for the body's anxiety symptoms and for relaxation. The alarm overactivates the bodily functions we need for *fight-flight-or-freeze* responses. Our heart rate goes up and our muscles tense. At the same time, the alarm shuts down other bodily functions not needed immediately for fight-flight-freeze. Relaxation, digestion, and sleep can wait until a crisis passes. For example, salivation is one of those things that can wait, so anxiety often results in a dry mouth. Digestion can wait too, but not forever, which is why anxiety is commonly related to stomachaches, diarrhea, and nausea. The all-clear signal is responsible for a return to relaxation. No all clear means chronic stress, which keeps the body in crisis mode for way too long.

We often feel anxiety in our gut, chest, throat, skin, or muscles. This impact on the body is important even if your child's anxiety is mostly ruminating thoughts or pessimistic beliefs. That's because bodies, thoughts, and emotions are so intertwined that they can't really be separated. A scary thought changes the flow of blood in the body, making hands and feet cold because all the blood is going to the running and fighting muscles. Slow breathing changes the experience of a scary thought, taking away its power to frighten. Drawing a picture of a fear is a physical act that turns an abstract thought into an artistic expression, which can transform the fear.

Take a few minutes to tune in to your own body. Slowly scan your sensations from head to toe. What did you notice? If you didn't notice anything, go back and take more time. Scan more slowly. How often do you slow down your busy life? Do you get enough rest or sleep? When was the last time you paid attention to your own breathing? Do you have muscles that are twisted into knots? As you increase your awareness of your own body, you will be better able to help your child's anxiety. If you have high anxiety, you will probably want to try the ideas in this chapter yourself, or establish some of them as everyday activities to do together as a family. Don't be alarmed if these ideas are harder in practice than they seem on paper. Anxious people tend to have a lot of resistance to relaxation and other ways to reduce stress and worry. Later in this chapter I will present some ideas for overcoming that resistance.

THE FEAR-O-METER

A mother sent me a picture of a drawing she made with her son. Labeled the Fear-O-Meter, it was shaped like a thermometer, with a scale from one to ten. One was marked "piece of cake," six was "getting tough," and ten was "out of control!" I use some version of a scale like this whenever I work with an anxious child (or adult). Sometimes the scale is from zero to one hundred, and sometimes it has no numbers at all. Instead of numbers, there might be faces representing "just a twinge" and "about to explode," or a color code from green to red. For children who don't understand the idea of a step-by-step scale, you can use hand gestures to signify low and high distress or big and small distress.

In the language of behavior therapy, this type of scale is called a SUDS, which stands for *subjective units of distress scale,* but I like to have children name the scale themselves. SUDS are subjective because they capture a person's inner experience. When an airplane hits some turbulence, I might be at eight, but the person next to me might barely be at two. When I am at eight I might hyperventilate and break into a cold sweat. Someone else might experience those symptoms at five. It's highly individual, and that is what makes it a powerful tool. I have seen many parents try to argue with their children about their Fear-O-Meter number. Don't! It's the *child's* subjective experience that counts.

Notice that the "D" in SUDS stands for "distress" instead of a more specific word such as "fear" or "anxiety." This is deliberate. It gives children the chance to define their experience for themselves. Some children prefer to link their scale to a specific emotion, like the Fear-O-Meter. Others use a high number on the scale to refer to any strong unpleasant feeling, such as worry, anger, upset, or panic. The low end of the scale is also deliberately vague. Low distress can mean complete calm, total relaxation, or happiness. The simple act of creating a Fear-O-Meter or SUDS together can help you and your child find a good way to talk about anxiety, worry, and fear. Let your child take the lead in naming the scale and labeling the points.

What's Your Number? is the simplest way to use the SUDS to lower anxiety. Once you have the scale ready, just ask children to rate their current level of distress. It's that easy. Even if the number is high, the act of searching inside for the answer to that question helps reset the Security System. When a person is anxious, the alert and alarm functions are highly active, while the rest of the brain isn't doing much. Assignment of a number on the Fear-O-Meter activates different pathways of the brain, and that helps turn down the alarm.

Identifying the number on the scale is just the beginning. As children activate more of their brain they can lower their anxiety even more. That happens when children describe a feeling in detail, name it, or draw a picture of it. Unfortunately, it's hard to think when you're anxious. Fortunately, it's hard to stay anxious when you engage in certain types of thinking, such as numbers and creativity (unless, of course, you have math or art anxiety!). In most people, numbers and creativity flow through different pathways of the brain than anxiety does. Therefore, when we activate numerical or creative thinking, we lessen the hold of anxiety. Activation of the nonanxious brain can calm the alarm and boost the all-clear signal.

Parents often ask anxious children, "How do you feel?" or "What's the matter?" But children may not be ready to put their feelings into words. Try asking first, "What's your number right now?" Parents often tell anxious children to calm down. But that can feel like a criticism. Instead, try saying, "Let's see if we can get that number down to where you want it to be."

A conversation about the SUDS number can also prevent unpleasant arguments. Many parents tell their children, "You are anxious or stressed." The goal is to raise the child's awareness, but it can backfire when the child retorts: "You don't know what you're talking about!" Instead, try it this way: "Hey, I just noticed my number is getting up around five or six. What's yours?" If the child's number is high you can begin a good conversation about bringing it down, with no arguments. If their number is low you can express genuine curiosity: "That's so funny, I would have guessed it was higher. Do you want to know what I saw that made me guess that?"

The Fear-O-Meter or SUDS is a useful way to measure the effectiveness of any antianxiety technique. A drop from eight to six on a ten-point scale is a tangible achievement, which gives children confidence that they can lower it even further. The goal is movement down the scale—don't worry if it moves slowly. I remember one girl who announced proudly that she had lowered her distress from 97 to 96¾! Remember that your child "owns" the scale. If your daughter says she is at ten, don't say, "You can't be at ten, ten is a complete meltdown, you must be at seven." If your son says he is at ten million, just take that number as the upper end of the scale: "Wow, ten million! That is *enormous*. I wonder if you can lower it to nine million nine hundred ninety-nine thousand nine hundred and ninety-nine?"

Take some time to create your own family version of the Fear-O-Meter with your child. You will use it for many of the activities that follow in this chapter and other chapters as well.

RELAXATION

Once you have developed your own SUDS or Fear-O-Meter scale, it is time to apply it to relaxation and stress reduction. The scale gives immediate feedback as to whether the techniques are working—did the number go down? The scale also guides you to the right techniques, because the top of the scale requires different strategies from the middle. Marsha Linehan, the psychologist who developed Dialectical Behavior Therapy, notes for example that warm water and soft music are good for deep relaxation, while cold water and loud music are more effective in a crisis.

For simplicity I will use the one-to-ten scale, but you can adapt it to whatever personal scale you and your child create. The high end of the scale—roughly the eight-to-ten range—is the area of crisis, panic, and extreme anxiety. Children at this level of distress need immediate relief. The middle range— roughly from three to eight—includes techniques for lowering stress, self-soothing, grounding, and centering. Most of the work of resetting the Security System happens in this middle range. The low end of the scale—below three—is the zone of deep relaxation and tension release.

Eight to Ten

For extremely anxious children—at eight to ten on the SUDS— physical comfort is usually best. Talk less and cuddle more. At this level of distress words may even interfere with soothing. Try rocking, humming, or gentle massage. You may have to experiment to find the right type of contact to provide the most comfort. Let children know you are there, and that you will not judge or criticize what they are feeling. Some children become agitated when you get too close. Step a few feet away but still send love and affection. Back in the 1960s we called it "sending good vibes."

Shaking on Purpose is a good technique for children who freeze or collapse when they are very high on the scale. Encourage them to scream, jump up and down, and make their whole bodies shake. Add exaggerated scared noises, from a high-pitched eek to a low-pitched moan. It seems a bit odd, but high anxiety can shut off a child's natural expression of fear. Shaking on Purpose lets out some of these blocked feelings in a safe way, which can bring down the anxiety level quickly. Some children are embarrassed to make noise and tremble or shake, so it helps to do it with them (or do it first to get them laughing at you). As always, make sure they don't feel teased.

Children who are already screaming, sweating, crying, or shaking in terror don't need any help expressing themselves. They are spontaneously releasing their overloaded feelings. I call it Getting Unscared. It isn't always pleasant, but it is healthy. These children need your *calm, loving presence* nearby so they can slowly recover a sense of ease. It can be quite uncomfortable to listen to a child's intense feelings without trying to stop them, especially if no one ever listened to your feelings when you were young. Try not to hush children when they are getting unscared. Don't tell them that the situation is too small for such big feelings. They are communicating something important. There is no need to rush these children to "use their words," because they are already experiencing emotion on a more direct level than language. If they have a problem you can easily solve, they will tell you; you don't have to pressure them with "What's the matter, what's the matter, what's the matter?"

Ice-Cold Water can be great for the panic end of the Fear-O-

Meter scale. If you plunge your head or body in very cold water, your heart rate slows. Of course, always ask children's permission before dunking them in cold water! You can get a pretty good effect by splashing ice water on your face or temples. The benefit lasts just a few minutes, but that often lowers the panic enough to open the door for other techniques.

My favorite panic-attack interrupter—The Reminder—might surprise you, because it is so simple. Just write on a piece of paper, *I'm having a panic attack. It's not life threatening. It will pass.* Keep this paper in your pocket, and when you feel a panic attack coming on, take the paper out and read it to yourself a few times. The words on the paper are a gentle reminder that your life is not in danger, no matter what it feels like, and that anxiety always passes eventually. Panic leads people to believe that the terrible feeling will never end and might kill them. One girl who used this piece of paper called it "my panic-attack counterattack."

Three to Eight

The middle range of the Fear-O-Meter—roughly from three to eight on the scale—is where real change happens for anxious children. Since they aren't in extreme crisis or panic mode they can absorb the lessons of relaxation. Each time they lower their distress from eight to three they reset their whole Security System. The simplest method is Counting Down. Ask children for their number on the scale, then have them count slowly from that number down to one. When they are done, ask for the new number. One countdown rarely provides full relief, but it almost always brings the number down a little. Repeat the countdowns until they become boring or you get down to three.

There are numerous variations of Counting Down. You can

count while you visualize walking down a staircase. You can count out loud or silently, with your eyes open or closed. You can add words between each number, "Seven, deeper and deeper relaxed, six, deeper and deeper relaxed, five, deeper and deeper relaxed . . ."

Some mid-range techniques are more physical. Vigorous Exercise is one of the most widely used and most effective anxiety reduction techniques. The key to using exercise for anxiety is to work the body very hard in a rhythmic activity such as running or jumping jacks. As one mom said, "I took my daughter out to run the other day when she was too keyed up to eat her dinner. She liked the challenge and ran really fast. It also helped me relax!" Vigorous physical activity that takes more brainpower—such as obstacle courses or challenging yoga poses—can also be good for lowering anxiety.

Rhythmic activities that aren't vigorous, such as pouring water or sand back and forth between containers, can be quite relaxing as well. Preschool teachers know that pouring is a fun activity that teaches children about volume and gravity while also promoting calmness and self-regulation.

The Bounce is when you stand and bounce gently up and down on the balls of your feet. Your heels rise and fall, never quite touching the ground. Add a little shake of your hands, as if you are shaking water off them. Just a few seconds of this can provide a good amount of anxiety relief. Note that some children spontaneously flap their hands when they are anxious or excited, and that's not the same thing. The relaxation benefit comes from doing it on purpose.

Numerous yoga poses promote relaxation. I'll describe a few that are especially easy for children to learn and to use. Mountain is a simple standing pose, arms by your sides, with back straight. Look straight ahead or close your eyes, and imagine the crown of your head lifting upward, as your feet remain firmly planted. Try it in shoes and barefoot, standing on different surfaces, to increase the awareness of solid ground under your feet, which is often missing in anxious children. Just a few deep breaths in this posture can provide a strong sense of feeling "grounded."

The Challenge is a variation of Mountain. While your child is standing in Mountain pose, tell her you are going to give her a little push against her side. (Don't push too hard!) The first time, ask her to think about something that makes her anxious, then push. You will both notice that she is easily pushed off balance. Next have her think about being a mountain, connected to the bedrock of the earth. Have her think about her own inner strengths and resources. Give the same push, and see if she stays steady this time, swaying a little but not losing her balance. This game teaches children the difference in their bodies between the off-balance feeling of anxiety and the power of being "centered." Another variation is for you to be the mountain, while your child tries to be a storm or wind to knock you over. Hold your ground for a while, then fall over in a funny way so you can start the game again.

Some children aren't interested in stillness. If your child always has to be on the move, try OBOM (One Breath One Movement), which can be done with a variety of movements. The idea is to match each motion to an inhale or an exhale. For example, you might start in a high push-up position, exhale into a Downward Dog pose (it looks like an upside-down V), then inhale back to high push-up position. Move back and forth between these positions as you inhale and exhale a few times—it gets tiring faster than you might think. You can do OBOM with Mountain, raising your arms high overhead on inhale, lowering them slowly to your sides on exhale. For neck tension or headaches you can slowly turn your head to one side on inhale, return to center on exhale, and turn to the other side on the next inhale. Do the same thing nodding your head yes, and then tilting your ear toward each shoulder.

Three to Minus Three

After I introduce the one-to-ten number scale to children, I surprise them by saying that there are ways to lower their number to *negative three*. These are techniques for deep relaxation. For children who don't understand negative numbers I say, "Imagine being as relaxed as you can be. Now imagine being *even more* relaxed than that." Many anxious children have never experienced that level of relaxation. Perhaps you never have either.

Minus three is *very relaxed*. You probably don't want your child to be below zero very often—certainly not when it is time to get dressed in the morning or during a dance recital. But all children benefit from the ability to lower their number to minus three on the scale when they choose. Spending time in the negative numbers resets the Security System in a powerful way. Keep in mind, however, that if your child is at five or eight, they will not be able to instantly practice a deep relaxation technique.

There are many methods of Deep Relaxation. Experiment with a variety of techniques, some sensory (a warm bath, gentle music, massage), some using imagination (guided visualizations), and some physical (deep breathing). Remember that your children may relax differently than you. Deep relaxation takes practice and repetition. Children who relax regularly find that they don't get highly distressed as often, and when they do, they can calm themselves faster.

Progressive Muscle Relaxation is based on the idea that you can't use willpower to force muscles to relax, but you can easily will them to tense more. Ironically, this idea was popularized in a book called *You Must Relax!* Like many deep relaxation techniques, this takes some time to do fully, anywhere from fifteen minutes to an hour. However, once you have done it several times, you can use a two-minute version that provides a good amount of anxiety relief.

Start with your right hand. Tense it as tightly as you can into a fist for a slow count to five. Isolate the muscles so that only that fist is tightened, not your neck or face. Now slowly release the tension as you count backward from five. Count backward from five once again, releasing even more tension. Your hand will probably be less tense than it was when you started. It's as if deliberately tensing teaches muscles how to let go. Repeat the sequence with your left hand, then with every muscle group in your body that you can isolate. It can be fun to find muscles that you don't usually think of, such as scrunching up your whole face before you relax it, or opening your eyes wide without moving any other muscles on your face.

My Hands Are Heavy and Warm is even simpler. Get comfortable, close your eyes, and repeat silently to yourself, "My hands are heavy and warm." You can warm a young child's hands in yours while you say the words out loud. You can just keep saying that phrase, or you can alternate it with "My feet are heavy and warm." Most people feel a heavy, warm, or tingly feeling after just a couple of minutes, while fifteen to thirty minutes usually brings very deep relaxation. That feeling is the result of increased blood flow to the extremities, which means that there is less blood in the "anxiety centers" of the gut, chest, and long muscles. I think it works because our minds and bodies are completely intertwined.

Guided Visualization is another simple technique for deep relaxation, where you paint a relaxing picture with words while your child vividly imagines being in that safe place. I like to develop the story collaboratively with children. Would they like to imagine lying on the beach, walking in the woods, or floating on a river? Guided visualizations often include walking down steps or into a cave to symbolize deepening relaxation.

Some children like stories at bedtime that begin as adventures and then ease into calm tranquility. One mother, Maude, starts the bedtime routine by having her daughter pretend to fly. She might be a dragon, a kite, or a fairy. Maude takes elements from her daughter's story and turns them into visualizations for relaxation. A lake, for example, becomes a place where all worries wash away. Bedtime is a perfect time for strategies that take your child below zero on the distress scale.

Anxious children may not believe it is possible to *choose* to relax. They tend to believe that they are stuck feeling their anxiety. With these techniques they can learn to take charge of their emotional states. Repeatedly moving down the number scale makes the alarm less sensitive and the all-clear signal stronger.

I like to teach children several techniques across the scale, and then let them pick a couple of favorites to practice frequently. It's good to choose some that take just a few seconds and some that are intensive, and to practice them during calm times as well as anxious ones. That helps the new skills become automatic, so children can use them even when they are anxious and have trouble remembering what they know.

THE BREATH: LESSONS IN ACCEPTANCE AND CHANGE

Often the best way to *change* our anxious bodies is to *accept* what is happening inside us. This section contains techniques based on acceptance—noticing and allowing whatever is going on in our bodies—as well as techniques based on deliberately creating a change.

The best place to start an exploration of acceptance and change is with the breath, because it's always there with us. We usually breathe without any conscious awareness. That's good, because we need our brainpower for more interesting matters. When we are anxious, anxiety takes charge of our breathing. That's a problem, because anxious breathing (fast, shallow, or holding the breath) keeps the alarm activated and interferes with the all-clear signal.

We can become aware of our breathing, and that can be good too. We might use that awareness to notice the breathing just as it is, moment-by-moment. Or we can change our breathing on purpose, making it deeper and slower, or breathing in through the nose and out through the mouth. Both actions— acceptance and change—have profound effects on our bodies, our mood, and our thinking. When our nonanxious mind takes charge of the breath, we are better able to turn off the alarm and signal the all clear. Psychologist Margaret Wehrenberg explains that both noticing one's breathing and breathing deeper activate different pathways of the brain than shallow respiration.

Even though our breathing is always with us, most of us don't know much about it. Breath Awareness can be a fun way for you and your child to be scientists or detectives getting to know how anxiety and the Security System operate. Take some time to study your breathing, when you are calm and when you are anxious. Do you gasp, gulp, or hold your breath? Is your breathing shallow or deep, fast or slow, steady or choppy? Is your inhale or exhale longer? What parts of your body move as you breathe? Just a few breaths can provide a lot of information. That's fortunate, because most children don't like to sit still for long periods of mindfulness meditation.

If your child is open to watching the breath for a longer period, maybe ten or fifteen minutes, sit next to each other in a comfortable position, with eyes open or closed, and start to focus on the breathing. Notice the in-and-out flow, the changing sensations at the tips of your nostrils, the movement of your chest and belly, and so on. Just notice, with no effort to change it. It may change on its own as you notice it, or it may not. Your mind will certainly wander; that's completely normal. As soon as you realize you've wandered, gently turn your attention back to your breathing. That's all there is to it—at least to get started. Some people study mindfulness for years, so don't confuse this very brief introduction with a complete course.

Mindfulness of your breathing, without trying to change it, is one way to relax. Directly controlling your breathing is another way. The possibilities are endless. Three Deep Breaths is self-explanatory: "Let's take three deep breaths!" If your child hyperventilates, say, "Let's take three *slow* deep breaths." Dragon Breath adds make-believe: Take a big dragon breath in through your nose—sniffing the air for anyone trying to steal your gold—then open your mouth as wide as you can and exhale like you are blowing fire. Pizza Breath is a similar idea: Hold your hand flat in front of you as if holding a slice of pizza. Inhale through your nose (smell your pizza), then blow through your mouth (cool your pizza). A number of other breathing techniques are included at the end of this chapter.

THE ANXIOUS BODY FROM HEAD TO TOE

Stomachaches and headaches are common childhood anxiety symptoms, but anxiety can affect every part of the body. Anxiety tends to overly activate certain parts of the body and suppress others. Some areas become tense; others get hot or cold depending on where the blood flows. Anxiety in the body can also feel like a blockage, numbness, or hollowness.

The gut, chest, and throat. The gut has so many nerve cells that they are considered a separate nervous system, the *enteric nervous system*. I think that must be why we talk about "gut instincts," and we decide how we feel about something by doing a "gut check." Many anxious feelings are located in the gut. We might feel butterflies from light anxiety, a stomachache from moderate anxiety, and a churning or burning feeling from high anxiety. One way to soothe these uncomfortable feelings is to place your hand below your belly button and breathe deeply so that your hand rises and falls with each breath.

The chest and throat are also common locations for anxiety and tension to gather. Perhaps there is a physical reason, or perhaps it represents the symbolism of heartache, or not being able to breathe or speak. In the gut, chest, and throat, anxiety often feels stuck, caught, or blocked.

One way to get that blocked feeling unstuck is to Give It a Voice. Ask your child, "Imagine that the feeling in your belly (or chest or throat) has a voice. What does it sound like? Can you make that sound? Does it have words? What would it say?" There may only be sounds, and no words. Most relaxation techniques aim to quiet those feelings, but sometimes we just need to get them out.

The throat and vocal cords are closely linked to anxiety, especially in children who stammer or stutter. Some anxious children speak in a whisper—or don't speak at all. I try my hardest to encourage all these children to Be Loud. It sounds quite simple, but can be very hard for some anxious children. Let them scream, sing, roar, shout for help, or say, "Eek!" Since anxious children often avoid expressing themselves in a loud or angry voice, you may need to be a role model for them by doing it first. It's okay if they laugh at you!

The five senses. Many anxious children say, "People tell me I think too much." I think this means that they aren't firmly grounded in the present moment, but instead are preoccupied with thoughts about the past or the future: *We almost crashed! What if lightning hits?* The five senses are direct pathways to the present moment. Be Here Now is just noticing and accepting whatever greets your senses right this moment, without trying to change those sensations. It's named after a book written by the spiritual leader Ram Dass. Notice your feet on the floor, or your bottom on the chair, and the feel of clothes, furniture, or air on your skin. What do you see, hear, smell, feel, taste *right this moment*? Close your eyes and see if that changes how you take in things from your other senses. Children may be able to focus on this exercise for only a few seconds, but try it yourself for longer. One fun way to practice mindfulness of the senses is to eat one raisin or one section of an orange so slowly that it takes you several minutes.

Most people have a habit of jumping from experiencing sensations to telling a story about those sensations. For example, you may sense being cold, but then you tell yourself, "I am too cold, I can't stand it," or "I'll never be warm again." Those added-on thoughts turn ordinary sensations into anxiety triggers. Now you are unbearably cold and terribly anxious about it. Be Here Now counteracts that by keeping attention on the actual sensory experience.

Additional senses. We receive information from the outside world through sight, smell, hearing, vision, and touch. But we also have senses that give us information about our inner world. We have a *kinesthetic sense* that tells us about muscle tension. *Proprioception* tells us the position of our joints. The *vestibular sense* gives us our position in regard to gravity and velocity. These senses are closely connected to the Security System's overall feeling of safety or danger. Think about the sudden anxiety you feel if you are suddenly and unexpectedly falling.

Super Slo-Mo develops awareness of these inner sensations. Move in slow motion with your child, moving all parts of the body in every possible direction. Switch to Super Fast Motion for a few seconds—jump up and down and shake all over—then back to slow motion. As you play Super Slo-Mo with your child, you can bump into each other safely or engage in friendly mock combat, which increases the fun and the anxiety-reduction value of the game.

Some children fear the physical sensations of fear. *If I'm breathing fast and my heart is pounding there must be terrible danger.* A slight anxiety becomes a full-blown panic episode. One solution is to deliberately create those sensations—in a safe way—in order to get used to them. I call it Roller Coaster, because some people ride roller coasters in order to feel the very same sensations that anxious people avoid. Roller Coaster works by creating the physical symptoms of panic in a controlled setting, so your brain can see that they are just normal reactions, nothing to worry about. You can re-create specific sensations that are common in extreme anxiety if you spin in a swivel chair, breathe through a skinny plastic straw, hold your breath for as long as you can, do very hard exercise—or ride a roller coaster. Be sure that the child is in control of the experience and can stop at any time.

The skin. The skin is our largest organ and the gateway to the healing power of touch. Children can be so anxious that they can't pay attention to our words. Yet they can still sense our safe and loving touch. Some children become more agitated from touch. If so, try holding your hand a few inches or a few feet from their skin, as if you are touching a force field around the body. Usually there is some distance where a sensitive child can feel "touched" without feeling overloaded. You can even give a pretend massage or gentle pat from that distance.

Touch is crucial for security from the time we are born and throughout our lives. During World War II, for example, Mary Ainsworth discovered that children in orphanages who were fed and changed didn't thrive unless they were also held and cuddled. We don't always have someone nearby to give us a hug, but we can always give ourselves one! Francine Shapiro, the psychologist who developed EMDR therapy (eye movement desensitization and reprocessing), describes the Butterfly Hug: Cross your arms in front of you and pat your shoulders, alternating right- and left-handed pats. You can also alternate gentle squeezes of each shoulder. Shapiro has found that the right-left alternation reduces anxiety and helps recovery from trauma by activating both sides of the brain. Butterfly Hug works best if you get more of your brain involved by visualizing a safe place or silently repeating a word or phrase that represents security (such as "I'm safe" or "peace").

Comforting touch communicates *You are safe, you are loved, everything is all right.* Even though children grow up and seem too big to be in your lap, they still need to cuddle. Everyone does. Oxytocin—a substance the body releases during breastfeeding, hugging, roughhousing, and sex—has been nicknamed "the cuddle chemical." Not all cuddles are created equal when it comes to anxious children. One mom described that it took her years to figure out that a soft squeeze on the shoulder comforted her son, while a full hug made him more anxious.

The motor system. Our bodies were designed to move freely, but anxiety often freezes us up or makes us move in highly rigid and repetitive ways. Many forms of movement can help us shift from anxiety to calmness, such as The Antsy Pants Dance, in which you move your hands and feet wildly and shake your whole body. Some children prefer a Story Dance, where you move your bodies to act out an adventure, such as tiptoeing through a forest, swimming across a stream, chasing a rabbit, and dancing with a bear. Vigorous exercise also activates the motor system. I like to encourage anxious children to take up as much space as they can, spreading out their arms and standing on tiptoes, because they often try to make themselves small and inconspicuous.

Drawing a picture of one's fear is a powerful symbolic act—it gets a scary image out of your head. It's also effective because the simple physical act of drawing engages the body and the creative mind. For older children, writing in a journal can serve the same purpose.

Body language. The psychologist and trauma expert Peter Levine describes two different body languages of anxiety, one for the fight/flight state and one for the freeze state. In fight/flight the child has tight muscles, especially visible in the neck and shoulders. You will see jitteriness, jumpy eye movements, accelerated heart rate, enlarged pupils, shallow uneven breathing, and pale skin. The child may report having cold hands and cold sweat. In the immobilized condition you will notice a slumped posture, staring into space with smaller pupils, and very slow breathing and heart rate. The skin can be "a pasty sickly white or even gray."

In general, our task is to soothe the alarmed child who is stuck in fight/flight, and to activate the immobilized child who is frozen in fear. For soothing, use your most comforting voice and loving embrace, and suggest that your child use any of the more gentle relaxation methods, such as counting or slow breathing. When the body language shows shutdown or immobilization, choose methods that involve playful contact, movement, and loudness.

Fidgeting and nervous habits. Anxious children fidget. They have nervous habits such as nail biting, tapping, or constant movement. Many parents treat fidgeting as a bad habit and try to break it with rewards, punishments, or humiliation. These efforts at behavior modification usually end in failure, frustration, and shame, because fidgeting and nervous habits are extremely hard to change. Yet we don't want to just ignore these signs of anxiety.

All of the relaxation and body-focused techniques in this chapter will decrease fidgeting over time, but you may want to address it directly. Before you do, be sure to spend some time reflecting or talking with a friend about what your child's habit stirs up in you. Do you get annoyed, embarrassed, angry, or frustrated? Does the behavior or your reaction to it remind you of anything from your own childhood? It is quite important to get these thoughts, feelings, and memories out of your head before you try to help your child; otherwise your "helping" may trigger shame and humiliation.

Some fidgeting is simply excess energy, which is helped by increased exercise and more outlets for creative self-expression, such as art, writing, or acting out stories. Whenever you desire a child to sit still—such as for homework or church—let them run around or do jumping jacks first. Many classroom teachers and occupational therapists have discovered that some children concentrate better if they have a squishy ball in their hands to squeeze or can sit on a large ball instead of a chair.

Some fidgety behaviors are an attempt at self-comfort. These usually involve rocking, thumb sucking, or some other rhythmic activity. When you see this, increase the amount of cuddling time you spend with your children, even if they are older. Give children a massage, rock them in your arms, or snuggle them in your lap. If possible, make some gentle eye contact with children while they are engaged in their self-comfort, instead of forcing them to stop.

I believe that most nervous habits and movements are the mind's way of avoiding an unwanted or unpleasant emotion. You can get to the heart of that blocked emotion if you put your hand very gently on your daughter's hand as she bites her nails or sucks her thumb. Or place a hand gently on your son's jittering leg. Your job is to convey love and safety, not judgment or criticism: *You don't have to bury your feelings with this habit, because I am here to support you.* You can gently tug on a pacifier—not enough to pull it out but enough so that your child feels the tug. It is crucial that children feel your love and acceptance when you try this method, because you are asking them to uncover and express emotions that they have buried deep inside themselves. They can let those emotions out only if they feel very safe. If you have provided enough safety by being sure not to humiliate or shame them for having their nervous habit, then your gentle hand can bring a healing flow of tears or an angry outburst that reveals the feelings they have been suppressing with their habit.

Fidgeting and repetitive movements may also be signs that children are struggling with sensory processing problems, especially oversensitivity. They may be overwhelmed by sensory information—such as not being able to tolerate scratchy clothes or loud noises—and they use self-stimulating movements to calm down their nervous systems and cope with their environment. If you see your child reacting anxiously to certain sounds, touch, or sensations, an OT (occupational therapist) can often help tremendously. There are also many good books on sensory integration.

Roughhousing, or rough-and-tumble play, is the ultimate activity for anxious children because it gets them moving, builds bodily awareness, maximizes playful touch, strengthens relationships, and unleashes the "creative life force." That's my term for the exuberant childhood energy that gets blocked by anxiety. If children aren't used to roughhousing it can get a bit rowdy the first few times you try it, but that will pass as they reclaim their innate sense of physical confidence and power.

Siblings and friends can have fun roughhousing, but the best roughhousing play for anxiety is between parent and child. That builds a strong connection between you, which is crucial for security. Be sure to start and end every playful wrestling match or pillow fight with a hug or a high-five. Look for roughhousing games that build children's confidence, use their whole bodies, and let them go "all out," pushing you as hard as they can or pinning you to the floor while you playfully beg for mercy. Put up resistance to match the amount of energy they put out, but let them win in the end (until they ask you to try your hardest so they can test out how strong they really are). Avoid tickling, which can increase anxiety by making one's own body feel out of control.

There are endless variations on roughhousing games, and most of them are excellent for anxious children and their parents. Dr. Anthony DeBenedet and I spell out dozens of them in our book, *The Art of Roughhousing*, so I'll present just a few here. Anthony says that the only thing that really calms his daughters is physical play, especially a game they invented called Sleeping Bat. Start out face-to-face with your child, holding hands. Have your child climb up your legs and torso—keeping her head near your feet—until she is hanging upside down with her feet tucked under your armpits. Maybe it is all the blood flow to the head, or maybe it is the different perspective on the world, but hanging upside down like this can change a child's mood quickly.

One of my favorite roughhousing games for anxious children is Force-Field Hands. Start face-to-face with your child; you may need to be on your knees. Bend your elbows and hold out your palms so that they are almost touching your child's palms. Hold your hands close, but not quite touching, until you both start to feel a tingly or warm sensation in your hands. Then begin to "push" each other gently, using just that "force-field" sensation between your hands, rather than actual contact. You have to tune in to each other very deeply with this game, which makes it great for parent-child bonding. With practice, even young children can play.

You can shift from Force-Field Hands to Pushing Hands, in which your palms touch. As you push against each other, keep your elbows bent and gradually push harder and harder. If you exactly match your child's strength neither person will move or you will both move in a slow circle. Increase the intensity to-gether, noticing how much force you can use without anyone get-ting hurt or falling over. You can then add an element of competition, trying to push the other person off the mat or out of the room. Avoid sudden shoves and make it as much a dance as a competition. Many parents who have learned Pushing Hands say that their children start to ask for it as a way to calm them-selves when they are agitated.

Chase and Miss is a fun way for younger children to boost their confidence while building a strong connection with you. Chase after them and miss at the last minute. It works even bet-ter if you fall on the floor dramatically and make funny boasts: "Next time you will never get away!" Of course, next time they get away again, until they "let" you catch them.

Older children gain confidence by wrestling with you. Match their strength with your strength, so they have to work hard but don't feel overwhelmed or overpowered. Let them win after they have worked for it. Eventually they will ask you to wrestle your hardest, so they can discover how strong they are. Remember that the purpose of this wrestling is not to toughen a child up, but to instill confidence and security. If you never wrestled like this as a child or are afraid of it, try it anyway! Keep each wres-tling bout short, just thirty seconds or so, with a break before the next round. If you wrestled fiercely with your brothers or friends when you were young, make sure not to get too competitive with your child. I recommend this kind of roughhousing for every family, but it has a special impact on anxious children, boosting their confidence and their feelings of security.

OVERCOMING RESISTANCE TO RELAXATION

Reading this chapter won't reduce your anxiety. Reading it out loud to your children won't reduce their anxiety. I wish it would! Just reading about relaxation and play won't activate the parts of the brain useful for anxiety reduction. *You and your children have to actually do the techniques.* Practice them. Give them a fair trial. That's not easy, of course. Anxious children are famous for rejecting ideas without trying them, based on their IPMA (instant pessimistic mental assessment): "That won't work!"

I distrust "simple" relaxation strategies that don't acknowledge it's never simple to encourage an anxious child to try something new. Parents feel inadequate and children feel annoyed, but it isn't anyone's fault—it's just the nature of anxiety to resist relaxation and other anxiety-reduction methods.

It may seem odd that some people resist relaxation when they are anxious, but it's quite common. Christina Luberto, a doctoral student at the University of Cincinnati, has even developed a psychological test for sensitivity to relaxation. When I told my sister Diane that I was collecting relaxation techniques, she said, "I can't help you. I get nervous if I start to get too relaxed."

You may have experienced that resistance within yourself, or heard it from your child. I think it comes from a basic conflict of interest between the alarm and all-clear signals of the Security System. Both parts of the system try to keep us safe and secure, but they have very different methods. The alarm thinks that safety comes from being revved up, ready for danger, while the all clear prefers to lie on the beach with a glass of lemonade. We've already seen that in anxious children the alarm demands the last word, so say goodbye to the lemonade on the beach.

If you know you are safe, but you still feel anxious, then you may welcome a chance to lower your anxiety. If you believe you are in danger, however, then it would be foolish to relax. You need to be prepared to act on a moment's notice. That's why some highly anxious children angrily reject suggestions to relax. Abe, the boy who was so afraid of thunderstorms, once said to his mother, "Three deep breaths are not going to stop us from being hit by lightning!"

Another reason some anxious children resist relaxation is that slowing down and letting go of tension can open the door to feelings that have been buried or shoved aside. I learned this the hard way. I used to recommend yoga or meditation to every anxious adult who came into my office. Too often, however, my clients came back the next session angry with me, or worried that something was seriously wrong with them. The yoga or meditation had resulted in a flood of scary or painful emotions, and they thought they were losing their minds.

I still recommend yoga and meditation, but I add a warning that a flood of emotions may result when they let down their guards and relax. With guidance, these extreme emotional states can be tolerated and even welcomed. Some anxious people have a scary flood of emotion as soon as they slow down their hyperactive pace of life and come face-to-face with feelings they were trying to avoid.

Traumatized children have a special reason to resist anything that increases bodily awareness. Abuse or injury can lead children to believe that they are not safe inside their own bodies. They may have had out-of-body or dissociative experiences in response to an overwhelming threat to their safety. "Leaving" their bodies was like built-in anesthesia for unbearable pain. The problem is that once they leave, once they conclude that their bodies are a source of pain, it can become very hard to come back fully into the body. This protects us from certain types of pain, but also shuts out the possibility of relaxation.

Keep this in mind as I describe ways to overcome a child's resistance to relaxation. *Don't push too hard.* Your child may have a valid reason to resist. If that's the case, use other approaches, especially increased empathy and lots of physical affection: "I can understand that it's too scary to relax. Can I sit with you or hold you so you don't have to be scared alone?" It's especially important not to push too hard against resistance when there has been a big trauma. When the body is linked to intense feelings of terror, children need close connection with you through cuddling and play before they can relax. Survivors of trauma need to build up safety and security before they can tune in to their bodies.

Most anxious children, however, just need a little push past their resistance. As you push, keep in mind four basic principles:

- Do it together
- Let your child be in charge
- Make it fun
- Avoid power struggles

Relaxing together breaks down resistance. It also has an added benefit—you probably need to relax as much as your child does. "*Let's* take some deep breaths" is much more effective than "*You* need to take some deep breaths." As one mother said, "Whenever my daughter needs to calm down, so do I! She's more likely to take a deep breath with me if she knows I'm actually doing it for myself and not just to get her to do it."

Many parents find that their children respond better when the child has ownership over the techniques. One young girl,

Lena, rejected all her mother's suggestions to relax until she took a yoga class at school. "My daughter learned in her yoga class that lying still on her back was good for when she was feeling upset. Since she loves her yoga teacher and has great memories of doing this pose with the teacher and her friends, I just remind her about that idea and (sometimes) she'll do it."

The next step to overcoming resistance is to make stress-reduction fun. It can even be so fun that children don't know they are relaxing! Brenda wanted to teach her children mindfulness—paying attention to and accepting the present moment. Anxiety takes us out of the fullness and richness of the here and now. But she had a hard time convincing four kids, aged five to eleven, to sit still and concentrate on their breathing. She had much more success with Candy Meditation. (It can be done with raisins, if you're not a fan of sweets.) "Have everyone in the family eat one M&M or other small candy. Once you've done that, everyone gets another piece of the same candy. This time, hold the candy in your mouth and slowly notice every detail: the size, shape, texture, and taste, and how those sensations change inside your mouth over time. Notice your thoughts: Do you have an urge to chew? Are you bored? Do you wish you had a whole bag of candy? Once everyone has eaten the second candy, we talk about what it was like, and how slowing down and paying attention can help you deal with things that upset or scare you, like teasing or a big dog. Telling my kids to be aware of their own breathing didn't work, but with the candy they learned that simply becoming aware of their own physical experience can take them out of their anxious mind enough to give them some relief."

Power struggles aren't very relaxing, especially power struggles over whether or not to relax! The best way to avoid them is to offer plenty of empathy and compassion first. Take some time to lower your own distress level and talk with a friend about your frustrations before you offer "helpful" suggestions. My friend Dustin doesn't ask his daughter anymore if she wants to relax with him, because she always said no. Instead, he just starts very visibly doing a relaxation exercise in the middle of the room, and often she joins in.

I recently watched an exasperated father—my friend Doug—try to calm down his seven-year-old son, Art, who was leaping around the room. Doug had just told me that he and his wife consulted a psychologist for some assistance with their son's anxiety and volatile emotions. Occasionally Art would "accidentally" knock into the seat where his baby sister was sleeping. I could see Doug struggling with how to handle the situation. He shouted at Art, "Think about your special quiet place!" Art kept leaping.

I could see Doug was ready to explode. I imagined he was thinking, *I tried the calm approach we learned from the therapist, and it didn't work. Time to scream and make a threat.* Doug was offering a great idea, but it was a technique suitable for a child at number three on the Wild-O-Meter, not eight or nine. The gap from wild leaping to peaceful tranquility is too big. I said to Doug, "I think it might be too big a step for Art from crashing into things to visualizing a special quiet place. I wonder if there are any steps in between." Doug was able to see an in-between step right away. He invited Art to play a rowdy game with him away from the sleeping baby—it involved Art showing off complicated flips and tumbles on a big mat. After Art did his flips he sat in Doug's lap and talked quietly with him until the baby woke up from her nap.

Babel-Um

Marilyn and her eight-year-old son, Connor, solved a very frustrating form of resistance. One of Connor's big fears was that something bad would happen to someone in his family. If his father was late coming home, Connor's anxiety would escalate to extreme levels. In our first few sessions together I shared a few relaxation ideas and Connor enjoyed doing them. The resistance began at home when Marilyn urged Connor to use the relaxation techniques he had learned. Connor refused, and insisted instead on talking about how many minutes late Dad was, what might have happened to him, and what would happen to the family if he died. The tension escalated. Now, in addition to Connor's anxiety, they were both angry and frustrated.

When we met again and I heard about this power struggle, I said to Connor, "You think the problem is *Dad's late* and your mom thinks the problem is *Connor is anxious*. Then you have a big argument about that, which is a brand-new problem." Connor thought about this and said, "Let's call it Babel-Um." He explained that the story of the Tower of Babel was about people speaking different languages, and he and his mother were speaking different languages to each other. The "Um" was because he often felt during these arguments that he didn't know how to say what he really wanted to say.

Now that they had a name for the problem, it was easier to solve. Either Marilyn or Connor would say, "Babel-Um!" and they would stop their argument and agree to speak the same language. Sometimes Marilyn would gently reassure Connor about his dad. Other times Connor practiced his favorite relaxation skill, which was My Hands Are Heavy and Warm. Or they did five minutes of each. They both said it didn't really matter which language they spoke, as long as they weren't caught in Babel-Um anymore.

"What's the point, it won't help." Is that a familiar phrase in your house? Hopelessness can sink in to children who feel anxious, and hopelessness brings even more reluctance to try something new. Whenever I hear "It won't help," I tell children one of my favorite jokes: At a funeral, during a moment of silence, a voice came from the back, "Give him some chicken soup! Give him some chicken soup!" Everyone looked around and saw that it was an elderly woman, sitting alone. No one knew what to do as she kept shouting, "Give him some chicken soup!" Finally, someone went to her and said gently, "But lady, it wouldn't help." She shrugged her shoulders and said, "It couldn't hurt!" I can't promise you or your child that any particular technique will help, but I believe they are all worth trying as an experiment.

CALM BODY, CALM MIND

Parents try very hard to engage children's thinking brains. We reason with them, talk to them, and explain things. We urge them to use their words because we know how smart our children are. But anxiety can't usually be solved with more thinking or more talk.

Like it or not, we have to deal with the physical body, because anxiety clouds the thinking brain. To alleviate some of the suffering of anxiety we need to provide affection and cuddling, increase playful physical contact, and help children practice breathing exercises and relaxation techniques.

If you managed to read through this chapter without stopping to actually do any of the games and activities, please go back and try some! Anxious children often reject relaxation techniques because the *idea* of the technique doesn't instantly relax them. Of course it doesn't! When your child says, "I already know it won't work," you will be more persuasive if you have tried it yourself. You and your child will discover that something profound happens when you actually get out of your head and into your breathing, out of anxiety and into awareness of your body, out of worry and into acceptance of your moment-to-moment experience.

ADDITIONAL BODY-BASED TECHNIQUES

Blow Out the Candle. A grandmother from England taught me this fun deep-breathing idea: "First we make a cozy place for us both to sit in a sea of cushions on the floor in front of the coffee table, then I light a candle in the middle of the table. We have to blow out the candle just by exhaling deeply. After these deep breaths we're ready to snuggle in our cozy nest and read a book." If you are worried about fire safety, you can use a feather and blow it off the table.

Hands-On Breathing helps children notice their breathing as it is, and also helps them deepen and slow it down. Put one hand on your chest and one hand just below your belly button. Notice how each hand moves as you breathe. Can you get the lower hand to move? Next, exert gentle pressure with your hands, pressing the breath out with each exhale then releasing the pressure to invite a deeper inhale. You can also place your hands on your side ribs, and try to breathe so that both hands move outward with each exhale. Most of us aren't aware that our lungs fill to the sides as well as to the front.

Solar (Plexus) Power. Place one hand in the center of your chest as you breathe. Imagine that your hand is sending warmth into the solar plexus (which after all was named because the muscle looks like the rays of the sun). Warmth in the solar plexus is a signal to the body to relax. This technique provides a powerful experience of "mind over body," as the thought of warmth creates actual warmth.

Warm Hands, Cool Heart is a way to shift excess energy away from the gut and chest where anxiety tends to get stuck. Since anxiety affects blood flow in the body, you can lower anxiety by deliberately changing the blood flow. When you rub your hands together briskly to warm them, or run warm water over them, they receive more blood. The mind interprets this change as a signal that all is well, and deactivates the fight/flight centers of the body. Strangely, when you run *cold* water over your hands— or hold an ice cube—you also trigger the body to send more blood to your hands, in order to stabilize the temperature. Either way, more blood to the hands or feet is an anxiety reducer.

Stimulate Your Senses. Anxiety blocks us from simple pleasures and from noticing small things in our environment. *If it isn't about danger, I don't need to know about it.* You can counteract this block by deliberately stimulating your senses. The most common examples are pleasant smells, beautiful pictures or scenery, delicious foods, peaceful sounds or music, and soft and silky textures to touch. Make sure to slow down and appreciate the full sensory experience.

It may take time to discover what sensory experiences help your child relax, but it's worth the effort. A father described his discovery that Weighted Pressure helps his child relax: "There are two ways that we do it. I put a heavy hand on his head or shoulders while we talk. He usually feels relief from this pressure, even if we are talking about something difficult. The more fun idea is Make a Burrito. He curls up on a blanket, then I roll him out flat. After that I put pretend fillings on him, with a motion to go with each one. Then I wrap him up in the blanket. He loves this, it relaxes him, and it gives us an opportunity to have some really nice contact. We always finish with a good feeling between us."

Playful Obstruction. When children are immobilized or shut down they need lots of love and affection in order to build safety. But they also need to be gently nudged out of the emotional corner where they are hiding. I like to be slightly annoying, move in a little too close, and stick my face very near to them. If they get too annoyed, I back off a little, but if they giggle I keep making this kind of contact, which Stanley Greenspan calls being "playfully obstructive." Children in this state are often "floppy," with low muscle tone. I like to gently bounce them around on my lap or in the air to activate their vestibular and kinesthetic systems and help them "reenter the world" and engage with other people.

Rabbit/Turtle/Snail is a game for children who can't settle down because they are too highly activated. I learned it from a woman in England who plays it with her grandson when he is too wound up to go to sleep. "It starts as a madcap running race (rabbits), then each round of the race is slower and slower (turtles) till we finally inch toward bed (snails), where we end the race curled up ready for sleep."

CHAPTER FOUR

The Edge:
Approach and Avoidance

*My son was scared of the eye drops he needed, so we played
the Stop and Go Game: I started across the room, then
walked slowly over to him with the eye drops as he told me
when to stop and when to go. Every time I stopped he laughed.
This was amazing because before, anytime he saw me with
eye drops, he panicked. When I got close I said, "What if I
just drop one drop on your nose?" He agreed and laughed
because it tickled. He let me put one drop in one eye, and then
said I could do the other eye too! Yay!*

—A mother of a four-year-old boy

My sister Aliza recently took me to a scenic view above a waterfall in the Catskill Mountains. When we got about fifty feet from
the edge she said that I should go the rest of the way by myself. I
hadn't known she was afraid of heights, and I offered to help her
with that fear. She agreed, then instantly changed her mind. I
told her we wouldn't go one step farther than she was ready for. I
stood close to her and asked if we could take one tiny step nearer
to the edge. She began to tremble and laugh nervously. We were
still very far away, but the anxious mind only understands one
thing: *We are moving closer to danger.* We paused after each tiny
step for more laughter, with some shaking and arguing thrown in

every few steps. Whenever she said, "That's enough, let's go home," I said, "That would feel safe but let's just stay right here until you feel safe." A few times we needed to take a small step backward, but before long we were lying on a rock with our heads over the edge, looking down over the top of a waterfall. Later that summer she was able to go up a mountain on a gondola and keep her eyes open as she rode down a steep, winding road.

To overcome a fear, we need to spend time at the edge. The edge of our fear isn't always an actual cliff, of course. More often the edge is metaphorical. How close can your daughter get to a dog before feeling panic? How many minutes before school does your son's anxiety begin?

In chapter one I introduced four children who each experienced a different variation of anxiety at the swimming pool. The youngest boy, buried in his mother's lap, was right at the edge. He felt safe in his mother's arms, but one inch closer to the pool was too much. The swimming instructor gently tried to help him find a new edge closer and closer to the water. The six-year-old girl was able to get right in the pool and was happy until water splashed into her face, sending her instantly over the edge. The boy who insisted that he hated swimming (even though he had been looking forward to it all week) was past the edge, flooded with terrified feelings that came out as anger. He desperately wanted to go home so he could be far away from the edge. The diver was close to the edge, feeling just the right amount of tension to help her concentrate on her dive. Then a glimpse of her competitor sent her over the edge. Some children are so anxious that they never get to the pool. Their edge is at the front door, so they sit at home with a head full of worried thoughts. They protect themselves from high anxiety, but they also miss out on fun and an important life skill.

The edge is the place where we face our fears, where we feel afraid but do it anyway—or at least take a small step closer. Many children at a swimming class have no fear of the water or of separation from their parents. They may actually seek out an edge, for example by seeing how long they can stay underwater. Thrill-seekers go a step further, and enjoy being over the edge. Some other children are a little bit fearful. Jumping into the water is a big deal, and they feel some fear at the edge of the pool, but they aren't overwhelmed by it. These children end the day with a sense of accomplishment and the knowledge that next time it won't be as scary.

APPROACH AND AVOIDANCE

There are children who avoid the pool completely, children at the edge, and children who jump right in without a second thought. Then there is a small group of children who force themselves to swim or dive but are too tense to enjoy it. I call this "white-knuckling" because of the way a person's knuckles turn white from gripping tightly. The grip is a way to endure the unendurable. White-knucklers get through it, but they don't learn that it's safe—or fun. Therefore they are just as scared, or even more scared, the next time.

If something is scary you have four choices:

• *Avoidance* is when you stay far away from the thing that scares you. If your avoidance is "successful" you won't feel any anxiety, but you won't experience life either—you avoid both the situation and the feelings.

• *Flooding* is when you try unsuccessfully to avoid a situation and become overwhelmed by the feelings.

• *White-knuckling* is when you approach the situation—either on your own or because an adult forces you—but you avoid the feelings by gritting your teeth, clenching your fists, and tensing your muscles.

• Finally, *facing-and-feeling* is when you approach the situation and feel the feelings. This is sometimes called *exposure,* and is the essence of most therapies for anxiety.

To help children with anxiety, we need to help them spend more time in the face-and-feel zone. Some children need extra soothing when they are flooded or white-knuckling, while some need an extra push out of avoidance. It reminds me of a saying I learned from my colleague David Trimble, who heard it from his father, a minister: "My job is to comfort the afflicted and afflict the comfortable." Let's look at each of the four states in more detail.

Flooding

Children flooded with emotion are overwhelmed and have little access to logic or reason. They may cower in a corner, frozen in terror or trembling with fear. They may rage, be extremely agitated, or "bounce off the walls." Children who are flooded usually can't maintain eye contact, and some like to bury their heads in their parents' laps or clothes, or hide under the covers or even under the bed. Others are aggressive, especially if they are pushed forcefully toward their fears when they are already flooded.

If flooded children can speak at all, they fixate on danger, usually repeating the same fearful phrases over and over, such as: "Make it stop. . . . I can't stand it. . . . Something bad is going to happen." In this flooded state children can't function very well. Flooding is a terribly distressing state for children, and quite frustrating for parents. Flooded children are very hard to reach. Reason and reassurance don't work, and suggestions to relax are likely to be rejected. Flooded children may even reject offers of love and affection. Learning doesn't occur very readily in this state. That's why flooded children can make it through something and still not learn that it is safe, even if nothing bad happens. (Nothing bad besides the flooding, that is.) The part of the brain necessary to make that new connection—*This is safe, not dangerous*—isn't available.

We usually think of nudging children *toward* the edge, as I did with my sister above the waterfall. But children who are already over the edge need to be pulled back to safety before they can make any more progress. How can you push someone toward the edge when they are already past it? Flooded children need to be held and comforted, loved and validated, respected and shown empathy. Don't worry, they will find the edge again.

Avoidance

Aside from a few daredevils, most of us have things we are scared of that we avoid. I have overcome many fears, but I have no intention of ever skydiving. Anxious children avoid too much. This excessive avoidance creates two problems: They miss out on life, and their anxiety gets worse. Children need experience to develop confidence and a sense of safety and security. That's why a common antianxiety slogan is *Avoid Avoidance*.

Avoidance is not the same as running from danger. In the flight response we know what we are running from, we know that we are scared, and our fear helps us survive. In avoidance we don't like to think about what we are avoiding, we may not even be aware that we are frightened, and our survival is not threatened. We aren't really avoiding danger, but the *feeling* of danger. Avoidance is why so many anxious children refuse to accept the idea that they are anxious.

Sometimes avoidance feels like "nothing," because feelings are avoided so thoroughly. In fact, the numb, hollow, and empty feelings that can come along with avoidance are often worse than whatever the person was trying to avoid!

A colleague shared an extreme example of avoidance with me from his work with a U.S. Army veteran. One day Wayne mentioned to his therapist that he drove an hour to and from work, even though he lived nearby. My colleague was curious about this, but Wayne wasn't. Curiosity and avoidance are opposites, so it can be hard to inspire curiosity in someone who is avoiding.

Finally, the therapist convinced Wayne to look together at a map of his route. It turned out he was driving miles out of his way to work every day, but he had no idea why. They eventually realized that the direct route would take Wayne past a cemetery where a close Army buddy of his was buried. Without even being aware of it, he rerouted himself to avoid that reminder. Over time he had to go farther and farther out of his way in order not to be reminded of his friend's death. Of course, somewhere in his mind Wayne had to know what he was avoiding; otherwise he wouldn't have been able to avoid it so well! But he was not conscious of that knowledge. Avoidance interferes with people's lives by creating detours around anything that might be a reminder of something upsetting.

Avoidance also prevents us from gaining new experiences that teach us about safety. The Security System doesn't get the information it needs to make a good assessment. There may not be intense fear, but there isn't real security or calmness either.

The "treatment" for Wayne's avoidant commute was for him to drive right past the cemetery and realize he could survive thinking about his friend. It was very painful, but it was possible. With the pain came an unexpected bonus: a return of positive memories about his friend.

The strangest thing about Wayne's story is that he managed to avoid the cemetery without even knowing he was avoiding it. The same thing happens with nervous habits. Nail biting, shirt chewing, and finger tapping often begin when an unwanted thought or emotion is about to intrude on the person's awareness. Some deep part of the mind notices the intrusion and quickly offers an avoidance strategy. That part, sometimes called the hidden observer, makes sure the thought or feeling remains well buried.

The result is that people with nervous habits are often completely unaware that they are nervous. I was discussing fear of the dark with a friend, who said she wasn't afraid of the dark. As we kept talking she added, "I always sleep with a light on." I laughed. Of course she isn't scared of the dark. She doesn't have to be! I asked her what she would feel if she wasn't able to have a light on, and she couldn't answer. (No one likes to have avoidance challenged.) She insisted that she wouldn't be afraid of the dark because somehow she would find a light.

Avoidance likes to disguise itself: "I'm not afraid of parties, I just don't like them," "I don't feel like going to swimming class today," or "I enjoy driving the long way to work." To recognize avoidance, look for a pattern. Does your child repeatedly have a burst of enthusiasm and then a loss of interest? Does your child dislike every new activity? Does your child have a major meltdown when avoidance is challenged, or can you have a calm and reasonable discussion?

Avoidance can't last forever. It always has an expiration date. Eventually avoidance breaks down and we end up flooded with feelings. The more we avoided, the stronger the flood. It's like shoving unpaid bills into a desk drawer and forgetting about them. Those bills always come due, with interest.

Avoiders are hard to reason with or reassure, just like children who are flooded. Avoidant children don't want to be reminded of whatever they are avoiding. When they are pressed, they often respond with anger or irritability as a protection against the breakdown of avoidance. Anything to avoid the full force of exposure.

Despite my obvious bias against avoidance, it's necessary sometimes. It can even be healthy. We need to rest and relax. We can't face our fears all day every day. There is a reason that therapy is usually one hour a week, not forty or eighty hours. A little distraction is fine, as long as we don't distract ourselves so constantly that we can't accomplish our goals in life.

White-Knuckling

White-knuckling refers to enduring something scary by tensing your muscles, gripping the arm of the chair, or gritting your teeth. The name comes from the way that blood leaves the knuckles when you make a tight fist, leaving them paler. If you have to get through something just once, white-knuckling might work. But if you really want to conquer a fear, white-knuckling won't help you. You don't get any of the benefits of successfully completing the experience. You don't learn that it was scary but safe. This is why parents of anxious children often find themselves saying, "I don't understand. You did this last week and it was fine—you even enjoyed it. Why are you scared all over again?"

Ezra, an adult client of mine, was afraid to fly, but had to travel frequently by plane. Before every flight he distracted himself with loud music on his headphones until the last possible moment to board, then raced to his seat and gripped the armrest (or his wife's hand, if she was traveling with him). He held his breath so much during the flight that he felt light-headed. Every safe landing was a fluke, rather than a sign of the overall safety of air travel. That's white-knuckling.

My own most vivid white-knuckling experience came on a rock-climbing trip in the Joshua Tree desert. I was nervous at many points in the trip, but when it came time to rappel down a cliff, I was terrified. I remember standing with my heels hanging over the edge, my back to the void behind me. The instructor told me to get into a sitting position with my body and trust the harness and ropes. I said, "Okay, I am sitting." The instructor laughed. I looked down and saw that I was still standing perfectly straight. I had "told" my body to squat down, but I hadn't budged. I was so tense I didn't even know that I hadn't moved. Finally, I made myself bend into the right position, and white-knuckled my way down the side of the cliff. At the bottom I suddenly relaxed. Someone asked if I had seen the hawk's nest on the way down. Of course not! I was too busy fighting the fear to notice anything. I wanted to go down again, and actually enjoy the experience this time. But I didn't have a chance. That's the downside of white-knuckling.

In white-knuckling the situation can't be avoided, so there is a doubled attempt to avoid the feelings. But the experience is hardly peaceful or relaxing. At one level, the feelings are avoided, but at another level the anxiety is still there, it is just buried away. Some antianxiety drugs, such as the benzodiazepines, work very much the same way as white-knuckling. You make it through the scary event, but you don't get the benefit of facing your feelings. If you have a severe snake phobia and you take enough of these drugs, you can sit completely relaxed with a ten-foot python around your neck. As soon as the drug wears off, however, you still have your snake fear, which may be even stronger because now you remember—without the drugs—what that snake felt like around your neck. You endured the experience, but you didn't update or reset your Security System.

White-knuckling can go unnoticed until it is named and described, then you start to see it everywhere (and notice yourself doing it). One girl, Clara, loved that there was a name for this, because she had used it to get through many anxiety-arousing things in her life. Like avoidance, it can be a lifesaver if used sparingly. Clara knew that white-knuckling didn't help her deal with anxiety on a long-term basis, however, and she wanted a new approach.

Facing-and-Feeling

One afternoon a college student named Ethan came into my office and told me that he just had the best week of his life. As a boy he had been cruelly abused and he was having a hard time coping in school. I wasn't sure if therapy was helping him so I was glad to hear he had a good week. He said that for several hours a day he cried, shook with fear and rage, and sweated through his clothes. I asked him what was so great about that. He answered, "Don't you see? I started feeling emotions that were just words to me before." That's the power of facing one's feelings. I have worked with many people who have discovered that they can survive the most painful emotions and memories, but I have never met anyone besides Ethan who enjoyed it so much.

Ethan let his emotions flow, rather than being overwhelmed by them, and that is what makes face-and-feel different from flooding. Face-and-feel can be uncomfortable, but it isn't intolerable. During face-and-feel, children can maintain eye contact and accept emotional support from parents. This emotional connection—so crucial to maintaining safety and security—is nearly impossible in the flooded or white-knuckle states.

Remember Ezra, who used typical white-knuckle responses—distraction, gripping the armrest, and holding his breath—to endure a plane trip? To get him to face-and-feel his fear instead, I suggested that he take everything very slowly and deliberately on his next flight. He was horrified by the idea, but to my surprise—and his—he tried it. He made sure to be first in line to board, but right before his turn he pretended he forgot something and went to the back of the line. As people joined the line behind him, he breathed slowly and steadily, looking around and noticing people's faces, without listening to music on his headphones. When it was his turn again he stepped to the back of the line another time to expose himself even more to the scary (but safe) boarding process.

Once he finally got on the plane, Ezra walked very slowly to his seat, making eye contact with as many passengers as possible on the way. In his seat, he practiced tensing then releasing the muscles in his hands and checked on his breathing. He imagined getting off and reboarding the plane all over again, and that thought amused him. The realization that he was smiling astounded him. Since then, flying has been easy. His idea to make eye contact with people and notice their facial expressions was particularly wise. A neuroscientist might say that he "activated his social brain," which counteracted his anxiety by providing the emotional safety and security that comes with human connection. Ezra said that noticing other people helped him see that they weren't afraid, and that calmed him down. In other words, the other passengers were his calm second chickens. Unlike Ethan, he didn't exactly enjoy these feelings. He found them extremely unpleasant. But he felt them, and then they were over. Exposure without white-knuckling while knowing you are safe— that's the essence of using the edge to overcome anxiety.

Many children feel annoyed when we advise them to face their fears. I think that's because we make it sound too easy. It's actually very difficult. Anxiety primes us to turn away (avoidance) or tense up (white-knuckling). Fear of flooding makes it even more tempting to avoid or white-knuckle. On the other hand, "face your fears" is generally good advice. How can we help children stay in face-and-feel mode so they can overcome their anxiety?

First we have to stop rewarding avoidance and stop pushing them into a flooded or white-knuckled state. We don't mean to do this, but it happens all the time. For example, "You don't have to if it scares you" supports avoidance. Forcing children to do something that terrifies them supports flooding. "Just do it without all that crying and whining" promotes white-knuckling. "Don't be a crybaby" is an especially cruel way to humiliate children for being in a flooded state.

From Wild to Mild

People with post-traumatic stress disorder (PTSD) swing wildly between flooding and avoidance. Memories of trauma return in a flood of unbearable thoughts and feelings, so survivors of trauma feel a desperate urge to avoid. They may even repress their memories completely. Avoidance can't last forever, because scary feelings, memories, and thoughts press to come out. Eventually everything that has been shoved aside comes bursting through in nightmares, flashbacks, or overwhelming waves of emotion. This flooding is so awful that survivors avoid even more dramatically, with numbness, loss of interest in life, substance abuse, or detachment from other people. Avoidance creates flooding, which creates avoidance, which creates flooding. . . .

Less extreme anxiety can also swing between flooding and avoidance. My friend's daughter, Audrey, was caught in this trap. She was eager to take gymnastics class, but every week she was so anxious that she refused to leave the car. If her mother forced her to go to the class she would scream and cry—flooding. If they drove away without going to class Audrey's anxiety disappeared—avoidance. As soon as she got home she burst into tears over missing out on her class—more flooding—and begged to have another chance to go. Throughout the week she forgot she was scared and made no plans to cope with the fear—more avoidance. Each week the cycle repeated.

The solution is milder swings. Face the feelings for a little bit, then rest, relax, and distract. After this break you are more able to handle a moderate level of fear, and after facing something scary you are ready for another rest. I like to talk to children about drastic avoidance versus gentle avoidance. Hiding under the bed the day of the school play is a drastic avoidance method. Distracting yourself with music is a gentle method.

In order to face-and-feel, a person has to tolerate some uncomfortable emotions, but these will be less intense than a flood. "If we go home now you will feel better immediately, but you won't get past this fear. If we stay you'll feel pretty awful. I think it's a level of awful you can deal with. I've seen you deal with things that are just as upsetting. Would you like me to remind you of some of the ways you have handled tough feelings like this before?" If children still flood, that just means they need more safety and comfort before they are ready to try again.

PARENTS AT THE EDGE

Children need to stay at the edge long enough to work through their fears. That can be extremely uncomfortable for parents. When we push children to confront their fears—to "feel the fear and do it anyway"—it can seem like we are being cruel. This is the spot where many parents lose heart and let children avoid. I don't blame them. Why subject your child to unnecessary agony? It is so much easier to say, "You don't have to go to the party (or the class, or the pool, or to school)." Unfortunately, supporting avoidance abandons children to their anxiety and fear.

How do we support children without supporting avoidance? Stay with them as you push, to help prevent flooding. Keep pushing gently, to prevent avoidance. Hold their hands, stand side by side with them. Say, "We're going to go in, but I'll hold you for as long as you want until you're ready." As you walk together toward something scary, pause frequently to cool down. But then take that next step. You won't prevent every episode of avoidance or flooding, and that's okay. Just keep aiming for the face-and-feel zone.

Some parents shove their children past the edge out of anger or frustration. Perhaps their parents threw them in the deep end of the pool to toughen them up when they were little. It wasn't right then, and it isn't right now. Children who are forced past the edge have to white-knuckle it or else become flooded. At that point they may face more anger or punishment from parents for crying or throwing a tantrum as they try to recover. So don't throw children heartlessly into their fears, just because you "know" that they will be glad you did. I know some parents believe the face-and-feel approach is too soft on fearful children. All I can say is that I don't believe a hard shove over the edge brings children and parents closer, and I don't think it offers real internal strength and confidence.

As you hold children at the healing edge between flooding and avoidance, they may pour their hearts out in tears, sobs, trembling, or even angry tantrums. This is healthy. In fact, it is often a key to significant progress in overcoming anxiety. Welcome these feelings and just listen. That description of a healing release of feelings sounds a lot like flooding, so how can you tell the difference?

After a healthy outpouring of emotion children are cheerful, relaxed, feel closely connected to you, and are ready to play or to drift into a deep, restful sleep. The flooded state leads to disconnection and cranky exhaustion. You may not know which is which during the tears or shaking. That's okay. Just offer loving affection, gentle cuddling, and kind words. Try to get some eye contact but don't be too forceful about it. With your support your child will either continue a healthy release of emotion, or the flood will subside.

As a worried father, I got this all wrong when Emma was little. I shouted, "What's the matter? What's the matter?" in a desperate tone of voice whenever she was upset. That sure didn't help her feel secure! It took me a long time to realize that if she had something to tell me in words, she would. Otherwise all I needed to do was comfort her as she cried.

What would it mean for you to stay at the edge with your child, without promoting avoidance or pushing too hard? Here's a one-question quiz to help you think about it. Imagine your child is scared of something and begins to panic. Which of these are you most likely to say?

a) "You don't have to go."
b) "I'll give you a whole bag of candy."
c) "Just do it and stop being a baby."
d) "You liked it last time you went, and look, everyone else is there already and they are having a good time, and besides, nothing bad is going to happen."
e) "Just grit your teeth and it will be over before you know it."
f) "I don't want to hear another word out of you about this."
g) "I can feel you trembling. I know it's scary. I'll hold you for as long as you like, and when you're ready we'll go together."

Every parent, myself included, has tried most of these from time to time. But I recommend the last one. The first two choices—skipping the event or distraction with gobs of candy—promote avoidance. The next two—pressuring children to ignore their fear—are likely to result in flooding. "Grit your teeth and keep quiet" is a recipe for white-knuckling.

Let's look again at the last response, the one that I recommend: "I can feel you trembling. I know it's scary. I'll hold you for as long as you like, and when you're ready we'll go together." Does that seem too weak, too cruel, or just right? If you usually push your child to the flooded or white-knuckle state, this kind of response probably sounds weak. Try it anyway, and see how it goes. If you usually "protect" your child from all suffering by supporting avoidance, my suggestion probably sounds too tough. Try it anyway, and see how it goes. It's only fair that we move out of our own comfort zones if we expect our children to leave theirs.

Separations and farewells are an opportunity to practice face-and-feel instead of avoidance, flooding, or white-knuckling. Every day—at schools, preschools, daycare centers, and at home—parents have to figure out how to handle farewells. Some sneak out the door while the child is sleeping or paying attention to the babysitter or a television screen. The idea behind this sneakiness is to not upset the child, but it promotes avoidance (and often backfires into flooding when the child discovers that the parent is gone).

Some parents worry that their children are flooded when they are just expressing some sad feelings about saying goodbye. Of course they are sad! Other parents never leave, which deprives the child of growth and independence. Instead, offer some comfort, then say goodbye, trusting that the teacher or babysitter will continue to offer comfort. If you aren't sure whether your child is truly flooded or is releasing a normal and healthy level of feelings, ask the teacher. She has likely seen enough separations to know the difference.

You have to use your instincts to find the right balance between avoidance and flooding, as my friend Magda discovered when her son Hank was ten. Hank was selected to sing in a special choir performance in another state, and Magda knew that he would have trouble sleeping. He was a boy who was fiercely independent during the daytime, but needed comforting and reconnection at bedtime. Magda was especially worried when she found out the children would be sleeping in single rooms. When she raised her concerns with the choir director and organizers, she was met with advice to avoid ("He should stay home if he isn't ready"), or advice that she knew would lead to white-knuckling or flooding ("Stay out of it and he'll be fine").

Magda opted for a middle way. This involved careful preparation and emotional support. Before the trip she and Hank practiced visualizations for relaxation and restful sleep. Since it was his first trip away from home he needed to internalize his mother's safe and nurturing presence. Each night during the trip they had a planned phone call. In the first call, Magda guided Hank through turning on his flashlight, switching off the overhead light, then turning off his flashlight for longer and longer periods of time until he could sleep. She had him notice that even without the flashlight there was light coming under the door. He slept very well.

Hank gained confidence on this trip, and the next summer he went on another choir trip and did not need any extra assistance sleeping. Magda summed up her approach: "I knew some parents would have thought it was too much, that I was helicoptering, but I knew my kid. I was just giving him tools. Others said he wasn't ready to go, but he was ready, he just needed some help at night. I had to trust myself in the face of other people questioning my instincts."

THE STOP AND GO GAME

When my daughter was little, she was scared to have her fingernails trimmed. Trying to force her didn't work, because she would squirm around too much for it to be safe. I learned a game called Stop and Go from a friend, and I decided to use it with Emma. I started about ten feet away from her, holding the nail scissors. I told Emma that as soon as she said stop I would stop immediately, and I wouldn't go again until one of us said go. If she didn't say go after a while, I would say it myself. I moved forward very slowly, stopping instantly every time she told me to. My slow forward movement kept her right at the edge, where she could feel just as much of the fear as she could manage, without avoidance or flooding.

Sometimes I went too far or too fast, and I had to take a step backward until I reached the safe side of the edge again. Then I slowly inched forward once more. At one point I had to add a rule that she couldn't just say "stop-stop-stop-stop-stop" real fast— there has to be a "go" in between every stop.

Eventually Emma's nails were cut without the usual fights or frustrations. The fact that I stopped when she said stop built up her trust that I wouldn't hurt her or overpower her, and the fact that I followed each stop with a small step forward meant that I wasn't giving in or giving up.

Another version of the Stop and Go game is played side by side, like when I walked closer and closer to the cliff's edge with my sister. You can walk together toward anything scary, such as the big dog down the street or the front door of a new school. Stop instantly when your child says stop, then move forward together after a short pause. The best part of the side-by-side game is that you can be right there to offer comfort and encouragement. If you go slow enough and tune in to your child's emotions, you may actually *feel* the edge when your child hits it. It's like a force field at the exact midpoint between avoidance and flooding.

At the edge children may talk rapidly about all their experiences with whatever scares them. They may tremble and sweat or try to escape to a safer place. Be a comforting presence, but resist the false protection of avoidance. Patty Wipfler, the founder of Hand in Hand Parenting, notes that when playing this kind of game it doesn't matter how close you get to whatever is scaring your child. Just enter the zone of face-and-feel and stay there for a little while. Sometimes, she says, all you have to do is *suggest* that you are going to move toward the scary thing. That's enough to bring your child to the healing edge.

Wipfler also talks about a different kind of avoidance, when anxious children bury their heads in their parents' laps or clothes. This kind of burying may seem like close connection, but more often it's an avoidance of feelings. She suggests a gentle push toward eye contact, perhaps saying, "You need to see I'm not scared and I need to see your fear." In between the avoidance of burying one's head in a lap and the panic of flooding there is an edge where the child feels scared *and* secure. That's where healing occurs.

Stop and Go is very similar to games that children play naturally and spontaneously. Babies love peekaboo, which is a game that plays with the edge between a scary separation and a happy reunion. Toddlers explore a little, right to the edge of their safety zone, then come racing back to Mommy or Daddy for a dose of safety and security. Hide-and-seek gets its excitement from these same themes.

Owen Aldis, who studied animal play, noticed that baby lambs have a "zone of safety" around their mothers. A little way out from the zone of safety, but before the danger zone, is a "play-fear" area. The lamb will trot out to that area, then look startled for no apparent reason and race back to Mom. Sound familiar? Aldis believes this is similar to the way humans engage in thrill-seeking—such as roller coasters and horror movies—in order to stretch their safety zones.

As you play the Stop and Go game you can ask at each step for the child's SUDS or Fear-O-Meter number. (See chapter three for a full description of this number scale.) On a one-to-ten scale, you might stop whenever the child is at about seven or above, then use your favorite relaxation techniques until the number goes down to three or four. Then take a small step forward and check the new number. If the number stays under seven, keep moving forward step-by-step. If it shoots up, take another pause. Again, it doesn't matter how far you get. The most important thing is to spend time together at that healing edge. If your child is at nine or ten on the scale, shift to flood-management: comfort, affection, and connection.

The String game starts with an invitation: "You know how you hate being away from me? Let's find out how exactly far apart we can be before it's too much." Curiosity is the complete opposite of anxiety. While hugging your child tightly, ask, "How is this? Do you miss me?" That is sure to bring some giggles. Then separate just a few inches, a few inches more, and so on. Use a string or tape measure to measure the distance you can be apart before the first twinge of anxiety. You can hand one end of the string to your child and have her go as far as she comfortably can, or you can step away, counting off the distance as you go. Make sure to keep some tension in the string so your child can feel your presence at the other end. Always stop at the edge, before flooding, and reconnect with a hug after each measurement. If your child wants to avoid completely by rejecting this game, just chase her around the room with the string in a funny way to get her laughing. The great thing about the string is that it lets children feel a physical bond (the string you are both holding) while they experiment with more and more distance. Tossing a ball back and forth is another great way to experience both connection and distance at the same time.

Secret Mission is a similar game for older children who are afraid to stray too far from their parents. Send your child on a secret mission to get something or to take a picture of something in another room. Start with places very close, and build up to greater distances. Be sure to make yourself a "secure home base" where your children can return for refueling, security, and a new mission. Some children love certificates of achievement for each mission they accomplish, like the Lion in *The Wizard of Oz* who didn't realize how brave he was until the Wizard gave him a medal.

THE IMAGINED EDGE

Many anxious children have a strong imagination. This is both a blessing and a curse. It's a curse because vivid imaginings of disaster set off the alarm system just as much as real danger. But imagination is also a blessing because it makes possible a game called Think It, Feel It, Do It. That's my name for systematic desensitization, the most commonly used treatment for anxiety. It's a lot like Stop and Go, but it all happens in your child's imagination. Children vividly imagine something that scares them (*Think it*). That pushes them to experience as much of the fear as they can handle (*Feel it*). Then they relax and repeat the cycle. After a number of repetitions, the child can actually confront the fear in real life (*Do it*).

Sensitization is when the Security System overreacts to safe things as if they were dangerous. Desensitization is the unlearning of that link. The all clear finally signals the alarm to stop. The technique is systematic because it moves step-by-step, with each step big enough to bypass avoidance and small enough to avert flooding. This technique can be challenging because children flood easily and they frequently retreat into avoidance. Your job is to help the child stay at the edge, in the zone of facing-and-feeling where real change occurs.

You'll need two things before you start: a SUDS or Fear-O-Meter scale and a relaxation technique that works well for your child (both described in the last chapter). Using a one-to-ten distress scale, the goal of Think It, Feel It, Do It is to gently flow up and down the scale from around three to around seven and back to three. With each repetition, anxiety is lessened a little bit. Don't worry if your child ends up a bit higher or lower than these numbers. They are only rough guidelines. It isn't a technique for when your child is in the middle of a panic, but for when things are relatively calm and relaxed.

The final thing you will need is a list of things that are a little bit scary, kind of scary, and very scary. This is usually called the *ladder*. It might include seeing a dog, petting a dog, and being jumped on by a dog. It's very important to make this a joint project with your child, instead of just making the list yourself.

Once you have the ladder ready, ask for your child's current SUDS number. If it is high, use a relaxation technique to bring it down (I use Counting Backward most often, from the current number down to one). The idea of this technique may have aroused a significant level of anxiety, so take as long as you need to bring the number down. Be patient!

Once the SUDS number is low, your child is ready to imagine the first rung of the ladder. If it is imagined vividly enough, the number will go up. That's good! You want to gently alternate between raising the number and lowering the number. That repetition helps children turn down the alarm signal and boost the all-clear signal.

Once the anxiety goes up, spend however long it takes to

bring it back down again using your child's favorite relaxation strategies. Once the anxiety is low, boost it up again by having your child imagine the same rung of the ladder one more time. When that stops being scary, move to the next rung. The goal isn't to always be at a low number. The goal is to experience over and over the mind's power to raise and lower anxiety. A typical session of Think It, Feel It, Do It with a child might last from five to thirty minutes and contain anywhere from two to twenty shifts from high anxiety to low anxiety. You may need a number of sessions to see results, and you may need to vary the relaxation techniques if they lose their effectiveness. Over time, this resetting of the Security System in imagination will generalize to real life. If imagination doesn't ever bring the number up, then you can switch to the Stop and Go game. The real-life scary situation will bring the anxiety up high enough for the repeated up-and-down flow.

"I DON'T WANT TO TALK ABOUT IT!"

Most parents of anxious children are used to hearing children shout, "I don't want to talk about it!" when they raise any topic related to fear or anxiety. That's usually because extreme avoidance feels to children like the only way they can prevent flooding. (It can also be because we are anxious when we start the conversation and our children don't need any more anxiety!) The reason we push for a conversation, however, is that talking is one of the best ways to lower anxiety. Louis Cozolino, a neuroscientist and psychotherapist, notes that trauma victims need to tell their stories to recover, but anxiety interferes. Telling the story triggers the alarm, but only telling the story can turn off the alarm. The result is that trauma can literally be unspeakable. Cozolino explains that stories integrate the different pathways of the brain. Talking about scary events—big and small—keeps them from haunting us.

We *need* to talk when we are anxious, but we *avoid* talking when we are anxious. The answer, once again, is the edge. In this case, it is the edge between not talking at all (avoidance) and being overwhelmed by the topic (flooding). Play can help children find that edge. Here's an example from a playful parent about a boy who didn't want to talk about a trauma until some play made it safe enough:

"My friend's six-year-old son, Andre, fell from a tree onto his head and was badly injured. He recovered physically, but became timid and fearful. His parents couldn't get him to talk about the experience. Three weeks ago, I visited that family and Andre watched as my kids jumped off the couch. We had made it very safe for jumping. I said, 'Oh, no, I just cannot watch, it is way too dangerous! What if somebody falls and breaks his ears, or his tongue will come out like this?' I made a funny face, and everyone laughed. I asked, 'Is there anyone in this house who knows what it means to break a head?' Andre said, very seriously, 'Yes, me!' 'Oh, really! I heard about a boy with a broken head,' I said. Then I told a story that was half silly and half based on the procedures I knew Andre went through. All the children laughed, especially Andre. He became very wide-eyed when I said that this make-believe boy shouted at the doctors to stop hurting him. Then he told us his story from the hospital, how his mother was not quick enough to catch him, and so on. Once he could talk about it he was much less fearful in his life."

Daniel Siegel is a psychiatrist and a pioneer in integrating neuroscience with parenting skills. His technique called "the remote control of the mind" offers a creative approach to "I don't want to talk about it." He writes, "When a child is reluctant to narrate a painful event, the internal remote lets her pause, re-wind, and fast-forward a story as she tells it, so she can maintain control over how much of it she views." It's perfectly okay for a child to skip over the tough parts. A variation of this game is for you to tell the story instead, while your child uses the imaginary remote to pause you, rewind you, or fast-forward you to a happy ending. An element of play can help children face even the most difficult events.

Make Your Own Metaphor. Metaphors are another way to help children overcome their reluctance to talk about their fears. Metaphors are powerful because they combine the rational and the emotional sides of language. They allow a child to speak deeply about emotions even when the details are "too hot to han-dle." Garth was nine when he related this extended metaphor to me about his anxiety: "It's like I'm the captain of a ship. The first mate was always yelling things at me like 'we're going to crash!' That upset me, so I gave him a new job, to go way up into the crow's nest to look for pirates. If he thinks he sees one, I send two other men up the ropes to check it out—because he has lots of false alarms. I have a new first mate who tells me everything is going to be okay. He reminds me to look at the clouds and the stars."

The Troll and the Dungeonkeeper is a metaphor that I fre-quently share with children who never get angry or who have episodes of explosive rage. The suppression of anger is a common source of childhood anxiety. Since everyone has anger inside, I assume that a child who never gets angry is suppressing it. It takes a great deal of mental energy to keep those feelings locked up inside. Like avoidance, suppression of emotion can't last for-ever, so it eventually comes out in destructive ways.

The story is simple: A dungeonkeeper locks an angry troll in the dungeon. After all, an angry troll is dangerous. The problem is that the longer the troll is locked up, the angrier it gets, and the more it tries to escape. Every time it tries to escape, the dungeonkeeper puts more locks and bars on the dungeon door. That makes the troll angrier. At some point, the dungeonkeeper decides to give the troll a chance. Maybe it's only angry because it has been locked up so long! Freedom for the troll does not go well at first. The troll is awfully angry about being locked up, so it causes some mischief and needs to be locked up again. Over time the troll becomes less angry and the dungeonkeeper becomes more trusting. Eventually the dungeon is no longer necessary. The dungeonkeeper gets a retirement party, because he was trying all along to keep everyone safe. Some children immediately make the link between this metaphor and their own emotions, while others just enjoy the story. Either way it can help children find a healthy edge between suppressing and exploding their emotions.

The Projectionist is another metaphor that I use to help children talk about their anxiety. The projectionist flashes pictures and thoughts across our minds. The anxious projectionist specializes in doom and gloom. I like to ask children to imagine walking into the projection booth to confront the projectionist about its choices. "Why are you sending me *those* thoughts and images?" Often children will speak back to the projectionist in a very commanding voice, and demand that the projectionist present a more balanced or a happier set of images.

Some children make the confrontation into a dialogue, one that sheds a lot of light on their anxiety. One anxious girl, for example, had her projectionist say, "I was only trying to keep you safe, keep you prepared, keep those bad things from ever happening to you again." She returned to her own voice to respond,

"Thanks, but it's not helping me, it's just making me miserable. I can be safe without thinking of bad things all the time."

The Oops-Bonk-Waah Game. Some children are too young to tell you in words how they have been hurt or scared. You can tell the story for them. The story is even more healing if you use a lot of emotional expression. When my niece Lila was a year old, she crawled over a pillow on the floor and bonked her head. She began to cry and held on tightly to her father, buried into his shirt. She wanted to leave the room and looked like she'd never let go of him. I said, "Oh, no! You were climbing and you went oops, bonk, waah." I acted out each part as I said it. She peeked out at me. I told the story again, with more exaggerated emotion and with a funny bonk to my own head with the palm of my hand. She said, "Again." I shortened the story to "Oops, bonk, waah," and told it several more times as she laughed. Then she squirmed out of her father's arms, crawled to the exact spot of her fall, and reenacted it in slow motion with a serious expression. She looked at me and made a face that clearly meant, *Tell that story again.* I did and we all laughed. This approach, which I now call the Oops-Bonk-Waah game, can help prevent young children's injuries or upsets from becoming lasting anxieties.

Even when children are old enough to talk they may not have the words to convey their deepest emotions. Kim told me about her daughter, Judy, who suddenly developed fear of a large-size furry doll of Cookie Monster. Kim tried to talk about it but Judy refused to talk. When she realized talking it through wasn't going to happen, Kim grabbed Cookie Monster and threw him into the garage, shouting in a funny voice, "That's it, you're not going to scare my little girl anymore!" Judy laughed and then proceeded to tell her mother that Cookie Monster was very scary. Her fear continued, however, so the next day Kim said to Judy, "I wonder if Cookie Monster wants some water." Judy was wide-eyed with curiosity and walked to the garage door with her mother, but wouldn't go in. Over the next few days they visited Cookie Monster frequently, bringing him water, food, and even underwear. Each time Judy stepped farther and farther into the garage. Finally she went all the way in and started carrying the doll around. She kept Cookie Monster in his underwear, probably to keep him less scary. Kim didn't force Judy to talk—has anyone ever successfully forced a child to talk about feelings if the child doesn't want to? But Kim did keep the "conversation" going through play. By being lighthearted she was able to keep Judy at the edge long enough to resolve her fear.

"I *DO* WANT TO TALK ABOUT IT."

Some children do want to talk about their anxieties—endlessly. They talk, but they don't get anywhere. Instead they are stuck in a repeated loop with no progress toward facing their fears. These children need to be gently pushed to expand the conversation in new directions. You can help if you make it clear you are genuinely interested, but that you want more details, not just a repeat of what you have already heard. You can ask:

- "What are you feeling in your body as you talk about this?"
- "How scared are you, from one to ten?"
- "Do you have any ideas for what to try next?"
- "Can you imagine any possible happy endings to this situation?"
- "What is the scariest thing about this?"
- "What's the worst thing that could happen?"

Parents often avoid these questions out of a fear of increasing the child's anxiety. But the answers to these questions *decrease* anxiety by integrating the thinking brain with the emotional brain.

Another way to take dead-end talk in a valuable new direction is to make your child the expert. You might say, "My friend's son is very scared of swimming (or making friends, or dogs, or monsters under the bed). I know you've thought a lot about that, so I wonder if you have any advice I can give my friend." Most children are eager to be seen as knowledgeable, especially about an area in which they struggle. And in fact they are the biggest experts on their own anxiety. With younger children you can pretend to be the voice of a stuffed animal that is afraid to go to bed or a doll that is afraid to go to school. You may be surprised by the responses your children give to these characters.

MORE PLAY, LESS TALK

I've described the power of talking and some ways to get a good conversation going, but the fact is that some parents talk too much and ask too many questions. I should know; I'm one of them. Anxious children have a hard time listening. They tune out our words because they are preoccupied with their inner worries. These children need something more fundamental than talking, such as hugs, quiet soothing, and play. Just about any form of play will do, but here are some playful ideas that are especially designed for anxious children when talking doesn't help.

Role Reversal games help children manage their fears and worries by letting them be in the more powerful position. Children may do this spontaneously, or they may need help. Either way, reversing the roles releases tension through play. After getting a shot at the doctor's office, most children come home and play doctor, only this time *they* have the syringe. After an earthquake children will line up their toys on a table and shake it until all the toys fall off. After the attacks of 9/11, my friend who directs an after-school program told her staff, "Bring out all the planes and blocks you can find." Some of the parents were horrified, but she knew that the children needed to play out their fears in order to recover. It's role-reversal play, because in the make-believe world they are not helpless victims.

You can help children tap into the power of role reversal by taking on the role of a weak and helpless character, letting them be strong, competent, and brave—or scary. You can be Chicken Little while they are the Lion, or you can be scared to step off the couch until they come to rescue you.

A great role-reversal game is for you to loudly brag that you are big and strong and not afraid of anything. Then as soon as your child gives you a tiny push or a funny look, shake with fear or hide under a blanket. Make sure, of course, that your child doesn't feel that you are making fun of him with this game. Often children will ask you to be a monster, but be sure to be a bumbling, incompetent monster. Act surprised when the child slips away from your grasp. Alternatively, your child can be the monster or big scary dog that chases you. Exaggerate your pretend fear in a silly way (I know that's hard for some highly dignified parents). Letting children scare you, catch you, tackle you, or wrestle you to the ground is a great way for them to build confidence.

Scientist, Detective, and Spy. Curiosity promotes exploration and discovery instead of avoidance and flooding. Scientist, detective, and spy are three roles that thrive on curiosity. Anxiety can be a bad guy that the detective has to catch in the act, the problem that the scientist has to investigate, or a sneaky spy that the child can outfox by being even sneakier. Children tend to feel helpless in the face of anxiety. In these make-believe roles they can feel more powerful. They might hunt for clues, decode secret messages, or draw and write in a special notebook. While they are playing they are also learning the ins and outs of their anxiety and developing counterstrategies. Some children prefer to be a superhero when they role-play. Help your child create imaginative superpowers designed to vanquish the arch-villain Anxiety.

For example, Paulie uncovered these "tricks" of his anxiety when he started thinking like a detective: "Anxiety sneaks in at night right before I fall asleep, and keeps me awake. I think it wants me to be tired the next day so I won't have any fun. It tries to tell me things that aren't true, like that my mother is going to disappear or something bad will happen to her." He came up with the idea to sneak into his bedroom a few minutes before his bedtime and hide beside the bed. He held a butterfly net and "caught" his anxiety as soon as it came in to try to keep him awake. He ran out to show it to his parents, who pretended to put it in a jar and save it for him to draw a picture of the next day. The picture was quite horrifying, but Paulie wanted to put it up on his wall, after he drew a giant X across it.

Anxiety can often be managed better if children see it as something external to themselves, rather than a part of them that can't be changed. *I'm an anxious person* leads to feeling helpless, powerless, or cowardly. *Anxiety is trying to outfox me* lets children feel powerful and create successful strategies. Through roles such as scientist or detective, children can get to know their own anxiety in a way that is lighthearted instead of overwhelming.

Playing It Out. Adults are fond of telling children to "work it out" when they have a problem. I prefer to help them play it out. Inner conflicts, for example, are a common source of anxiety. The conflict might be *I want to hit my brother but I don't want to get into trouble*. Or it could be: *I don't want to remember the bad things that happened to me but I can't help thinking about them*. Adults deal with inner conflicts by talking them out. Children deal with inner conflicts by playing them out. When they play good guys and bad guys, for example, they are playing a game about the inner conflict between their moral side and their mayhem side.

Because of the tendency in anxiety to avoid, you may need to help children play out their inner conflicts. For example, you might pick up two dolls or two stuffed animals and have one of them say to the other one, "Hey, what happened?" The second one can say, "I don't want to talk about it!" Then the two of them can have a silly argument: "Please, please tell me!" "No way!" You can get your child involved by asking for help settling the argument. Another way to play it out is for you to represent the problem and have your child tackle you, pound you with pillows, or shout at you. You might be a tough math problem, a situation at school, or anything that makes your child feel helpless or anxious.

THE INTERNALIZATION OF SAFETY

We want our children to be safe. We also want them to have a strong internal *sense* of safety. That is the antidote to anxiety. Inner safety comes from being loved and held in safe loving arms, and from spending time at the edge, where children can face their fears and feel their feelings without avoidance or flooding.

Here are three ways to promote this internalization of safety and reset the Security System:

- Comfort children when they are flooded.
- Gently push them when they are avoiding.
- Guide them away from white-knuckling toward facing-and-feeling.

It's okay if you don't always know which of these your child needs. If you approach the situation with empathy and playfulness, you will figure it out together.

CHAPTER FIVE

Dr. Spock versus Mr. Spock:
Emotion Expressed and Suppressed

Mommy, I have a feeling I have never felt before. It's excitement, and joy, and anger that you never brought me here before, and unbelievability that something this beautiful can exist.

—A nine-year-old girl arriving in Venice, Italy

Pediatrician Benjamin Spock launched a revolution in parenting when his *Common Sense Book of Baby and Child Care* was published in 1945. The revolution was not about feeding, sleeping, or diapering, but about emotions. Dr. Spock believed in children expressing them and parents listening to them.

Dr. Spock invited parents to look underneath behavior to see the emotion driving it, as in this example about a child's jealousy over a new baby: "When [Mother] sees him advancing on the baby with a grim look on his face and a weapon in his hand, she must jump up and grab him. But then she can turn the grab into a hug and say, 'I know how you feel, sometimes, Johnny. You wish there weren't any baby around here for Mother to take care of. But don't you worry, Mother loves you just the same.' If he can feel, at a moment like this, that his mother is still on his side, that she is still thinking of him, it is the best proof that he doesn't need to worry."

Mr. Spock, by contrast, is the pointy-eared half-Vulcan, half-human character from the *Star Trek* television show and movies. He is known for suppressing his emotions to an extreme degree. He attempts to live his life purely by logic and reason, though he is occasionally overwhelmed by the emotionality of his human side. In one episode the highly expressive Dr. McCoy tries to tell Mr. Spock that the release of emotions is healthy. Spock responds, "That may be, Doctor. However, I have noted that the healthy release of emotion is frequently unhealthy for those closest to you."

Which Spock is right? Both! A balance between expressing and containing emotions—Spock versus Spock—is very important for preventing and lowering anxiety. Children need to learn how their feelings work so they can recognize them, express them effectively, and choose whether to act on them. They need to learn how to regulate emotions so they don't escalate out of control. Most adults never learned the basics of emotions either. The lessons many of us learned—Be nice, Don't cry, Never show fear—aren't very useful.

I experienced a Spock versus Spock showdown in the children's section of a bookstore in Denver. I had just finished a presentation about Playful Parenting when a woman who worked in the store said, "I know this is an unusual request, but would you mind settling an argument between my coworker and me about the message to children in this book?" The book was *Smile a Lot!,* by Nancy Carlson, a picture book featuring a frog with a giant grin. The text advises children to smile heartily in response to life's difficulties, whether it's being served oatmeal with prunes for breakfast or being taunted by bullies. The frog's big smiles are offered as a more positive alternative to whining, complaining, giving up, or having an emotional meltdown.

The controversy between the two clerks at the bookstore was obvious as I flipped through the book. From one angle, you could say the book was full of helpful advice to look on the bright side, have a positive attitude, and think about ways in which a smile may actually get you what you want—whereas a meltdown or a tantrum may just dig you in deeper. We all know people who could use this advice, people who make an art form of misery, whining, and complaining.

From a different angle, the book seems to advocate an unhealthy suppression of feelings: Fake a smile and squelch your real emotions. That advice is not so useful. Excessively suppressed emotions build up inside. We are all familiar with uptight people with plastered-on fake smiles who are completely out of touch with their emotions, or people who explode with rage or implode with depression once their feelings can't be repressed anymore.

When I was asked to resolve this dispute at the bookstore, I found myself agreeing with both sides. I thought of people who might be happier if they chose to put aside their painful feelings and act cheerful instead. But I also thought of people who already smile too much, even when they are feeling something very different inside. These are people who need to get real and show how they truly feel. If you grin and bear it too long, at some point you may not be able to bear it anymore. You may also fool yourself into thinking that you don't have the feeling you are trying to hide.

In the end, I told the feuding booksellers that smiling a lot is great advice, as long as you also get a chance to truly express angry, sad, or hurt feelings. After my carefully diplomatic reply, each of the two employees said to the other: "See, I told you so!" What could I do? I just smiled.

Many people are unaware of their feelings, and unaware of how to express them effectively. Anxious children, for example, may complain of stomachaches and headaches, with no awareness that anxiety is involved. Many adult men discover that they have panic attacks only after they show up in the emergency room thinking they are having a heart attack. Why mostly men? Because the majority of us men are conditioned to be so out of touch with our emotions that we aren't aware we are anxious— even after our pounding hearts and soaking sweats bring us to the ER. For children and adults alike, understanding emotions is a key to reducing anxiety.

Start with yourself. What are you feeling right now? How do you know? Does the feeling include physical sensations? Thoughts? Facial expressions? What is the feeling urging you to do? Are you going to do it, or not? Is the feeling changing as you pay attention to it? If you can't identify a current feeling, what was an intense feeling that you experienced recently? Describe it in detail. The answers to these questions reveal how complex emotions can be.

Paul Ekman, a psychologist best known for his work on facial expressions and deception, proposed six basic emotions: anger, disgust, fear, happiness, sadness, and surprise. Other scholars of emotion count them differently. Some researchers reject the idea of basic emotions, suggesting instead a range of feeling from joy to sadness or anger to fear. The psychologist Marsha Linehan, who developed Dialectical Behavior Therapy, distinguishes between primary emotions and secondary emotions. Primary emotions are automatic, such as anger if someone hurts us, or sadness if we lose someone close to us. Secondary emotions are feelings *about* feelings, such as guilt about being mad, or shame about being afraid.

Since scholars disagree on naming emotions, I tend to follow the lead of another set of experts—children. Some like to keep it simple: mad, sad, glad, and afraid. Other children prefer a different name for every nuance of emotion: anger, aggravation, annoyance, hatred, and irritation. Some like to invent their own emotional language, like the boy I knew who made a fine distinction between "madder than a wet hen" and "madder than a wet hen in a haystack." Since he grew up on a farm and I didn't, I took his word for it about how mad a wet hen can be.

I asked a group of children to define anger. Here are some of their responses:

- "Anger is when someone hits you."
- "When you feel like hitting somebody."
- "It's like this." (Child makes tight fists and squinches up her face.)
- "Anger is yelling and screaming at someone."
- "It's not nice to get angry."
- "My sister gets me mad all the time."
- "Anger is when you're mad inside."
- "I get angry when something's not fair."
- "When I get mad I count to ten."

Yes! Anger is all of those things. Every emotion contains physical sensations and facial expressions (the tight fists and squinched-up face). Every emotion is triggered by a situation (someone hits you) or by a thought (it's not fair). Every emotion has what Marsha Linehan calls an action urge (the urge to hit someone or to scream), though that urge may not be carried out. Every emotion has an overall impression (feeling mad inside). And every emotion can set off new thoughts and feelings. For example: Anger might lead to the thought, *It isn't nice to be mad*, triggering guilt; or anger might lead to the thought, *My sister makes me mad all the time*, intensifying the anger. We can sustain the emotion, or we can try to change it (count to ten).

For sadness, the physical sensations might be an empty feeling inside, heaviness, and heartache. Sadness is often triggered by a loss. The action urges for sadness are usually to seek comfort and to cry, or sometimes to seek solitude. The overall feeling impression might be acute anguish or lingering mourning. The sad emotion can set off new thoughts and feelings (for example: *I can't stand it*, which leads to hopelessness; *It's my fault*, which leads to guilt; or *I miss him so much*, which leads to renewed sadness).

Now it's your turn. Consider a few other feelings, such as fear or joy, and think about the physical sensations, the typical triggers, the action urges, the overall feeling impression, and the thoughts and feelings that are likely to follow. You can do this exercise on your own or with your child.

When children are highly emotional, we often demand that they use their words. I avoid this, because I want children to understand all the different layers that make up an emotion— the name of the emotion is just one small layer. We eventually want children to use their words, but if we jump to that single word too quickly it can close the discussion instead of opening it up. During a strong emotion I like to ask children the following questions instead of telling them to use their words (but be sure not to pepper them with too many questions at once, and wait until they are able to talk before you ask!):

- "What are you sensing in your body?"
- "What sparked that feeling?"

- "What thoughts are you having about that feeling?"
- "What do you want to do next?"
- "What do you think will happen if you do that?"

All these questions help children integrate their thinking with their feelings—their Mr. Spock brain with their Dr. Spock brain. After you have explored all those layers, you can finally ask, "What would you call that feeling?" If you are talking about a feeling after it has cooled down, you can still ask all those same questions to increase emotional self-awareness.

THE FLAME MODEL OF EMOTIONS

The Flame Model of Emotions brings these ideas about feelings together in a way that children can understand. Every emotion begins with a *spark,* a thought or event that lights the *flame,* which is the emotion itself. If you are already having a bad day, that puts extra *fuel* on the fire, and the same spark will create a bigger flame. The flame metaphor is especially fitting for anxious children, who often treat their feelings as if they are too hot to handle. Fortunately, they can learn to pour *water* on the flames. The water is anything that cools down an emotion, such as counting to ten, breathing deeply, thinking about something different, or talking to a friend.

The flame of an emotion usually includes a physical reaction, such as hot or cold skin, crying or screaming, tense muscles, or butterflies in the stomach. The flame also includes an overall inner sense of a feeling, such as fear, anger, happiness, or sadness. This overall sense might be a metaphor, such as a trapped or sinking feeling. The emotional flame usually includes facial expression, verbal expression, and body language. The person having the emotion, however, might not be aware of any of these bodily reactions. Another part of the flame is the action urge, the drive to do something with that feeling. For anger it may be to shout or hit, for fear it may be to run, for sadness it may be to curl up in a blanket or seek someone to provide comfort.

Imagine that someone steps on your foot and you immediately feel a surge of anger. That's the spark and the flame. The size and shape of the flame depends on the spark. You will probably feel angrier if you think *He did that on purpose* than *It was an accident.* Now imagine you hear a banging noise and you feel startled. Your fear will be greater if your thought-spark is *It's a burglar* than *It's the wind.* Now imagine that you have painful memories related to alcoholism and it was a drunken person who stepped on your foot. Imagine that you were recently in a car crash when you heard the loud banging noise outside. Emotionally loaded memories add fuel to the fire.

Emotions *seem* to be sparked by outside events, but they are usually sparked by our own thoughts. In other words, the exact same event can create completely different emotional reactions, depending on the sparking thought. Suppose you tell your child that she can't have candy. If she thinks *I want it so badly, I'll just die without it,* then her emotion will probably be sadness. If her thought is *That's not fair!* then the emotion will probably be anger. If the thought is *It's okay, I'll have one tomorrow,* then there will be no strong emotion. A child with a fear of thunderstorms may believe that the fear is triggered by storm clouds, but it is actually triggered by scary thoughts about death and danger.

Beliefs about one's self and the world are a common source of fuel. Some beliefs that make anxiety more extreme: *Bad things always happen to me, Something bad is going to happen soon,* or *You can't trust anyone.* When a small upset leads to intense feelings, you may be able to understand why if you draw out the underlying subtext that added extra fuel to the fire. Beliefs can have a positive effect as well. *The world is generally safe* and *Someone will help me* are underlying beliefs that help prevent anxiety from escalating.

When children are tired, hungry, or bored they are more likely to have extreme emotional reactions. That's because these states are a concentrated source of extra fuel. As every parent knows, in these situations a small spark can become a giant flame. Unfortunately, we can't just tell children, "You're only reacting so intensely because you are hungry." That just adds even more fuel to the fire! The only real solution is to stay ahead of the game, preventing children as much as possible from building up that extra reserve of explosive fuel.

If all we had were sparks, flames, and added fuel, every emotion would escalate out of control. Fortunately, we have water to quench the flames. (It only *seems* that your child's every emotion escalates out of control!) In the Flame Model, water represents the thinking mind cooling the emotional flame.

Rating the intensity of an emotion from one to ten is one example. Drawing the feeling or making up an imaginative story about it also cools the emotion. Strong emotions overactivate certain pathways of the brain. Language, numbers, and creativity activate different pathways, so that Mr. Spock and Dr. Spock can find a healthy balance. Activating more of the brain seems to lower the flame in many anxious children. Another way to activate more of the brain is to describe in detail the physical sensations of an emotion: "I feel tingling in my arms and hands, my chest is tight, my heart is beating fast." A broader perspective also lowers the flame: "I'm having an anxiety attack, it isn't dangerous, and it will pass." Physical activity activates completely different pathways of the brain, which is why exercise, dance, and yoga can be so effective in reducing the intensity of strong painful emotions.

The thinking brain can step in to pour calming waters on an emotion's action urge:

I'm so mad that I want to hit you, but I would rather not get into big trouble, so I won't.

I'd like to laugh at my friend's haircut but he'll be offended and upset and I don't want to jeopardize our friendship, so I won't.

I want that bicycle, but stealing is wrong, so I won't.

Parents and teachers often say, "It's okay to be angry, but not to hit." That's true, but I don't think it captures what children need to hear. It leaves out a key step—the urge to hit. In order to say no to that urge, children need it to be acknowledged: "It's okay to be angry, and I understand that being so angry made you want to hit, but it's not okay to hit. It's hard sometimes, but you can always choose not to hit."

Not all action urges are created equal. Some make sense to act on, others don't. Wise or useful action urges are probably the reason we have strong emotions in the first place. Emotions galvanize us to run from danger, turn to confront a threat, speak out against injustice, seek a shoulder to cry on, and shower affection on those we love.

Do I really have to? is an exercise that I learned in a yoga class. It reinforces the idea that we don't have to act immediately on every action urge. Try it yourself, then coach your child through it. Take a few deep breaths. On an exhale, empty all the air from your lungs. Then wait before breathing in. Notice your first impulse to breathe, notice how intense it is, but don't inhale until your *body* signals you that you really need to. There is usually a gap of at least a second or two—if not longer—between the panicky impulse and the real need.

Maturity is knowing that many action urges are not so wise. We all know adults who have never grown up in this way, who act on every urge they have. But we can help children understand what to do if an action urge doesn't make sense. For example, they can imagine it without really doing it (just about everyone has had a revenge fantasy that they would never actually carry out). Marsha Linehan describes some things people can do when they are experiencing a powerful action urge that isn't wise to act upon. One is to do the "opposite action" to the urge. If you feel ashamed and want to hide yourself under your blankets, find a trustworthy friend and count on her to listen to you with compassion. If your heart is racing and your breathing is rapid and shallow, take slow deep breaths. If your fists are clenched, slowly open them. Avoidance is a common action urge for the emotion of anxiety. Avoidance is usually a lousy idea, so consider the opposite action—approach whatever scares you.

When doing an opposite action, make sure you aren't forcibly suppressing your emotions, but rather choosing in a gentle way to influence your emotional state. You can also choose an alternative action, not following the urge or doing the opposite, but something completely unrelated, like taking a walk or reading a book. Opposite and alternative actions are powerful ways to pour water on the flame of an insistent action urge.

When we are overwhelmed by an emotion it's easy to think, *This is going to last forever* or *This feeling might kill me*. These thoughts can easily become the spark to a new flame—adding anxiety to the original emotion. Linehan's solution for this escalation of emotion may seem strange: Just notice the first feeling and let yourself experience it. With practice, acceptance can cool even the most intense emotional flames. When you watch your own emotional flow with no effort to change it, you realize that you can endure it. What's more, you will most likely notice that the feeling lessens or changes over time. When we fight against our emotions, they intensify and linger. When we let each one be what it is, the emotion passes more quickly.

The discovery that everything changes has to come from within. It doesn't ever help to scold a child by saying, "Just let the emotion pass, don't get so upset by it." Instead, you can ask, "Do you notice any change at all in the feeling as you sit with it? Does it get stronger or weaker, do the physical sensations move to different places in your body?"

Many parents try to cool off a child's emotions by saying, "You shouldn't feel that way." This seldom works, because emotions don't listen to shoulds. Sometimes we don't realize we are giving shoulds to a child's emotion. When a child cries or hits after another child bumps into him, we are likely to say, "It was an accident." This really means, *You shouldn't be sad or mad.* But guess what? The child *is* sad and mad, and it doesn't matter to the emotional brain whether it was an accident or not, at least not at that moment of peak emotion.

Most parents are surprised to discover that empathy is actually a better way to tone down emotions: "You are really upset that she bumped into you." Parents fear that this kind of empathy will inflame the emotion more. Understanding and validation are actually the best paths to soothing and comfort.

Anxious children may try to block or eliminate all emotions, like Mr. Spock does, or just block the scary ones, such as anger. This doesn't work. I watched my niece tense up during a suspenseful scene in a movie. I asked if she was scared. "No," she said, "it's only a movie." I think she meant, *I'm not supposed to be scared, so I'm not.* Her emotional brain, however, didn't care that it was only a movie. She was scared anyway. The main problem with applying shoulds to emotions, where they don't belong, is that children can end up feeling ashamed or guilty that they have a feeling they aren't supposed to have. Meanwhile, they still have that unwanted emotion because shoulds don't make it disappear.

I've described the spark, flame, fuel, and water. But that's not the full story of an emotion. After we have a strong emotion our minds are in a different place than they were before. One child who understood the Flame Model very well called this "getting cooked or getting burned." She said the feeling can burn you up (if it overwhelms you or causes big trouble), or the heat can cook something (if the feeling leads you to do something constructive, such as solving a problem or escaping harm).

The flame of one feeling can also light a new flame, like lighting a candle with a match. You can feel shame about being sad (such as a boy who is humiliated for breaking the no-crying "boy rule"), or you can be scared of your own anger. You can feel joy or pride at having handled an emotion in a healthy way, or you can pass your feeling along to someone else (such as the upset child who hits a younger sibling, and now that sibling is the one who is upset).

Another way that an emotion changes us is that we are now more likely to notice and remember things that are in line with that emotion. Have you ever noticed this? Someone cuts in front of you in line or in traffic, and you are instantly filled with anger. Before your anger can fade you run through your mind all the other times that similar things have happened to you. These memories become new sparks that keep renewing and refreshing the angry flame. You also notice every annoying thing in the world around you. This is called selective memory and selective attention, and it can keep us stuck in a painful emotion for a long time.

Selective memory and attention explain why it doesn't usually work to insist to our anxious children that they think about positive things: "Just think of something happy!" The fear makes children selectively remember and notice only scary things, and there is no room for happier memories for a while. We have to help them finish that first emotion and let it fade before we can expect them to put their minds on fresh thoughts that are outside that emotion. Happy thoughts are usually too big of a leap. As a child starts to cool down, however, you can use neutral thoughts such as numbers or colors as stepping-stones: "Can you find three blue things in the room? Can you count backward from fifty by fives?" The message with this technique is to convey that the child can choose to emerge from that painful emotion, not that you need the child to hurry up and be finished with it.

I urge parents to teach the Flame Model, or a similar outline of emotions, to their children. This knowledge helps prevent emotions from causing so much anxiety and distress. Awareness of how the system operates gives children more control over the spark, the flame, the added fuel, and the cooling water. After you teach children the Flame Model it can become a way to talk about emotions without judgment or criticism: "I noticed that you were still tired from your nap, and then when your sister took your toy you got extra upset because you were thinking, *That's not fair!* Maybe you were thinking about other times when she took your toys too." You can also reflect on the action urge, the decision to act, and the consequences of the action: "It looked as if you were wondering what to do with all those mad feelings, then you thought about hitting her, then you decided to go ahead and hit her, then you got in trouble." The idea is to help slow down the process for children, because emotions happen very fast.

RUMI VERSUS RUMINATION: WELCOMING ALL EMOTIONS

Rumi was a Sufi mystic poet born in Persia in AD 1207. Yet "The Guest House," one of his best-known poems, feels very modern in its call to welcome every emotion, even those we consider negative or painful. Why welcome awful feelings? Because anxiety is often the result of blocked emotions. *"This being human is a guest house,"* Rumi writes, *"Every morning a new arrival. A joy, a depression, a meanness. . . . Welcome and entertain them all! Even if they're a crowd of sorrows."* Rumi goes on to urge us to greet even the most undesirable emotions with laughter and gratitude.

We often refer to "good feelings" and "bad feelings," but this confuses children. They think it means that certain feelings are right and others wrong. It's true that some feelings are pleasant and some are unpleasant, but none are *bad*. Of course, some emotions are harder to welcome than others. As psychologist Harriet Lerner says in her aptly named book, *Fear and Other Uninvited Guests*, "Feelings are a package deal, and you can't avoid or deny the painful ones without also forfeiting part of your humanity. If you are never fearful, you may also have trouble feeling compassion, deep curiosity, or joy. Fear may not be fun, but it signals that we are fully alive." That sounds to me like a lecture Dr. Spock might give Mr. Spock!

Rumi probably wouldn't be surprised by recent research on attachment and emotion, which shows that mirroring of *all* emotions is essential for children to learn who they are and what they feel. Mirroring teaches children that emotions can be shared and understood and don't have to be dangerous or destructive. The best way to convey this to children is to reflect all their emotions back to them, beginning when they are babies and continuing as they grow up. Match—and even exaggerate—their facial expressions, while naming the emotion: "Wow, you're really mad!" "Eek, that was scary!" Don't frighten them with your intensity. Just let them know that you understand what they are feeling. It's easy to mirror a smile or laugh, but make sure to mirror *every* feeling, not just the ones you like! It may be hard, because you probably didn't have all of your feelings mirrored when you were young.

ANXIETY AND UNWELCOMED EMOTIONS

Anxiety follows the same path through the Flame Model as any other emotion. The spark is a worried thought or perceived threat. The flame represents the direct experience of anxiety in the body and the mind. A temperament that is highly reactive to anything new and different provides anxious children with an endless fuel source. All of the strategies in this book—from the second chicken to relaxation to finding the edge—are ways to douse anxiety's flame with cool water.

Anxiety also arises when other emotions, such as anger or sadness, get stuck and don't flow in a natural way. The flow of emotion means that we cry when we are sad; we shout and stomp our feet when we are angry; we tremble, shake, and sweat when we are scared; we laugh and smile when we are happy. The opposite of anxiety is welcoming every emotion into the guest-house.

Flow also means that we follow each emotion's action urge, as long as that action is healthy and effective. We speak out when we are angered by injustice, for example, as long as it is safe to do so. When our emotions flow in a healthy way, we don't act on urges that are destructive to ourselves or to others. So we don't whack someone over the head every time we want to, only when our survival is at stake. Emotional flow means that we hide when we need to, fight when we must, and seek out comfort when we are lonely and sad. Healthy emotional flow means that we feel remorse when we've acted badly, but we don't plunge into self-hatred. We seek out intimacy without clinginess or excess neediness. In short, we feel what we feel and we express it freely, but responsibly.

Stuck emotions and frozen action urges arouse anxiety. If we don't allow ourselves to feel our feelings, they get stuck "halfway in and halfway out," which may be why so many people feel anxiety in the gut, chest, and throat. Many adults, especially men, tell me that their eyes hurt when they cry, but I think their eyes hurt from fighting so hard not to cry, because crying is "forbidden."

Even fear can get stuck and turn into anxiety (this is an example of how our language about emotions gets complicated). Healthy fear leads us to run, hide, or fight when we are truly in danger, so we can reach safety and find comfort. Afterward we "shake off" the fear, recover our balance, and return to a calm state. If the fear gets blocked, we freeze. Healing is blocked, and anxiety can result.

To prevent this anxiety blockage, the psychologist and trauma expert Peter Levine encourages people who survived a trauma to complete any action that was left unfinished because of fear. For example, they might move their arms in slow motion as if they are protecting their faces, because they were unable to protect themselves when they fell off a bicycle. They might run, throw a punch, or shout at a pretend attacker to finish an action that was stopped short by threat or terror. These movements are best done in slow motion to help the person shift from immobility to action to safety.

You can usually tell when children's emotions are blocked, because their expressions are flat when you would expect to see a strong feeling. They may say they feel numb, shut down, overwhelmed, or even dead. Suppression of feelings can lead to feeling fatigued, bored, or lethargic. As time passes, children have to suppress more and more to keep their unwanted emotions from pressing into awareness. Children with blocked feelings may also look aggressive or hyperactive. When one emotional channel is blocked, the emotional energy comes out in other ways. Put a tight lid on a pot of boiling water and steam will escape violently from the sides.

Children who are shut down, children who are overly nice and never get angry, and children who explode with rage all need encouragement to express anger in a healthy way. Dramatic play is a great way to help them, because you can introduce characters who are extra-aggressive, extra-nice, and extra-unemotional, like a robot. As you and your children play with these characters, they learn that anger doesn't have to be dangerous or scary.

Some children confuse parents because they are both anxious *and* angry. They swing wildly between rage and fear, or they feel both at the same time. I believe that when anger and anxiety go together, children are not accepting their more tender or vulnerable emotions, but they can't get rid of them either. The tender emotions—sadness, loss, and fear—are often seen as weak or shameful. But those feelings are still there, pressing for release. Such strongly rejected and conflicted emotions are a recipe for explosive anger and high anxiety.

Jonah, at age five, was extremely anxious, easily frustrated, and frequently angry. If he was upset with a friend he said, "I hate you, I'm not your friend anymore." Then he felt lonely and rejected. His anxiety and anger seemed to feed each other. If he was nervous about a game, for example, he tried to hide it with anger. After he exploded he became more anxious as he worried how others would react. Jonah's teachers described him as an excellent student but fearful of making a mistake. He had several losses in his life, including the death of a close grandparent, but he never talked about his feelings. Instead, he bottled everything up unless he was in explosion or panic mode. What helped Jonah was for his parents to mirror his angry feelings without moral judgments ("That's a very strong way to show that you're mad," instead of "No one is going to like you if you act that way"). They also helped him describe the intensity of his anxious feelings, such as rating the fluttering in his stomach from snail speed to train speed to rocket speed. This helped him regulate his anger and anxiety, but it had an unexpected result as well: He became aware of his buried feelings of loss and sadness and began to talk about his grandfather.

Children often cry for a minute or two and then suddenly stop, as if a gate has crashed closed. This may look like a good sign: They are done crying. But they probably aren't done; they have just become afraid of the release of their feelings and shut them off. Children also seek out sugary foods or television to close off their emotions. They need us to make an extra effort to let them know that their emotions are welcome to us, and not dangerous to them.

Children become especially anxious when they start to feel

"forbidden" feelings, most commonly anger and sexuality. Unlike Jonah, most anxious children never show anger. The result is always anxiety, because everyone feels angry sometimes. Boys who never cry are also likely to become anxious, because they can't help but be at the edge of tears now and then.

Sexuality can be a hidden trigger to childhood anxiety—hidden because it is so hard to talk about. I have seen young children who are quite anxious about feeling vaguely different from others. They can't put into words just how they are different, and it doesn't seem to have anything to do with sexuality. Years later, however, their anxiety lowers when they realize that the reason they felt different is that they have a gay or lesbian sexual orientation. Of course, if their families or peers reject them, their anxiety will increase tremendously, not decrease.

Lately I have noticed many parents scolding children for being "mean" to their stuffed animals or dolls, saying, "You hurt its feelings." What? I think the parents are afraid their children will become bullies, but the message is that all aggression is unnatural and needs to be eliminated. But aggressive play isn't violence, it's play! Children understand the difference—they know toys don't have feelings—it's adults who get confused sometimes.

You might wonder what's wrong with closing the door to these unpleasant or adult-only feelings. Anger can be dangerous, and sexuality is too grown up for children, right? No, because suppression is even more dangerous. It's easy for children to feel ashamed if their age-appropriate sexual feelings are denied. As much as we might like to believe that our sweet and innocent children have no sexual feelings, the fact is that all children want to know where babies come from, are interested in the differences between male and female bodies, and notice that it feels extra good to touch certain places. If we shame children for having these feelings, the result will be anxiety, as suppression fights against the natural urge for expression. It's much more effective to be matter-of-fact about sexuality and offer accurate information geared to each child's level of development.

Parents would love for children to always use their words to express their anger. I'll never forget the mother who told me what happened when she requested that her young son use his words instead of hitting. He proceeded to swear and curse, using the foulest language she had ever heard! She had no idea he had been exposed to those words, but he sure knew how to use them. She could hardly tell him to stop, since she had just told him to use his words. We often see only two choices with anger: violence or complete suppression. But we need another way. It's easy to take advantage of a person who never allows herself to be angry. When there is injustice, unfairness, or a threat, we need to stand up to it. That requires the energy that comes from anger.

At the same time, we can help children by not exposing them to violence or sexuality that is beyond their capacity to understand. It's not healthy for children to go to sexually explicit or ultraviolent movies. We might think sexual movies are okay because children won't understand them, but they become overwhelmed and confused by the images and emotions portrayed on the screen. The result is often a compulsion to try to understand what they have seen by acting it out with peers or younger siblings.

However, we do want to expose children to the full range of human feelings, even anger and sorrow. If we try to protect children from knowing our true feelings, they will sense that we are hiding something and that will make them more anxious. On the other hand, if we yell and scream and rant and rave or cry inconsolably we can easily frighten our children. So be a role model by expressing your own emotions freely, but not in a scary way. Use your words! Children benefit greatly when they see their fathers or other men shed tears when they are sad, and when they see their mothers acting assertively.

Emotions are so important that our bodies rebel when we try too hard to suppress them. A group of therapists coined the term "affect phobia" to describe fear of one's own emotions. Some people react to any unwanted feeling with "bodily tightness, tension, withdrawal, panic, fear, and inhibition." The solution is to emotionally move step-by-step toward each scary feeling. Pause frequently to face-and-feel the emotions. This is very similar to the games described in chapter four, such as overcoming a fear of dogs by taking baby steps toward a friendly dog.

Some anxious children are very sensitive to the idea that they might show the "wrong" feelings, such as laughing when someone is hurt or crying at their birthday party. Of course these aren't wrong feelings at all, because there is no such thing as a wrong feeling. Let me repeat that, because anxious children have trouble with this concept: *There is no such thing as a wrong feeling.* People often laugh nervously when something bad is happening, and many children cry when they feel overwhelmed, even if they are being overwhelmed with positive attention. We feel what we feel.

For children to welcome all of their emotions, *we* need to welcome their emotions. Before we can do that, we need to welcome our own. When we block off areas of feeling in ourselves, it is simply impossible to acknowledge or encourage those same emotions in our children. I know this is a challenge. I have never met an adult yet who grew up with every one of their emotions welcomed by the adults around them. As a result, we constantly give children messages to tone their feelings down—"Don't be mad, he didn't mean to take your truck, he's just a baby." Welcome feelings instead with a simple reflection: "Wow, you are really mad."

One controversial topic in regard to welcoming emotion is whether or not to encourage a child to release anger physically—but safely—by pounding pillows or shouting. In some situations, such as road rage, it seems that the release of anger just increases the anger. But in other situations, such as playful roughhousing or a friendly pillow fight, this release can be calming and beneficial. I think the key is whether the child feels a strong connection with a safe adult when they are releasing those feelings physically. If they do, then the anger releases instead of recycling and escalating, and balance is restored. But if they are "seeing red," hurting people, or unable to notice your warm presence, then the release will probably do more harm than good.

Most adults have a hard time welcoming *every* feeling, but some even feel the need to tone down children's joy! When my daughter was little, we were visiting friends who lived in a large apartment building. Walking down the hall, the girls were laughing and giggling. Someone came out of an apartment and said that the children were "laughing too much." She even filed a complaint with the building management. Fortunately, the managers could not find anything in the rules against laughter, and the matter was dropped.

If you want to take the "advanced course" in emotion, try this: For a half hour, Welcome Every Emotion that comes into your own mind (and body), as Rumi suggests in "The Guest House." If that's too long, try it for a few minutes and build up slowly. If you notice a feeling that you'd like to avoid, step toward it instead. Take your time. Go deeply into that avoided feeling. You can give it a number for its intensity level, and you can name it. In addition to naming it with one word, such as anger, sadness, or jealousy, think of a metaphor to describe the feeling. Do you feel trapped, sinking, or like you have been punched in the stomach? Do you feel like a volcano about to explode, or like a doll abandoned on the side of a road?

Welcoming every emotion goes by many names: mindfulness, radical acceptance, or willingness. I have taken you through this exercise so that you can see just how challenging it is. Stick with it, because we can't really help our children welcome feelings if we can't do it ourselves.

Another exercise for parents is to Write Your Own Emotional History. What did you learn about emotions when you were a child? Take anger, for example. How did each different person in your family express anger when you were growing up? Were you allowed to show anger? In terms of sadness and sorrow, did you ever see a grown-up cry? What kind of comfort (or rejection) did you get when you cried? Did you get any help naming and managing your feelings? Don't forget to write about the family history of anxiety.

Moving to the present, what feelings within you are hard to accept or to bear? What feelings in your children are hard to accept or to bear? Do you cheer your children up relentlessly? One time when I picked up my daughter from preschool I could see she was having a bad day. She made it very clear that she didn't want to talk about it, so I dropped the subject. Absentmindedly I started to sing as we walked down the stairs. She asked me suspiciously, "Are you trying to cheer me up?" I answered, "I wasn't thinking about that, but would you like me to cheer you up?" She said, "I'd like to see you try!" As you write your emotional history you will gain more perspective on your current struggles as a parent of an anxious child.

Listening to children and welcoming all their feelings does not mean "giving in" or "spoiling." You can say, "I will listen to you for as long as you need me to, and you can cry and be really mad, but I am not going to change my mind about that candy." Both parts of this sentence are crucial: You aren't going to change your mind because of the feelings (unless you realize you made a mistake, in which case you can correct it). But you aren't going to add rejection and humiliation on top of the sadness and anger they already feel.

Often children don't know what they feel, and aren't able to express their emotions in words. Or they may simply be too young. If you have a pretty good guess about what your child might be feeling (jealousy of the new baby, perhaps, or nervousness about a new activity), then you can speak it for them. Just make sure that you are somewhat tentative. "I think maybe you are feeling _____." The psychologist Mona Barbera calls this being a spokesperson for a neglected feeling. For example, if a child is frequently scared but almost never gets angry, you might stand up tall and yell out the window, "Go away, storm! You don't scare me! Grrr!" Then you can encourage your child to join you.

Anyone with high anxiety will tell you that it is exhausting. I think a big part of the exhaustion comes from the nonstop fight to suppress feelings. Welcoming feelings can be scary. The relief, the lowered anxiety, and the increased energy are well worth it.

THE YAWN-A-THON: HEALTHY RELEASE OF EMOTION

The Yawn-a-Thon game counteracts the pressures on children to suppress emotions. The game works best in a group. Have everyone pretend to yawn. This always brings on real yawns, because yawns are so contagious. Then have everyone fake laugh. This brings on real laughter, because it's fun to fake laugh. Keep going through all the emotions you can think of: fake crying, fake trembling and teeth-chattering with fear, fake storming around with anger, fake gasps of surprise. Most of these pretend emotions will bring more laughter, partly because it's funny, and partly because everyone is breaking the "rule" not to show too much emotion without a good reason.

The Yawn-a-Thon also teaches that we don't always have to *do something* about our feelings. We can just feel them and release them from our bodies with tears or giggles, shakes or yawns. The game gives people control over this release of emotion, which helps counteract the fear that emotions will spin out of control. Adults in therapy often say, "I am afraid that if I start crying, I won't be able to stop." I always ask them if they have ever seen that happen to anyone. No one ever has. There is no "world's longest cry" in the *Guinness World Records*.

Have you ever sought out a sad movie or sad music to give yourself just the right amount of sadness to release some backed-up tears? Children often seek out things that are a little bit scary so they can feel just the right amount of fear. Of course, often they miscalculate, and get overwhelmed by the scary movie or the roller coaster that they thought would be just-scary-enough.

My favorite example of deliberately scaring oneself comes from *The Lion King*. Two hyenas are talking about Mufasa, the fearsome king of the lions. One says, "I just hear that name and I shudder." The other one says, "Mufasa" and the first one shudders, then says, "Ooh, do it again." Then one hyena says, "Mufasa, Mufasa, Mufasa" as the other one shakes and laughs, releasing the pent-up fear.

Once a child's feelings start releasing, they need us to stick around and listen to them until they are finished. Parent educator Patty Wipfler, founder of Hand in Hand Parenting, calls this *staylistening*. It's the exact opposite of "Go to your room until you can have a smile on your face. . . . No one wants to listen to that. . . . You are ugly when you pout."

Listening can happen whenever a child is upset, but it can also help to set aside Feelings Time. This is a regular time, usually at the end of the day, for parent and child to share feelings that have built up and haven't had a chance to be fully expressed. It could be something that you know about: "Do you have any leftover feelings about what happened at the park today?" It could be something that you don't know about: "You seemed a little upset at dinnertime, but I'm not sure why." Feelings Time builds closeness and promotes emotional awareness. You can share your own feelings too during this time, as long as you don't overwhelm your child with adult concerns or extreme emotions. Over time your child will come to count on that time, and use it to share feelings that are harder to put into words.

Overall, children need a balance between expressing their emotions freely and putting their attention on positive thoughts. During Feelings Time the focus is on expression. Since you are probably tired at the end of the day you might be tempted to dismiss feelings that don't seem important or serious to you. Resist that temptation! Every emotion is important to the person feeling it. In fact, if you want children to tell you important things, then you have to listen attentively to *everything*, no matter how trivial it seems to you. I like to say, "That's an important thing to be sad (or mad) about." This helps me control my frustration, which is urging me to say, "I've got better things to do than listen to you talk about this triviality."

Children need to learn from us that they can handle any emotion they happen to feel, even ones that seem forbidden, overwhelming, or unwanted. When children can't put their feelings into words we need to offer them other ways to express themselves, such as drawing, pounding on pillows, wrestling, or curling up in our laps (even if they seem too old for this). At times children will insist, like Mr. Spock, that there is "no point" in sharing feelings because it won't change what happened in the past. Push back against this belief. The point of emotional expression is that speaking out and releasing feelings eases the grip of the past and clears our minds to enjoy the present moment.

Sometimes children know what they need to say, but are scared to say it. Unspoken truths are a major source of anxiety. The Gestalt therapist Fritz Perls developed the Empty Chair for adults who have something to say—but the other person isn't available or isn't likely to listen respectfully. This technique can be used with children also. Bring over an empty chair and have your child pretend it holds the neighborhood bully, the math test, or their grandmother who passed away and left them so sad and lonely. Encourage them to say whatever they want to say, without any worry of reprisals or hurting anyone's real feelings.

Another great use for the Empty Chair is to have children pretend that their anxiety, or some other emotion that troubles them, is sitting in it. They can speak to the anxiety about how angry they are that it limits their lives, or they can tell it to stop sending scary pictures to their minds. If your child wants, you can sit in the chair and pretend to be that emotion. Let your child direct you and give you a script. For example, one boy asked me to be his anxiety and say things like, "I'm not going to let you sleep or have any fun." Then he made angry faces at me and threw pillows at me while I pretended to be very scared and promised to leave him alone.

EMOTION OVERLOAD

Not all anxious children suppress their emotions. Some have extreme outbursts of sadness or frustration. They may cry frequently without the tears providing any release or healing. These children have trouble regulating their emotions, rather than trouble releasing them. They need to understand their own emotions in order to express them in healthier ways.

To prevent emotional overload, ask children to rate the intensity of their emotions from one to ten *before* it gets up to the top of the scale. Children who escalate rapidly into extreme emotional states usually don't notice the buildup. The number scale helps children tune in to their emotions when they are easier to express with words or nondestructive actions.

Children learn more about their own emotions when adults avoid judgmental or critical language. For example, one nine-year-old boy, Scotty, became extremely agitated whenever his mother told him that he was "out of control." Even though to some extent this was true, those words made him feel ashamed and humiliated. That made him act even more out of control. When his mother started to say instead that he seemed to be "heading up toward one hundred on the Angry-O-Meter," Scotty could acknowledge his feelings and brainstorm with her about ways to lower the intensity of his emotions.

Some children like to imagine that their feelings have a dimmer switch, rather than an on-off switch. Others pretend to turn down the flame on the stove from boil to simmer to warm; or they imagine anger as a wild bear that has gotten loose from the zoo and has to be tamed. Sometimes children will suggest that their anger or anxiety has to be shot or destroyed. I always push back against this image. On the one hand, children need to choose their own metaphorical language. On the other hand, eliminating feelings is impossible, and locking them up is unwise. I try to gently steer children toward a new metaphor such as making peace with the feeling, taming it, or harnessing its energy. These images promote a healthy balance between expression and regulation.

When feelings are especially strong, words aren't enough to allow for their full expression. Children also need to use their bodies to share their deepest feelings. You can encourage them to roar like a lion, dance, run, make themselves into a sculpture that represents how they feel, or crash into a pile of sofa cushions.

My favorite physical activity for regulating emotions is Faster, Slower. Have your child run in different directions and at different speeds based on your rapid-fire instructions. "Run left, run right, run to me, run backward, run fast, run slow, run in super slow motion, run real fast!" You can do this with any rhythmic activity, such as jumping jacks. And you can do it with volume, as in the Isley Brothers song "Shout" ("A little bit softer now . . . a little bit louder now"). I don't know exactly how it works biologically, but physical games with quick changes like this seem to translate into more manageable emotions.

So should we encourage children to smile a lot and whistle a happy tune, as Anna sings in The King and I? Or do we encourage them to release all their emotions? Dr. Spock and Mr. Spock were both right to some extent. Mr. Spock is right that sometimes people's emotions get carried away to extremes. But overall, I believe we need to lean more toward Dr. Spock. In his discussion of childhood fear, Dr. Spock wrote, "Don't make fun of him, or be impatient with him, or try to argue him out of his fear. . . . This is a time for extra hugs and comforting reminders that you love him very much and will always protect him."

Emotions are a natural reaction to situations and thoughts, and everyone has the right to experience each and every one of their emotions. But passions are sometimes so strong that they get in the way of reasonable thinking or happy relationships. We need to feel our feelings, express them, and also regulate them. When we do that, our emotions are much less likely to trigger anxiety. Children need to express their true feelings, and adults need to welcome those feelings warmly. But we can also help children take charge of their emotions by choosing how much to fuel them and how much to cool them.

CHAPTER SIX

"What If" versus "What Is":
Challenging Anxious Thoughts

Mom, what if you are on your way to Stop & Shop and there is a huge, weird rainstorm and you die?
—A twelve-year-old girl

A man was trying to sleep on an overnight train ride. Just as he drifted off, he heard a voice moan, "Ohhhh, am I thirsty. Ohhhh, am I thirsty!" He tried to ignore it but the complaint continued, louder and louder. He couldn't sleep, so he stood up, walked to the water fountain, filled two cups, found the elderly woman who was moaning about being thirsty, and gave her the water. She thanked the man graciously and he went back to his seat. The train car was finally silent and he was just drifting off to sleep when he heard, "Ohhhh, was I thirsty!"

This joke is a reminder that anxious people live a large part of their lives in the past, ruminating about close calls or missed opportunities. Anxious people also live in the future. Ziggy, the always-worried cartoon character created by Tom Wilson, says, "I try not to worry about the future—so I take each day just one anxiety attack at a time."

I call this anxious focus on the past and future the "What Ifs." *What if we had hit that car? What if you don't pick me up at school? What if I left the door unlocked? What if Dad doesn't come home on time? What if we miss the plane? What if dinosaurs aren't really extinct and they come into my room? What if I don't get into college because I got an A– on a sixth-grade math test?*

Of course, anxious thinking about the past or the future doesn't always include the words "what if": *If only I had studied more for that test. How could I have made such a terrible mistake? We could have crashed! Are you sure there aren't any monsters under the bed? I don't know what to do. Am I going to die? Are you going to die?*

The joke about the thirsty woman on the train demonstrates a special skill of anxious people: The ability to create "What ifs" about *anything.* My favorite example comes from the narrator in a Dave Eggers novel: "Ella Fitzgerald was singing from a small speaker over our heads. Maybe Sarah Vaughan. I worried briefly that they, Sarah and Ella, knew that I didn't know the difference, and were angry."

What ifs are at the heart of three common symptoms of anxiety:

- indecisiveness (*What if I make the wrong choice?*)
- perfectionism (*What if I make a mistake?*)
- overpreparation (*What if this happens or that happens or the other thing happens?*)

What ifs also reveal the bias toward pessimism of the anxious brain. It's always *What if we hit that tree?* and never *What if everything goes perfectly?* One reason anxious thoughts focus on the past or future is that the present moment can be hard to accept: *Why me? This can't be happening. The store can't be closed— what are we going to do?*

People with low anxiety also have what ifs, but milder ones

that reflect simple curiosity or a passing feeling. Relaxed what ifs can even lead to positive changes or important learning experiences. Worry can be useful as long as you stop when you find a solution, or when you realize you aren't going to find a solution by worrying harder. As psychologist Margaret Wehrenberg says, "Worry well and only once."

Anxious what ifs are repetitive, strained, stressful, and don't lead to creative ideas or useful solutions. Instead, they create as much terror as a real danger: *What if monsters are real? Oh, no!* They are alarm sirens with no all-clear signals to stop them. They just keep ringing and ringing. Alarmed what ifs race through the mind or repeat in endless loops. When parents offer reassurance to anxious children, each reasonable thought triggers a new what-if thought:

> *"The party will be fun."*
> "What if I don't know anyone?"
> *"You'll know Ruthie and Louise and Evelyn."*
> "They all like one another more than they like me."
> *"You said yesterday that Louise is your best friend, and you are her best friend."*
> "What if Louise doesn't to come to the party?"

Shoulds and *Shouldn'ts* are another type of anxious thinking. Of course, we need a healthy level of shoulds and shouldn'ts. They guide us to act morally and ethically. Shoulds and shouldn'ts create anxiety, however, when they are too harsh or too shaming: "I should never have done that. What's the matter with me? What on earth was I thinking?" It's pretty obvious where these harsh inner voices come from—all shoulds and shouldn'ts start out as parental commands. Shoulds and shouldn'ts cause the most anxiety when they demand the impossible: *I should get a perfect score on every homework assignment. I shouldn't ever get angry. I should always be happy, generous, and kind—even in my thoughts.*

Magical thinking is very common in anxious children: *If I am good then nothing bad will happen. My grandfather died because I was bad. If I touch the lamp three times before I turn it off then I will be safe. After seven more cars come around the corner then the next car will be Mom's.* Magical thoughts represent an attempt to control the future or change the past. That's impossible, of course, but it doesn't stop anxious children from trying. The world is an uncertain place, and uncertainty can be scary.

Even young children struggle with existential questions about the meaning of life, death, suffering, and why bad things happen for no good reason. These can easily become anxious thoughts: *Why did Grandma have to die? Did I do something bad?* Human beings have a wonderful capacity to find meaning. It's not so wonderful when we can't stop searching for answers to unanswerable questions, or when we blame ourselves for things that aren't our fault.

Anxious thinking can lead children to be certain about things that are uncertain: *I know that I'll be bored and no one will talk to me.* Children with social anxiety don't think, *I hope no one stares at me.* They think, *Everyone will stare at me.* Anxiety can also make children uncertain: *I know dinosaurs are extinct but maybe they could come back and get into our house.* In other words, anxious children tend to get certainty and uncertainty exactly backward.

Nonanxious children don't spend much time worrying about things that are extremely improbable or far into the future, such as an asteroid hitting the Earth or the Sun burning up in a billion years. Anxious children do. Adults dismiss these kinds of fears—"Don't be silly"—but they are a reflection of how the anxious brain works. The alarm system responds to images and emotions, not statistics. A mental picture of the world blowing up is more vivid than a mathematical statement about low probability. Anxious brains don't have a very good sense of time either, which is why children can be very anxious about things that already happened or things that might happen far in the future. The intensity of the thought makes it real right now, even though nothing scary or dangerous is actually happening.

In the Flame Model of Emotions, described in the previous chapter, beliefs fuel emotion. Certain beliefs are especially common in children with high anxiety: *The world is a dangerous place; I can't trust anyone; I have no one to keep me safe. I'm responsible for my parents being happy.* If you look underneath your child's what ifs, you may well find evidence of these troubling beliefs. Children can gradually develop new beliefs that sustain security and calm once we increase our efforts to create a secure and safe "home base" for them.

A great deal of anxious thinking revolves around reviewing the past and rehearsing for the future. Children can use up all their mental and emotional energy this way, leaving nothing left for the present moment. These reviews and rehearsals often focus on conversations. *I should have said _____. When I see that person again I am going to say _____.* Reviewing the past can be useful—it can help us learn from our mistakes. Rehearsal is extremely valuable if you are preparing for a play or a speech. But to rehearse every possible variation of every upcoming conversation is a huge waste of time and energy. Anxious thinking can be exhausting and all-consuming. Preoccupied with the upsetting past or the disturbing future, children miss out on the real-life present moment.

The term "anxious thinking" resists easy definition but it may be helpful to think of these examples:

- Anxious thoughts are thoughts that trigger anxiety. After the thought, *There are monsters under the bed*, it's hard to relax.
- Anxious thoughts are thoughts that are triggered by anxiety. In a state of high anxiety, every noise leads to thoughts of burglars or kidnappers.
- Anxious thoughts are thoughts that try to magically lower anxiety. *If I check the doors and windows three times, I will be safe.*
- Anxious thoughts are mistaken conclusions about the world. If I have a random panic attack in an elevator, my anxious brain might explain these feelings with the mistaken conclusion: *Elevators are dangerous, stay away from them.* Next time I'm in an elevator my anxiety will rise and "prove" the conclusion is true.

BEFORE YOU CHALLENGE A CHILD'S ANXIOUS THOUGHTS, READ THIS

The solution to what ifs and other anxious thoughts is to challenge them. Recognize their irrationality; talk back to them; and live firmly in the here and now—the world of *what is* instead of *what if*. But anxious thoughts don't like to be challenged.

Have you ever wished your child's anxious thoughts would disappear in the face of your logical arguments? "There is no such thing as monsters." "Oh, okay, thanks for letting me know. Good night." That's a lovely fantasy conversation, isn't it? Sadly, logic doesn't make anxiety disappear. Anxious thoughts are very resistant to reason. So we need a few guidelines in order to challenge anxious thoughts effectively, without stirring up resistance:

• Start with acknowledgment and empathy. Children can't hear your challenges to their anxious thoughts unless they know first that you understand how they feel.

• A challenge is *not* the same thing as an argument. If you are arguing, then the thought is not being effectively challenged— even if you are "right."

• Challenges from within are always more powerful than challenges from outside. Invite children to develop their own challenges rather than imposing yours.

• Before you challenge your child's what ifs, reflect on your own.

If a child asks, "What if you die?" you might answer first with an empathic acknowledgment, such as, "That would be awful," "That sounds like a scary thought," or "Thank you for sharing your scary thoughts with me." Empathy is always a better first step than a direct challenge such as, "I won't die," "Don't worry about that," or "That's too far away to think about."

A friend told me this story about choosing empathy over a direct challenge: "Last night I was on the phone with one of my friends. I thought Tracey was asleep, but she came downstairs and said, 'Mommy, I'm feeling really nervous inside, and I don't know why.' My friend on the phone heard her and said, 'Oh, kids, they will do anything not to go to sleep.' I ignored my friend, ended the call, and let Tracey climb into my lap. She couldn't say what was wrong. I said, 'I am so happy you knew you were feeling nervous and came to tell me. You knew that was the right thing.' Five minutes later, she was asleep."

My friend did not dismiss her daughter's fear, even though she wasn't sure what it was about. She trusted that the feelings were valid, even though Tracey couldn't tell her the reason for them. It's hard to acknowledge feelings that are mysterious or seem to come from nowhere. It's even harder to acknowledge fears that seems trivial or silly, such as "What if my teacher turns into a werewolf?" Remember that underneath, all anxiety is about very important things, such as abandonment and security. It only sounds trivial because children can't put their deeper feelings into words.

Offer empathy whenever a child's alarm system is activated, not just when you think it *should* be activated. The Security System needs to be reset whether the threat is real or imaginary. If we tell children that they shouldn't be anxious over "nothing," they will ignore us, because it isn't nothing to them. It never helps to shame a child for being scared or for having an anxious thought.

Similarly, children ignore us when we say, "Don't worry, that won't happen." For them, the scary thing is happening *right now,* because they are imagining it so vividly. If we say it can't happen we must have no idea what we are talking about. Instead, appeal to children's natural curiosity: "Let's look around and see if what you are picturing is actually happening."

Children who are anxious tend to be very good at arguing. Their arguments may not be rational, but they are strong and repetitive. So here's a tip: Don't try to win an argument about an anxious thought! You will lose, no matter how right you are, because the anxious mind fiercely defends its anxious thoughts. That's why "I'm not worried" (the second chicken response) is more effective than "There is no reason for you to be worried." There *is* a reason. You just don't know what it is! Questions are another way to sidestep fruitless arguments: "Are there any other possibilities of why Daddy could be late, besides that something bad happened?" Wonder is also a natural antidote to anxiety. "I wonder how those anxious thoughts managed to slip in today. I wonder what you will do to challenge them. I wonder whether talking about it or deep breathing will lower your anxiety level more."

You can't change your child's anxious thoughts from outside. Effective challenges have to come from within. Imagine that your child is nervous about soccer practice and doesn't want to go. You remind her that she loved it yesterday. She ignores you. You get mad. You insist that she loved it yesterday. She gets mad. What just happened? Even though it is *true* that your daughter loved soccer practice yesterday, she can't use that fact to interrupt her anxious worry about soccer practice today. However, if *she* creates the challenge it has a different impact. You can inspire her to challenge her own anxious thoughts by asking, "What did you do to make soccer practice fun yesterday?"

I like to sit with children and write out a list together of the anxious thoughts that keep coming back to them, then ask them to think of their best challenges to each one. Resist the urge to offer your own "better" ideas for challenges when you help children make a list. Just keep encouraging them to come up with their own.

Karen was a girl with a lot of social anxiety who was fearful about returning to school after a long absence. Her list looked like this:

ANXIOUS THOUGHT	CHALLENGE
People will stare at me.	They are probably thinking about other things, not about me.
I won't know what to say if someone asks me where I've been.	I can just shrug my shoulders or say I was sick.

ANXIOUS THOUGHT	CHALLENGE
I shouldn't have missed so much school.	I did miss school; shoulds don't matter.
I'll never make a friend at this school.	I can't tell the future. I made friends at my other school.

Before you challenge a child's anxious thinking, take some time to recognize and challenge your own. What are your what ifs? If your child is a few minutes late walking home from school, does your mind leap to vivid pictures of kidnappings or car crashes? Or do you say to yourself that he probably stopped to hang out with his friends? Does the vividness of your worry make it seem real? If you are prone to anxious thinking, many of the strategies and techniques in this chapter may be helpful for you as well as your children.

Anxious thoughts are hard to change because they feel so real and true. Challenging them takes patience and compassion. Fortunately there are effective ways to deal with what ifs, shoulds, magical thinking, and other anxious thoughts:

- Playfully challenge.
- Shift from *what if* to *what is*.
- Activate more of the brain.
- Welcome—then transform—anxious thoughts.

CHALLENGE ANXIOUS THINKING WITH PLAY

Since anxious children have active imaginations, especially when it comes to disasters, they are usually expert at playing Fortunately/Unfortunately. In this game, one person—usually the parent—begins a story with something that is fortunate (Fortunately, it was a beautiful day). The other person continues with something unfortunate (Unfortunately, it started to rain). The two people continue alternating these fortunately/unfortunately sentences until the story reaches a dramatic conclusion. The idea of this game is to giggle away tension that children feel about expecting bad things to happen. This game provides a challenge to anxious thinking because it contradicts the deadly seriousness of what ifs and worries. It also provides an outlet for the anxious child's drive to create doomsday scenarios.

What If It Doesn't provides a more direct challenge to what-if thoughts, but still in a playful way. A lighthearted but respectful tone of voice is crucial. I learned this game from my friend Dana:

"My daughter is now almost twelve, so 'Mom, what if there is something under the bed?' has become 'Mom, what if you are on your way to Stop & Shop and there is a huge, weird rainstorm and you die?' I can no longer reassure her by checking under the bed, so I wasn't sure how to help her fear. Finally, one night I was sitting by her bed listening to another 'what if' tale of my demise. This one had to do with a shark swallowing me. I said, 'What if it doesn't?' I guess I stumbled onto the right phrase and the right tone of voice because she laughed and laughed. Now she says it to me: 'What if my teacher turns into a werewolf when he hands back my paper? I know, Mom, what if he doesn't?! Then I will just have to stare at my bad grade! I *know* my grade will be bad! I know, what if it isn't? But if it is I could eat my paper!' If she doesn't start the game I always listen for a while first before I say, 'What if it doesn't?' I think the key element is that we are joking together about heavy fears and that is empowering."

Silly Dancing challenges serious anxious thoughts because it is physical and a little wild. It is about as far as you can get from a logical argument. *Juggling the Jitters,* a children's book by Deborah Miller, contains a great description of a parent helping a child shift away from anxious thinking: "Let's silly-dance and sing those jitters away."

I've suggested imaginative play in other chapters as an antidote to anxiety, and it is especially useful for overcoming anxious thinking. Anxious children tend to be more imaginative than other kids. That's one reason they worry so much—they can vividly picture all kinds of dangers. In dramatic play, imagination becomes a tool the child uses to boost confidence, rather than a tool of anxiety.

Superhero and good guy/bad guy play are great for building confidence and exploring emotions through fantasy. Two other dramatic play ideas are particularly well suited to anxious thinking. One involves a scientist, the other a spy. In Spy vs. Spy, children pretend that anxiety is a sneaky enemy, and they get to be even sneakier. For example, a boy named Hugh told me, "My anxiety sneakily tried to get me to believe that I don't like soccer. But really I like it. I just worry sometimes that I won't be as good as my friends." So Hugh outfoxed his anxiety. "I told it I was going to a football game, so the anxiety should just stay home and take a nap." With a giant grin, Hugh explained to me that "football" is the word they use in Europe for "soccer," and that was how he tricked his anxiety into leaving him alone to play soccer with his friends.

The role of the scientist is the basis for a game I call Anxiety Lab, in which a child gathers important information: *When is my anxiety highest, when is it lowest? What is the anxiety trying to stop me from doing? What is it trying to get me to do? How does it make my body feel?* Since scientists do experiments, the next set of questions might be: *How will my anxiety react if I challenge it?*

What happens to my anxiety when I practice relaxation skills? In the role of a scientist or a spy, children use play to become experts on how their own stress levels operate. They soon discover that they have more knowledge about anxiety—and how to challenge it—than they ever imagined.

A girl named Daphne uncovered a set of strategies that her anxiety used against her to keep her from being able to have a sleepover with her friends. She gave these strategies funny names, which helped her feel a sense of mastery and control over them. One was called Doom and Gloom. This was the way her anxiety made her think about everything that could go wrong, and to forget everything that could go well. Sometimes Daphne's parents tried to talk her out of her anxiety, and she stormed into her bedroom and slammed the door. She called this Doom and Gloom in My Room. To outwit Doom and Gloom, Daphne kept a list of the most common negative thoughts that her anxious brain would present to her. Whenever she had one of those thoughts she made an x-mark on her list and said to herself, "Caught you!" She shared with me the "mean laugh" that she used when she caught her anxiety in the act of trying to scare her. It was a fake diabolical laugh like a cartoon villain, and it always made her really laugh.

Another strategy Daphne outsmarted was The Anxiety Illusion. She explained it this way: "You know how you think something is real just because you can imagine it so strongly? My anxiety uses that to trick me into thinking I'm in trouble when it's just something I'm picturing in my head. One Anxiety Illusion was that everyone would leave me out at Becky's party. It was so real in my head that I didn't even want to go." Daphne was right. The more vivid an image the more likely it will feel true. To challenge this illusion Daphne created The Reality Detector, which could see through anxiety illusions. It measured the truth of anxious thoughts and images on a scale from zero—Never gonna happen, to ten—Run for your life!

Older children who are too cool to play spy or scientist can learn to be skeptics about their anxious thoughts and images. *Does this make sense or is it the anxiety talking?* For example, Craig took a long time to realize that when he woke up in the morning and "didn't feel well," he was actually experiencing anxiety in a clever disguise. If he woke up and was aware he was anxious, he would know what to do (he had several effective relaxation strategies). But "I don't feel well" convinced him that he was sick, not anxious, so he needed to stay home. Craig enjoyed talking back skeptically to his anxiety: "You expect me to believe that it's just a coincidence that I don't feel well when there's a test that I'm nervous about?"

Anxious thought patterns such as Doom and Gloom or The Anxiety Illusion are sometimes called thinking errors. I stay away from that phrase because children might think it means they aren't smart. I explain to anxious children that they are smart, but their anxiety isn't very smart. It just has a few sneaky strategies it uses over and over. Children are smart enough to outsmart anxiety and its tricks. One of these tricks is WYSIATI, Daniel Kahneman's acronym for What You See Is All There Is.

Kahneman's theory is that the slow and logical part of our brain is kind of lazy and lets the faster and more emotional part of the brain run things most of the time. This automatic part of the brain takes shortcuts because it cares more about speed than accuracy. One shortcut is that the evidence right in front of you is all you need to know—WYSIATI—so there's no need to seek more information. Sometimes WYSIATI is fine, but it creates problems for anxious children. Their own anxious thoughts and feelings are all they see, so they think it's all there is. *I'm thinking a scary thought and feeling scared, so danger must be at hand.* They don't bother to look for evidence of safety, and they reject reassurance, because they already know all they need to know. When children become aware of WYSIATI they can choose to seek out and assess additional information. It's also fun to try to pronounce.

Talk Back to Anxiety is a technique that can be either funny or serious, but I include it here in the playfulness section because it is a form of dramatic play. You can start this game by asking your child to imagine or draw their anxiety—it may look like a big blob, a monster, or a person. Some children might prefer to use a stuffed animal or puppet to represent their anxiety. Then ask your child to speak to the anxiety. Try not to speak for your child. You may be surprised by what you hear. The words might be angry, sad, hurt, funny, or defiant—or a mix of all these. "Stop sending scary pictures to my mind! I know you are trying to keep me safe but I also want to have fun! I know your tricks!"

A lot of anxious thoughts take the form of negative self-talk. That is, children tell themselves everything that can go wrong, or everything they did wrong. Overcoming anxiety requires a change in this self-talk. But it isn't as simple as changing "I can't do it" to "I can do it." Anxiety can creep back into any new self-talk. In fact, tone of voice is even more important than the words. A *Saturday Night Live* character, Stuart Smalley, was famous for saying, "I'm good enough, I'm smart enough, and doggone it, people like me." The problem was that he always said it in such a helpless and squeaky voice that he didn't even believe it himself. New self-talk needs to have a new confident tone of voice.

We are so used to our own self-talk voice that we don't question it, or even notice it. Whenever I talk to children about their anxious self-talk, I always ask if they talk to themselves in the first person ("I better not make a mistake") or the second person ("You better not make a mistake"). I ask them to speak their thoughts out loud in the same tone of voice that anxiety uses inside their heads so I can hear what it sounds like. When I hear it, I can honestly say, "That must get irritating, having someone follow you around all day talking to you like that" or "I don't think I could sleep either with that in my head." I also ask if the voice is familiar to them. Please note that these "voices" are not hallucinations, merely the way everyone talks to themselves.

The goal is to bring self-talk out into the open, which gives children more control over it. When they have a little distance from their anxious inner voice, they can shift to more positive and confident inner language. As they get to know their self-talk better, I usually ask: "If someone else talked to you that way, what would you say back? What is that voice trying to get you to do, or stop you from doing? Is that okay with you?" The psychologist Francine Shapiro recommends a variation of this idea: Have children say their repetitive anxious thoughts out loud in a silly cartoon voice. That destroys the credibility of the anxious thoughts and lets children assess them more accurately.

CHALLENGE ANXIOUS THINKING WITH WHAT IS

One strong challenge to anxiety is to help children embrace what is, rather than focus all their attention on what was or what might be. When we experience the present moment we might feel sad, angry, or even scared, but we don't usually feel anxious. After all, if we are truly focused on the present moment and we are scared, that means there is immediate danger. We need to act, not sit around and worry. Embracing *what is* in the present moment is the basis of meditation and mindfulness, which even young children can learn. It doesn't require formal training, just a willingness to notice everything you can about your breathing, your physical sensations, your immediate surroundings, or the thoughts in your head—right at this exact moment. Even just a few minutes of this mindfulness can reset the Security System and ease anxiety. It seems like a paradox, but even what ifs can be part of this mindfulness exercise: *I'm having a what-if thought right now.* That awareness reduces the power of the what ifs.

Telling the Story. When people have a near miss, such as an accident that leaves them shaken but not badly injured, they often tremble and cry. That isn't anxiety. It's *Getting Unscared,* as I described in chapter three. They are simply releasing the overflow of feelings from the scary event in order to restore a sense of balance and a feeling of safety. They may also have an urge to tell the story, perhaps even to tell it over and over. This is a natural healing process that helps prevent scary moments from turning into lasting anxiety. Getting unscared and telling the story are most effective when someone listens with warmth and attention, without judgment or criticism. The caring listener helps the child balance the pain of what happened in the past with the comforting safety of the present moment. *That was scary but now I am safe. I was alone but now I am with someone who cares.* Each retelling may bring additional details and more shaking or tears. That's good—it is the release of tension and fear.

The Reality Check. The most direct challenge to an anxious thought is a reality check: "Let's check that thought against what's true." Don't impose your picture of reality on your children, because that just makes them defensive. Instead, invite them to take a closer look at reality themselves. I like to use two questions I learned from the self-help author Byron Katie: *"Is it true? Can you be absolutely sure it's true?"* You may not agree with your child's answer. That's okay. Don't argue.

Katie's questions—which she calls The Work—are especially useful for fears such as "Dinosaurs will get into my room at night." The first question invites children to compare their anxious thoughts with their knowledge about the world. If they still think their fear is true, the second question helps them reflect a bit more. Reality checks help children stay in the here and now— what is—instead of the anxious world of what if. Katie uses two other questions to challenge troubling thoughts: *How do you react when you believe it? Who would you be without the thought?* Since you can't prove or disprove most thoughts, you might as well have thoughts that don't make you feel bad!

No one can predict the future. Anxious children think they can! They have a highly exaggerated sense of their ability to predict what is going to happen and they *know* it's going to be bad. When something bad does happen, that proves it. When nothing bad happens, that doesn't prove anything. Anxious children imagine a future, believe what they imagine, then act on that belief.

An old joke captures this idea: A man was driving down a country road when he got a flat tire. He had a spare tire, but didn't have a jack to lift up his car so he could change it. He remembered a farmhouse a couple of miles back, so he started to walk toward it to see if he could borrow a jack. As he walked, he imagined walking up to the house, knocking on the door, greeting the farmer, and asking to borrow a jack. He imagined the farmer being very friendly, loaning him a jack, and even driving him to the car to help with the tire. Then he thought, *What if he doesn't have a jack? Then I'll be stuck. What if he has a jack and doesn't want to loan it to me? What a jerk. Why would he do that?*

By that time the man was at the farmhouse. He thought, *I can't believe he won't help me.* He pounded fiercely on the door. The farmer opened the door and the driver yelled, "Keep your stupid jack!" and stormed off.

The Risk Check. We can never know for sure how things are going to work out, so we have to be able to accept some risk and uncertainty. This is where anxious children have trouble. They often demand absolute certainty where none is possible: "Tell me that you are never going to die." "Prove that wolves can't get into our house." Dangerous things do happen, though not as often as an anxious child expects. It doesn't help to argue with anxious children about probabilities. A tiny chance of something terrible is still terrible. The second-chicken response can help: "Can you tell that I know that is a risk and I am willing to take that risk?" or "That would be truly awful, but it is such a low chance that I am going to take the risk." When parents insist there is no risk, anxious children become extra cautious. They don't understand why you are telling them they are safe when they don't feel safe. Far better to acknowledge the risk, then do a risk check: *Is it worth the risk?*

Stepping outside the door, riding in a car, and running across a field all involve some risk. We accept risks like this every day without a moment's worry. Try to see risk from an anxious child's point of view. Imagine that each of those activities felt highly risky. You might still do them, but you'd have a lot of anxiety.

On the other hand, even the most fearful children have areas of life where they take risks. Ask children about risks they take without even thinking about them, and risks they deliberately take. What do they do in life that is scary, fun, and safe? Point out that they do things every day that some people find too scary, just as other people do things easily that they find scary.

Some children like to read through a long list of phobias and laugh at the ones that they don't have, like epistaxiophobia (fear of nosebleeds) or lutraphobia (fear of otters).

"Be prepared" may be a good motto, but anxious children go overboard and try to be perfectly prepared for every possibility. Of course, life is too complex for that. Anxious overpreparation just leads to exhaustion, without making life any more predictable. I like to share another one of my favorite jokes with children who overprepare:

Alvin's lifelong dream was to appear on the stage, but he had always been too shy and too busy to pursue his dream. One time Alvin was on vacation in New York City. He ran into an old friend in Times Square who told Alvin he was a producer of Broadway plays. Alvin revealed his secret fantasy of being on the stage, and his friend said, "This is your lucky day, because I was just on my way to find an actor for the show tonight to replace someone who got sick. He's just your size, so the costume will fit perfectly." Alvin insisted he would never be able to learn his lines in just a few hours, but his friend said not to worry, there was only one line: "Hark, I hear a cannon."

Alvin couldn't believe his good luck, and ran back to his hotel, practicing his line the whole way: "*Hark,* I hear a cannon! Hark, *I* hear a cannon. Hark, I hear a *cannon.*" He practiced his line in front of the mirror a thousand times. Exhausted, he fell asleep, dreaming of his line. Waking with a start, he realized he was late and raced out of the hotel and onto the street, yelling, "Look out, hark I hear a cannon, get out of my way, hark I hear a cannon." Alvin ran into the theater, all the while practicing his one line. His friend yelled at him for being late and the stage manager threw the costume onto him and pushed him out onto the stage. As soon as he reached his mark, with all eyes on him, there was a tremendous "Boom!" Alvin jumped in the air and shouted, "Yikes! What was that?"

The *Belief Check* is a bit more difficult than a reality check or risk check, because the beliefs that lie underneath anxious thoughts are often invisible. It can take some careful listening and exploration to bring out those beliefs. For example, Kevin was a very bright sixth-grader who went into a panic when he couldn't solve a homework problem. I asked him my usual question: "What would be so bad about leaving that problem blank or getting it wrong?" (This question must be asked in a warm and friendly way.) Kevin said that then he wouldn't get the highest possible grade, so I kept asking (in a gentle way): "So what? What would be so bad about that?" Eventually we came to the underlying belief: *My entire future rests on getting into a top graduate school, and every homework assignment and test affects that goal.*

Uncovering this belief was very powerful for Kevin. Before that conversation he said, "I don't know what's wrong with me. I get so stressed over stupid little things." This self put-down didn't help his anxiety. After he realized the underlying belief, he said, "I understand why it bothers me so much, but my long-term goal is not at stake with every single math problem." In other words, he challenged his anxious belief instead of worrying endlessly about his homework. I told Kevin that he had uncovered one of the deep secrets of overcoming anxiety: *Don't believe everything that you believe.*

CHALLENGE ANXIOUS THINKING BY ACTIVATING MORE OF THE BRAIN

Louis Cozolino, a therapist and neuroscientist, introduced me to the idea of multiple brain pathways. A pathway is a large bundle of nerve cells that act together to control a major area of brain activity, such as memory, attachment, emotion, senses, language, and motivation. Cozolino explains that young brains develop best when children receive a great deal of love and affection and when many different pathways in the brain are activated at the same time. I always knew about the love and affection part, but the idea of activating multiple pathways was new.

Dramatic play is a good example of multiple active pathways, because it involves movement, language, imagination, and emotion. In contrast, children in an anxious state have one pathway—anxiety—highly activated. All of their other pathways are underactivated. Relaxation lowers the stimulation of the anxiety pathway. The techniques that follow increase the activation of other pathways.

A quick way to awaken more of the brain is to Get Sensory. Look around and find five green things as fast as you can. Close your eyes and notice the feel of the clothes or air on your skin. Notice what's under your feet or what you're sitting on. Hold an ice cube in your hand, play with mud, or touch as many different textures as you can. Give or receive a massage. The result will be instant activation of the sensory pathways in the brain. Don't forget inner senses as well, such as vestibular stimulation, triggered by spinning or hanging upside down. The field sobriety test (used to assess drunk drivers) is actually a test of proprioception, the sense of one's body in space. You can use the same test as a way to focus attention on this inner sense. Have children touch their nose with one finger, walk a straight line on the floor, and balance themselves on one foot, then do it all with their eyes closed.

Any of the various brain pathways can be activated to reduce anxiety. You can Get Physical by running around or roughhousing; Get Mathematical by doing arithmetic problems (as long as math doesn't increase your child's anxiety!); or Get Close by snuggling and cuddling. Silly Dancing, which I mentioned earlier as a playful antidote to anxiety, activates at least three important brain pathways at one time: movement, music, and the connection that comes from doing something fun and goofy together.

Most anxious people have discovered that they are less anxious when they are in a state of *flow*, where they are fully absorbed in a task or an activity. Also known as being "in the zone" or having a "peak experience," flow is a heightened brain state that is very different from the intensity of anxiety. Time disappears and the now moment seems to stretch. Instead of one small sliver of brain activity—what if, what if, what if—flow is full engagement with one's whole body and mind.

Of course, you can't just tell anxious children to drop their anxiety and flow! But you don't have to just wait for flow to happen either. Children can cultivate the experience of flow by engaging in creative activity or hobbies that are highly engrossing. One trick is to find things that are just challenging enough—too easy or too difficult and flow is broken.

Metaphors for anxiety activate more of the brain because they add layers of language, imagery, and abstract thought. The metaphor that I use most often to describe anxious thinking is The Projectionist. As I described in chapter four, the projectionist sends anxiety-arousing images, scenes, and thoughts to the screen of our mind. As a girl named Dora said to me, "The projectionist might pick what movies to play, but *I* get to pick whether to stay and watch them." I also like the metaphor of an inner thermostat, which automatically turns on a fan to cool off the brain when anxiety heats up.

Camille developed a unique metaphor that helped her cope with anxious thoughts—The Invitation: "I used to be really nervous that my mother would forget to pick me up after school. I really panicked a lot. Then I got the idea of invitations. When I start to worry I imagine receiving a fancy invitation from the Anxiety Society. On the outside of the envelope it says, 'OH, NO!' On the inside it says, 'If you accept this invitation, breathe fast and tie yourself in knots. You will have no fun, no independence, and you'll always be scared. If you decline the invitation, take a slow deep breath. You will remember that your mom always comes to pick you up, you will have fun with your friends, and you will be relaxed and safe.' I always decline the invitation when I remember to see my worries that way."

Thinking About Thinking activates a new brain pathway by adding language and reason to anxious thoughts. Several of the techniques based on the Flame Model of Emotions (chapter five) work this way, such as rating the intensity of anxiety on a scale from one to ten, describing physical sensations in detail, or identifying the spark, flame, fuel, and water. Thinking about anxious thinking is the basis for The Reminder, a technique I described in chapter three: Simply write on a piece of paper, "I'm having a panic attack. It is uncomfortable but not life threatening. It will pass." Carry that paper in your pocket and read it as needed, so the panicky thoughts aren't the only things going on in the brain.

CHALLENGE ANXIOUS THOUGHTS BY WELCOMING AND TRANSFORMING THEM

Children with anxious thoughts often fight hard to get rid of them, with little success. The solution is a paradox: Welcome and embrace anxious thoughts in order to transform them and really get rid of them for good. This welcoming of thoughts is very similar to the welcoming of emotions discussed in the previous chapter. Here are some ideas to help your child transform anxious thoughts by embracing them:

Worry Time. One common treatment for worry is to suggest that children set aside time for it. A regular worry time shortly before bed is best. Typically we avoid our worries as much as we can. Then they come crashing in uninvited, just as we are trying to relax or fall asleep. Worry Time is an anti-avoidance technique that breaks this pattern. Ten to fifteen minutes is usually a good length of time. All you have to do is worry as hard as you can until the timer goes off. You want the length to be short enough that it doesn't interfere with your child's life, but long enough that the what ifs and other worries start to get a bit boring. Children often insist that they can't worry on command. That's fine, they can just enjoy not worrying for ten minutes! The worries will return, of course, but when they do your child can say to them, "You had your chance, now you have to wait until tomorrow's Worry Time."

Worry Dolls are a Guatemalan folklore tradition for easing children's fears. These are tiny dolls who listen to a child's worries without judgment or criticism. The dolls allow children to speak worries out loud without the embarrassment of telling an adult. Some children prefer a box into which they can place their worries, or a ritual of writing out worries and burning them in a fireplace. A diary can serve the same purpose, with the added value that writing out worries can transform them into art, thereby making them less toxic.

Useful Rehearsal. Not all repetitive thought is anxiety. Some problems do benefit from worrying about them, or from rehearsing all the possibilities you can imagine. Your job is to help your child determine whether their thinking is productive, or just the exhausting spin of anxiety. For example, if a child says, "I was up all night thinking about *X*," you can ask, "Did you come up with any new ideas?" If they say yes, that's useful rehearsal. If they say no, encourage reflection about whether all that thought is useful: "Is it an unanswerable question? Is your thinking leading you to a decision or plan? Do you feel more confident after you spend time going over it and over it? Would you have more success devoting that energy to relaxation?" Don't ask all those questions at once!

Rehearse Success. Anxious children spend a lot of time reviewing the past and preparing for the future, but there is one type of useful rehearsal that they forget to do. They don't remember past times that they coped well, and they don't imagine themselves coping well in the future. To reverse this, encourage anxious children to Rehearse Success, the way nonanxious children do: "Yes, it will be challenging, so how will you handle it?" "That went really well, what did you figure out to do?" Many athletes visualize events in their minds before they start—and they always visualize victory. The good news is that anxious children already know how to rehearse, since they are so used to rehearsing past and future disasters ("what if" and "if only"). All they need is a friendly reminder to rehearse effective responses, active coping, and successful outcomes instead.

What else? An anxious thought can feel like "the whole story," because it fills up so much of an anxious child's brain activity. Let's say your daughter forgets a homework assignment. She thinks, *My teacher is going to be so mad at me.* She can't get that thought out of her mind. It's the beginning, middle, and end of the story. One repetitive anxious thought isn't much of a story! That's why I like to ask: "And then what will happen? And then what will happen after that?" You may discover deeper underlying fears, or your child may discover that it really isn't so bad after all. Another powerful question about an anxious thought is, "What does that thought reveal about what is important to you?"

This last question is based on narrative therapy, pioneered by therapists Michael White and David Epston. The answers open up the possibility of a richer story. For example, when I asked that question of Kevin, the boy who had so much anxiety about his homework, he said his panic revealed that getting into a good college was very important to him. With that opening, we could talk about whether obsession with his homework being perfect would help him get into college. He saw that the answer was no, and that relaxation exercises would actually be better for meeting his goals. That was a big breakthrough, because before that question relaxation seemed like a waste of time. He told me with total shock and surprise: "You know, I spend more time stressing than it takes to do a deep-breathing exercise." Yes, I knew that, but it was wonderful that Kevin finally knew it too.

After asking children what their anxiety reveals about what is important to them, you can ask another question: "What else is just as important to you, or even more important?" For Kevin, the answer was "having a life," which meant time having fun with his family and friends. This answer led him to see, for the first time, that anxiety—not homework—was his real problem. Try it on yourself: What do your anxious thoughts reveal about what's important to you? What else is important that your anxiety interferes with?

Psychiatrist Daniel Siegel is an expert on mindfulness and neuroscience. In *The Whole-Brain Child* he describes a father trying to help a child who can't sleep because of a fear of mummies. First the father dismisses and denies the fear: "There's nothing to be afraid of. Look around. There are no mummies in the closet or under the bed or anywhere in your room. Now go to sleep. You're safe." Then Siegel proposes a better alternative: "That can be scary, having those pictures in your mind. You know what you can do? You can change the pictures." The child asks how this works, and the father says, "Well, what if we made the picture less scary and more funny? Like, what if we put a tutu and a baseball hat on that mummy. . . ."

Jack, an eleven-year-old boy, came up with a very similar idea. He said that at first he tried hard *not* to think about scary things, and that didn't work at all. Then he discovered it worked better to change *how* he was thinking about them. That made the thoughts less scary, and they were less likely to pop back into his head. Jack said, "I used to just believe every anxious thought I had, and they made me very nervous. The more I tried not to have them, the louder they got. Then I realized they are just ideas—not every idea is a good idea. My friend Jerry has all kinds of bad ideas—mostly things that will get us into trouble—so I pretend that my anxious thoughts are some more of Jerry's bad ideas."

Safe Adventures. Safe adventures are a great way to challenge anxious thoughts. They are fun, safe, and just dangerous enough to be exciting. To retrain the anxious brain, children need to experience that life can be scary *and* safe *and* fun, all at the same time. The concept of a safe adventure is a revolutionary idea for most anxious children. Once they get it, however, they are usually very creative at finding activities that provide fun, excitement, and relief of tension, while maintaining a basic feeling of safety. Many children find this scary safety in outdoor physical adventures, such as climbing on rocks or crossing a small stream on a fallen log. Remember to challenge yourself to do things that you know are safe but feel very scary to you.

There's an old saying, *"The only exercise some people get is jumping to conclusions."* Anxious children have such a hard time with what-if thinking that it is hard for them to stick with what is. They are fixed in the past, or lost in scary speculations about the future. As parents, we can give them assistance in noticing what is real right now. Children are often skeptical that noticing reality or playing the games in this chapter will make them feel better. Of course, anxious children are skeptical about everything—except the truth of their own anxious thoughts! You can't force them to do any of these techniques, but you can present them as experiments that are worth a try.

Since I started this chapter with a train joke about preoccupation with the past—"Oh, was I thirsty!"—I'll end with another train joke about preoccupation with the future. Even though it is a bit morbid I think it is a great example of how *what ifs* can take over our thinking and make us treat our thoughts as facts:

A young woman couldn't decide whether to take the bus or the train to visit her sister. She thought: If I take the train I might have a seat by myself or someone might sit next to me. Probably someone will sit next to me. If someone sits next to me it might be a man or it might be a woman. It will probably be a man. If a man sits next to me he might be married or single. He will probably be single. If he is single I might want to marry him or I might not want to marry him. I'll probably want to marry him. If we get married we might have a child or we might not. We will probably have a child. If we have a child it might be a boy or might be a girl. It will probably be a boy. If we have a son he might serve in the Army or he might not serve in the Army. He will probably be in the Army. If he is in the Army he might go to war or he might not go to war. He will probably go to war. If he is in a war he might be killed or he might be safe. He will probably be killed. I think I'll take the bus.

CHAPTER SEVEN

From Monsters under the Bed to Worry Soup:
Tackling the Most Common Childhood Anxieties

*Are we seeing more anxiety these days? Yes! One boy falls
apart if his father is late picking him up. Another student
becomes agitated if anything happens that is different from
what she expects. We have children who chew on their clothes,
are afraid to go outside, or tear up every page of homework
that has a smudge. One girl who has trouble making friends
started to cry when someone complimented her new shoes!*
—A teacher in an after-school program

Previous chapters have focused on different areas of life affected
by anxiety: bodies, behaviors, emotions, thoughts, and relationships. This chapter divides things up differently, exploring playful parenting techniques for nine common varieties of childhood
anxiety:

- Attachment Anxiety
- Social Anxiety
- Monsters under the Bed
- Life's Dangers
- Traumatic Fears
- Inflexibility

- Excessive Anxiety to Please
- Matters of Life and Death
- Worry Soup

ATTACHMENT ANXIETY

I attended a lecture many years ago, when my daughter, Emma, was a baby. The slide projector broke and the lecturer announced, "I'm not too worried—someone is coming to fix it—but Stanley is very worried." We had no idea what she was talking about. She continued: "Stanley is my father, and even though he has been dead a long time I can hear his voice on my shoulder telling me this is a disaster, everyone is going to leave, and I will never be invited back to this conference again. All that anxious talk in my head used to make me panic, but now I just tell Stanley it's going to be okay."

I don't remember anything from that lecture except Stanley. But I vividly recall asking myself, *What kind of voice do I want to be on Emma's shoulder when she grows up?*

My hope for Emma, and all children, is that they will *internalize a nurturing and calming parental figure,* an inner voice of comfort and security. An anti-Stanley who can help them cope with upsets such as a short separation or a mild feeling of danger. That internalization doesn't happen overnight. It takes thousands and thousands of times that we meet children's needs, soothe them, and let them know they can count on us. Beloved blankets or dolls are called "transitional objects" because they are a transition between the real-life warmth and safety of a caregiver and that internalized sense of security. Children who don't have that internalized nurturing and confident inner voice are more likely to experience insecure attachment and separation anxiety. Children who were neglected or abused in their early years, or experienced a great loss, have extra difficulty internalizing comfort and safety. But even well-loved children can have trouble having that inner voice, especially if it is drowned out by anxious thoughts.

A little attachment anxiety is a healthy part of every child's Security System. Stranger anxiety, for example, is a sign that the child understands the difference between a familiar face and an unfamiliar one.

For nonanxious children, a little extra love, affection, and patience carry them through that burst of anxiety. They just need a gentle reminder that they are safe, and some games that build security. Peekaboo is a classic attachment game for babies, because it lets them play with the idea of missing you and finding you again, in a very safe and fun way. As children get older, hide-and-seek is a way for them to safely explore what it means to lose someone—or be lost—and find each other again. Another way children use play to become comfortable with separation is with games that include a lot of hellos and goodbyes. For example, you can pick up several dolls and stuffed animals and have each one say goodbye to your child, disappear behind your back, then quickly return and say hello again.

Children who suffer from excess attachment anxiety have trouble internalizing a sense of safety. Instead of brief periods of moderate distress, they have prolonged periods of intense distress. They need loads of extra comfort, especially cozy cuddling, no matter how old they are.

Sometimes the problem is not separation anxiety, but too much separation. Many children are away from their loved ones too long. Your children may simply need more time with you in order to lower their anxiety. When you do get home they need you to put your work down and play with them. Be prepared, however, for children to spend the first part of the reunion being sad or angry that you were gone. They may hide, ignore you, or pick a fight. Go after them to make a reconnection. They know you have returned. They are just showing you what it was like to miss you. Separation anxiety at bedtime may also be a matter of needing more connection rather than fear of being alone: "You had a good dinner that will last you until breakfast, and now I am going to fill you with enough love and affection to last you until morning."

At the other extreme, some parents try to protect their children from attachment anxiety by avoiding all separations. This is unworkable. Parents have places to go and children need their own activities. But the real problem with never leaving children with another trusted adult is that it deprives children of the chance to experience small separations that they can handle. It also deprives them of the joy of reunion when parents return.

If you fear that any separation will damage your child, make sure to look inside yourself, at your own feelings about separation. It may be you, more than your child, who feels out of sorts and at a loss when you are apart. Your wonderfully empathic child, picking up your distress, may then try to protect you by refusing to leave your side!

A friend of mine was reluctant to leave her son at preschool while he was crying, even though his teacher said he was always fine after a few minutes. My friend has never forgotten the wisdom of the teacher, who said to her son one day, "Crying is a good way to say goodbye to your mom." The mother understood that this message was aimed at her as well as her son.

Another friend described a game—*Let's push Mommy out the door!*—invented by her daughter's teacher to deal with drop-off anxiety. The teacher, holding the young girl in her arms, bumped gently into Mommy, and everyone giggled. A few more bumps and Mommy was out the door. Playful physical contact can be a great replacement for the clinging-to-the-leg that children use when they are in a panic about separation.

Speaking of desperate clinging, the attachment system in young children is all about getting someone by their side—it's called *proximity seeking*. That's why babies cry, and it's why adults can't stand the sound of babies crying. We want it to stop, so we rush over to give them what they need. Nonanxious children reset their Security System once their needs have been met: *All is clear; I can calm down and relax now.* Anxious children don't have a strong all-clear signal, so their proximity seeking never stops. Instead, they grab hold of your leg for dear life, melt into tears or tantrums when you try to leave, or make up endless excuses for why you have to stay. It's very annoying! Unfortunately, when parents get annoyed, children feel rejected and that only increases their clinginess.

Attachment panic is intense separation anxiety that includes an agitated state of confusion and frantic searching for comfort. Proximity seeking has not worked, and the child now feels all alone and terrified. You might actually be there, but the child can't process that fact through the panic. If you have ever dragged a child kicking and screaming into time-out, then you have seen attachment panic. Your child probably already felt disconnected from you, since most misbehavior comes from disconnection. Now your child is absolutely panicked by the impending separation. It doesn't matter how short the time-out is going to be or what the child did to "deserve" it. When you see attachment panic, switch gears immediately and give comfort. Keep giving comfort until they are fully comforted. There will be time to deal

with the child's behavior later. Some children experience attachment panic at bedtime or if parents are late picking them up ("I
thought you died or forgot me!"). Divorce of parents or death of
a loved one can also trigger attachment panic. Adults get attachment panic too. Did you ever lose track of your toddler in a busy
store?

My favorite game for children who cling is I'll Never Let You
Go. Reverse the roles and cling on to your child. Say, "I'm never
going to let you go—it might get a little messy when I have to stir
the soup or go to the bathroom, but that's okay, I'll never, ever,
ever let you go." Be lighthearted, not sarcastic! Very soon, your
clingy child will squirm away giggling. It usually takes less than
a minute, but if they keep clinging, you can be even more obnox-
iously clingy. By playfully overfilling the need for connection,
your child can return to a healthy balance between connection
and independence.

Another anti-clinging game, which I learned from a mother
with a very clingy child, is called The Worst Shoe Ever. If your
child grabs your ankle and won't let go, pretend that you are
wearing the worst shoe in the world, which can barely allow you
to walk. "Why did I buy this shoe? It's so heavy! And bony! And
there is only one!" This game allows you to express your frustration in a way that doesn't hurt your child's feelings, because the
things you say are embedded in play and are said with a smile
and a laugh: "I can't get anything done with this shoe on me! I
am going to scream."

The Worst Backpack Ever is a variation if your child clings to
your upper body instead of your ankle. Many of the games from
chapter four—such as sending children on secret missions to different rooms of the house, or seeing how far apart you can get

while holding two ends of a piece of string—are well suited to attachment anxiety.

Some anxious children can't seem to cope without you, even as their peers become more independent. They act helpless, hesitant, or younger than their years. This *anxious dependence* worsens when parents rescue too much. Children with anxious dependence need to be comforted, but not rescued. Psychologist Michele Borba asks parents to consider this question: "Would you say your response usually strengthens your child's independence muscle or weakens it?" Children need love, affection, and security, *and* they need to feel a little discomfort as they venture out into the world on their own. Don't expect complete independence all at once, but keep taking one small step after another. Balance every gentle push toward independence with extra time for your children to cuddle, snuggle, and fill their need for security.

Many fathers and grandparents feel rejected when their children only want Mommy. I always urge them not to take it personally. Children in a state of high attachment anxiety are unable to see people for who they really are. All they see is: *This is not Mom.* Until they have internalized an inner sense of security, they won't be able to relax and enjoy other loved ones. In the meantime, don't scold them for not being happy with you as a substitute. Empathize with their longing: "Mom will be back soon. You can tell me how much you miss her, or we can make her a special drawing as a welcome home sign." The purpose of the drawing is to rebuild the sense of connection that was broken by the separation. Once the intensity of the feeling has lowered, you might play a silly game of Where's Mommy? looking under all the cushions and blankets.

SOCIAL ANXIETY

The term social anxiety refers to shyness, timidity, extreme intro-version, and excess worry about what other people think. It causes a great deal of suffering. Social situations can trigger all the usual symptoms of anxiety, as well as specific problems such as avoiding eye contact, withdrawal or hiding, embarrassment, and self-consciousness. At the extreme of social anxiety, children may not speak to anyone outside their family or may refuse to go to school. A lack of social skills adds to social anxiety, and social anxiety makes it hard to develop good social skills.

We want our children to worry *a little* about what other people will think, however. That helps them participate in a community and be a good friend. Cathie asks her mother, "Do you think Sylvia will like the birthday present I got for her?" That mini-worry is a healthy midpoint between two extremes: "I can't go to the party because she might not like the present," and "I don't care if she likes it or not—that's her problem."

Children with social anxiety often rehearse and overprepare for every upcoming conversation and encounter. They vividly imagine social disasters. They don't think: *Maybe it will be okay* or *What's the big deal?* No, once they imagine those disasters, it's certain doom. Social anxiety most often involves the fear of being criticized, ignored, excluded, or humiliated. Some children try to be invisible. They pray that the teacher won't call on them, or cross the street to avoid meeting someone they know. One father I met does endless laundry because the tiniest stain triggers his daughter's refusal to go to school: "Everyone will see!"

Excessive social anxiety is painful, but that isn't the only problem it causes. Socially anxious children become lonelier and more isolated as they avoid more and more social contacts. With no chance to practice and improve their social skills, they struggle to make friends or join the group.

Are you socially anxious? If so, the single best thing you can do for your socially anxious child is to push yourself to face and overcome your own fears. I know it's hard! (Here's a secret: The techniques and strategies in this book are designed for children, but they work just as well for adults. Try them!) If you are resistant to working on your own social anxiety, consider the results of a recent study from Johns Hopkins University: Socially anxious parents were less warm and affectionate toward their children and more likely to express criticism and doubt. In addition to genetics, this might be how social anxiety gets transmitted from one generation to the next.

Are you outgoing, confident, and socially skilled? If so, you may be confused by socially anxious children. The best thing you can do is to be understanding and empathic. Your children don't just need to "try harder" or "get over it." They need two things from you: acceptance of who they are and a gentle push toward engaging socially even though it is uncomfortable. Remember, *gentle push*. Both words are important.

Slow to warm up. Many anxious children are slow to warm up to new people or new situations. They have a strong reaction to anything unfamiliar and take a long time for things to become familiar. This trait used to be called shyness, but many experts in childhood anxiety argue against using that word. The word "shy" suggests—incorrectly—a permanent problem. Psychologist Tamar Chansky recommends, "Begin to see your socially anxious child not as stuck in shyness, but as working slowly on a continuum toward connection. . . . Instead of telling people your child is shy, say that he 'needs time to warm up' and 'will be ready to play a little later.'"

Michele Borba suggests scheduling in warm-up time. I love this idea. It will help you not to be so annoyed when your child needs extra time on your lap—or extra time arguing with you—before finding the courage to venture forth. If you have an hour to spend at the playground, think of it as a half hour of lap time and a half hour of playtime (or fifty-nine minutes of lap time, then one trip down the slide together). That will lower your frustration level and will allow your child to fill up with confidence by your side. Once filled with security at "home base," a child can step out to explore. It's just like scheduling extra time to travel when you expect heavy traffic. Provide a safe and loving space for children to observe and to imagine participating for as long as they need. The payoff will be a long-term increase in their ability to warm up to new things. It just may take a good long time for that safety to internalize.

Each push out of a child's comfort zone needs to be balanced with extra support and encouragement. Stepping out of social anxiety is a big deal, and children need a loving ally by their side as they take even the smallest of steps. If a child has trouble making friends, one idea is to invite over a classmate and the classmate's parents—the kids may eventually find the adults boring and go off to play together. Of course, socially anxious parents are horrified by this idea!

Parents of slow to warm up or withdrawn children need to protect them from adults who come on too strong. I suggest finding a family friend (or therapist) who can take the time needed to gradually gain the child's confidence and build a relationship, drawing him or her out of isolation without shaming, humiliation, or impossible demands. It is important for socially anxious children to learn the value of saying "thank you" and looking people in the eye, but we have to be sure not to pressure them beyond what they can handle. Balance your gentle push with acknowledgment that these social niceties are not easy for them. You have more room to push if you do it in a lighthearted way. My favorite game with withdrawn children is to say "hi" until I get a response—even if it takes a hundred times. The key is to say it each time with a warm smile, as if it was the first time, not with escalating frustration.

Lacking social confidence and skill. Most socially anxious children don't get enough practice to develop social confidence and skill. Some children—such as those on the autism spectrum—might be neurologically wired to avoid faces, eye contact, or emotional interactions. Other children lack social opportunities because they are overly aggressive, usually as a result of exposure to violence or other trauma. Whatever the cause, children who lack social skills and social confidence need extra help.

Michele Borba breaks down social confidence into specific skills to practice, such as smiling, eye contact, speaking in a louder and more confident voice, introductions, taking turns in conversations, and friendly body language. Some other key skills are the ability to guess what other people might be feeling, to speak directly and clearly about one's own feelings, and to give compliments.

I like to use puppets or stuffed animals to practice these skills with younger children, to keep things less serious. Pick up an animal and give it a character—it might be superfriendly or supershy—whatever makes your child laugh most. Line up all the stuffed animals and dolls so that your child can practice speaking in front of a "group." When playing this way, remember that your goal is to evoke laughter. It isn't a quiz or lecture disguised as a game! It's using play to reduce the tension children feel about their social interactions.

A variation of this game is for you to be a totally clueless character, because children love to be the expert. For example, your character could say, "Should I look at the floor or the ceiling when I talk to someone?" Your child will say, "Look at the other person!" and you can act astonished to learn such a brilliant idea. Pretend your character doesn't know how to make friends or is reluctant to engage in social situations, and your child will enjoy teaching you social skills. They will even teach your character social skills you didn't think they knew. Of course, you may need to supply basic information ("I don't think he likes when you hit him over the head with that toy . . ."), but don't be heavy-handed with the teaching. Children learn better when they are laughing than when they are scolded, lectured, or criticized.

With older children you can use role-playing situations without the puppets. Let children tell you what role you should take, and exaggerate to get them laughing. With a child of any age, be sure to include a lot of cuddling and other affection as you play, because children are easily humiliated by their lack of social skills and confidence.

Some children spend most of their time alone but are not socially anxious. They are loners, with lower social needs than other children. Socially anxious children, however, might pretend that they don't need any friends, but they do. You might think that being lonely would motivate them to make friends, but it isn't that simple. They might even hide their loneliness from their parents, because they are afraid of being pressured to engage in social encounters that scare them. If you aren't sure if your child is lonely or a loner, ask him or her for a description of an ideal weekend, and notice how much social contact it includes. Another indication is when children say they are bored. This often means they are lonely, though it can also mean that they haven't learned how to entertain themselves because they are so used to being entertained by televisions and computer screens.

Remember to separate your memories of childhood from your child's experience. One mother told me that she spent years pushing her daughter, Ashley, to be more social, until she realized that Ashley was happy! She had just the level of social interaction she wanted, but her mother never would have been happy with that much alone time. As my mother used to say: *Put on your jacket, I'm cold.*

Fear of rejection or humiliation. Socially anxious children are highly sensitive to rejection, exclusion, and humiliation. They may believe that everyone is staring at them or that their most embarrassing secrets are tattooed on their foreheads for all to see. One playful approach to these fears is a role-reversal game, where you act out the voice of a "loser" stuffed animal or character that your child can reject and humiliate.

This game may appear to promote meanness and cruelty, but it doesn't. It reduces children's tensions about very tense areas of their lives. That will make them stronger and also make them kinder. Don't lecture your children that they are acting toward you just like the mean kids who reject and exclude them. That's the whole point of this game! They get to reverse the roles—in fantasy play—so they can overcome their fears. You will learn just how humiliated they feel by how viciously they tease you or the stuffed animal character. These games also help children develop a thicker skin, which is very important because socially anxious children often take playful teasing too seriously.

When socially anxious children are overwhelmed with a fear of embarrassment, parents can ease the worry by sharing embarrassing moments from their own childhood and adolescence—not as a lesson to children to "get over it," but to normalize the experience. You'll also share a good laugh together.

MONSTERS UNDER THE BED

With so many real dangers in the world, why are children afraid of imaginary or perfectly safe things such as monsters under the bed, dinosaurs, or flushing the toilet? One reason is that children's thoughts and imaginings can trigger exactly the same fear reactions as real-life dangers. This is especially likely when the images are vivid, and we know that anxious children tend to have vivid imaginations. Sensory overload also makes images more vivid, such as when a villain in a movie is accompanied by loud or scary music. Be sure to provide comfort just as if the fear was "real and important," because it *is* real and important to your child.

Another reason children have unreasonable fears such as monsters under the bed is that they aren't able to put their deepest fears into words. They might be lonely or scared of death, but they don't know how to tell you. They might not understand the root of their fear, so they pick something that sounds scary, such as monsters. They aren't being manipulative. Children are really and truly afraid of the monsters under the bed. They just aren't aware of the deeper levels of what their fear means.

My friend Margaret told me that when her son developed a fear of monsters in his closet she remembered that he had been telling her for weeks that he was lonely at night. She always told him he was fine and that he needed to go back to bed. It seemed that once he recognized that she wasn't going to listen to his real feelings, he decided to try something that she couldn't ignore—monsters. She said, "My sister told me he was just making up excuses to be with me. I told her that if he is going to all that trouble to be with me, he probably needs to be with me!"

"Silly" childhood fears can have a symbolic meaning to children that we don't understand, because we are grown-ups. For example, many children develop anxiety about their bodily waste being flushed down the toilet. This is a normal reaction for a young child who is trying to make sense of identity—*Am I the same person when I get my hair cut, when I put on different clothes, when I wear a mask?* As their waste flushes, they worry, *Is that a part of me? Am I still whole if it disappears?* Our job is to be sensitive to the feelings behind our children's fears, even when they seem silly to us.

Fred Rogers, the longtime host of television's *Mister Rogers' Neighborhood,* understood this sensitivity. He wrote a song about being afraid of being sucked down the drain of the bathtub, which included the refrain, "You can never go down / Can never go down / Can never go down the drain." In a tribute on *Time* magazine's website, James Poniewozik wrote, "Fred Rogers knew that childhood, which we misremember as carefree and innocent, is a time of roiling passions, anguish and terror. His show . . . was his professional way of doing what he had done as a boy in Latrobe, Pa., when he played with puppets to calm himself after hearing scary news reports."

Sometimes a silly fear isn't silly at all; we just don't know the whole story. A young boy named Anthony reacted with terror as soon as he heard the *Sesame Street* theme song. He was too young to explain why it scared him. If that was all you knew about the fear, would you try to talk Anthony out of being afraid of something so harmless?

Let's look at this same story again, with more detail. Anthony's mother told me that when he was two years old he saw *Sesame Street* for the first time. She writes, "I heard strange sounds from Anthony and went to check. He was standing in the middle of the room staring at the TV with a look of terror on his face. A giant boulder with eyes and a mouth was chasing two cartoon characters. I immediately picked him up and he began shaking like a leaf. I had never seen him scared like that before. He cried awhile until he seemed calm and okay again. Several months later—with no sign that this image still bothered him—we were sitting at the breakfast table and the *Sesame Street* theme started in the other room. He became frightened and wanted to be held. At that point I realized that he was traumatized by the cartoon and had been for months. I began to playfully help him work through it. One day I made a ball with play dough to look like the boulder, got a little man figure from his room, and had the boulder chase the little man. Anthony immediately used the little man to smash the boulder. We played that until he seemed satisfied and was tired of it. After that, his fear of the 'boulder man' (and the song) was gone."

Compare that full story to the abbreviated version, when you didn't know why a happy song caused so much fear. What a difference it makes when we know the reason, but that isn't always possible. When you don't know why a child is anxious, assume there is a good reason.

As you consider what deeper fear might lurk beneath a "silly" fear, keep in mind that the most likely possibilities for younger children will involve separation, danger, or being alone in the dark. For older children it may have to do with school, friends, or bullying. At any age children can pick up family stress—such as marital conflict, illness, or financial worries—and translate it into something more concrete such as monsters or kidnappers. One boy I worked with became terrified whenever his mother and stepfather had any kind of argument. He had already endured the breakup of one marriage in his life, and he was afraid of experiencing another. When he heard them raise their voices, he picked up all of his pretend weapons, put on multiple coats and sweaters as "armor," and went into their room to "protect them from bad guys."

Some families have found success with "monster spray" to clear out monsters under the bed, or some other playful tactic to overcome the fear. I think this can be effective as long as it is very clear to the child that you are playing a game. If children take monster spray to mean that you believe the monsters are real, then it can increase their fear. You can signify with your tone of voice and body language that you are playing a make-believe monster-elimination game, or you can keep it playful by dressing up in a silly outfit.

As with so many other anxieties, one great way to help children with unrealistic fears is to schedule regular roughhousing times. Ten minutes of playful wrestling or pillow fighting can boost children's confidence and rebuild their feelings of connection with you, and those are huge benefits in overcoming fear.

Monsters under the bed and other imaginary terrors often appear at bedtime as a way for children to express a fear of going to bed or a fear of going to sleep. These are two different things, though they sound the same. Fear of going to bed is typically about separation, being left alone in the dark, or FOMO (Fear Of Missing Out). Fear of going to sleep is usually about scary dreams or troubling memories and emotions. Sleep-related fears may also be a sign of existential dread, which is discussed in a later section of this chapter.

Sharing dreams in the morning can help children who resist sleep because of scary dreams. Older children may prefer a private dream journal by the side of the bed. You can also encourage your child to make up a happy dream during your goodnight ritual.

When children wake in the night with a nightmare or scary dream, validate their feelings first ("I can understand why you would be scared of that"), and then help them understand the difference between images and reality ("It was a dream"). I often ask children to draw the scariest scenes from their nightmares, and I am duly frightened when they show them to me. You can also ask them to make up a next chapter or a happy ending to the dream.

LIFE'S DANGERS

A friend told me that her two-year-old daughter, Libby, was startled by a car alarm and ran to the window asking, "What's happening, Mama? Is everything okay?" Her mother told her it was just a car alarm making "big noises" but everything was okay. Libby picked up her big stuffed hippo and told it, "Everything is okay, Hippo."

Obviously Libby is not an overly anxious child! She was able to take in her mother's reassurance, then reinforce her sense of security by sharing it with her stuffed animal. Children who are more anxious remain troubled by life's possible dangers even after they are reassured. They might clutch their stuffed animals in panic, but they aren't able to internalize safety.

Libby transmitted the all-clear signal to her hippo after she learned that there was no actual danger—it was literally a false alarm. One of the hardest things about parenthood is that we can't protect our children from all of the real dangers in the world. Sadly, kidnappers, bullies, illness, and accidents are all too real. How do we protect anxious children and teach them about safety without overwhelming them with fear? First and foremost, we have to recognize and deal with our own fear. We can't ask a child to look into our eyes for reassurance and comfort if we are overwhelmed with anxiety.

Peg Flandreau West was a pioneer in safety education for children. West's program, Protective Behaviors, went beyond the simplistic idea of frightening children about "stranger danger." She promoted three principles that I often share with children who worry about real-life dangers. Adults also find these ideas helpful.

West's first principle is to recognize your gut feelings, especially danger signals, safety signals, and the difference between what feels good and what feels right. This is especially important in protecting children from sexual abuse. It might feel *good* to be touched in certain ways, to keep an important secret, or to receive candy from a stranger, but it might not feel *right*. You have to be able to tune in to your instinctive awareness of danger and safety in order to be able to trust those instincts and avoid harm. I experienced the exact opposite of this advice once in the men's room of a movie theater. There was a long line that stretched out the door, so the door was half open. From outside a very anxious mother called out to her son, who was standing in the line, "Don't let anyone touch you!" A wave of panic shot through all the men in the line—were we going to be accused of child abuse? I can only imagine how scared the boy must have been. Any gut feeling of safety he may have had was overwhelmed by his mother's alarm.

West's second principle is "risking on purpose," which is similar to my idea of finding things to do that are scary, fun, and safe. Her third principle is that there is nothing so bad that it can't be talked about with someone, and that you can keep searching until you find someone who will listen. Children who are frightened by real-life dangers are often relieved when they have a plan for responding to danger, including how to seek help.

Children need accurate information and they also need to be protected from being overwhelmed with more than they can handle. It's confusing to parents when children beg to see horror movies or super-violent movies that give them nightmares. At first children have an urge to see these movies so they can feel grown-up. After the nightmares, their urge to see the movies again is even stronger, as they try to expose themselves to something *a little bit scary* in order to overcome their fear. The problem is that these images aren't a little bit scary—they are *extremely* scary—and they are hard to remove from the mind. Children then want to watch these movies *again and again* in order to desensitize themselves, but it doesn't usually work. One tactic that sometimes helps is to watch semi-scary films together at home, rather than a movie theater, so you can pause the movie frequently to share a hug, talk about what you've seen, and release some fear with silly screams or by acting out scenes in a goofy way. That can help the tension from building up so strongly that it becomes too much to bear.

As much as we need to protect our children from overexposure to media violence and real violence, we can't protect them from every reality. I was in Washington, D.C., shortly after the capture of two snipers who had randomly killed a number of people in that area. A mother of a five-year-old girl told me: "I was sure that my daughter had no idea what was happening. We shielded her from all the news reports and didn't talk about it in front of her. Like so many other people, we ducked and ran whenever we were in a public place, like going from the parking lot to a store. I told my daughter this was a game, and she never asked why we played that game. She never expressed any fear either. When I heard the snipers were caught, I excitedly shouted the news to my husband in the next room. My daughter said, 'Does that mean we don't have to play that game anymore?' I was so sad as I realized that not only did she know about the danger, but she felt that she couldn't talk to me about it because I was trying to keep it secret to protect her." Children absorb insecurity and need to know the truth in order to make sense of it.

My general rule is that if you are worried about something, then your children have probably picked up that worry from you, so you might as well address it directly. But there is no need to create fears where there weren't any before. Many children's books address particular fears, such as going to the dentist. These books can be very useful to help children deal with that fear. But sometimes children never think about being scared of the dentist until they read a book about overcoming that fear!

Children whose anxiety focuses on real-life dangers tend to be in a constant state of high alert. This hypervigilance can interfere with their daily activities, and can create so much tension that it interferes with sleep as well. They get angry when you tell them to relax, because their anxiety-logic tells them that relaxing their guard would be dangerous. Imagine telling a Secret Service agent who is guarding the president, "Hey, buddy, you look nervous, why don't you relax a little bit?" What kind of response do you think you would get?

The real solution is to take over the vigilance for them, to let them know, in a serious way, that you will be on guard so that they don't have to be. It may seem strange, but I experienced this with my dog, Hunter, who used to bark for a long time every time someone came near the front door. Telling him to stop barking didn't work. Then I read that it helps to thank dogs for alerting their human companions to possible danger. I said "Thank you" to him the next time and he stopped barking right away! He didn't understand the words, I am sure, but he must have understood that I appreciated his effort to sound the alarm, and he trusted that I would take over from there. In fact, when I thank him he stops barking, but when I thank him and also tell him I am going downstairs to check the door, he is very happy.

Parents often tell me how exhausted they get from endless discussions with their children who worry about real-life dangers. "Exactly how likely is it that X could happen?" These discussions are rarely reassuring to anxious children. Pillow fights are much more effective. Yes, surprisingly enough, pillow fights give children a sense of mastery, security, and connection with you that they don't get from verbal reassurance. Ten minutes a night of pillow fighting or other fun roughhousing can make an enormous difference. Perhaps it nonverbally says *Things must be safe and secure if Mom or Dad is doing this fun stuff with me.* Or maybe it just takes the bottled-up "worry energy" and translates it into action, easing the tension.

Children's need for love, safety, and security makes them very sensitive to tension between their parents. When a ten-year-old client of mine told her friends that her parents were getting divorced, they all said to her, "That's my worst nightmare." Parents who live together need to work on their relationship, so that children will have firm ground to stand on. Parents who are separated or divorced need to provide that firm ground to their children as well, which is why bad-mouthing an ex-spouse and high levels of conflict are so damaging.

When a major world tragedy hits the news, such as a school shooting, natural disaster, or terrorist attack, all children (and adults) are unsettled. Anxious children are especially vulnerable to worries, nightmares, and insecurity at these times. When parents ask, "What should I say to my child," my advice is always the same: Listen more than you talk. Ask children what they already know, and answer any questions they have. Keep your answers honest and brief. Focus on reminders of the essential goodness of humanity, such as relief and rescue efforts. Psychologist Aureen Wagner adds that parents can "Help the child (if old enough and so inclined) to show caring and empathy for victims—to donate clothes or toys, collect money, write letters, attend a prayer service or organize a relief effort. Such actions lessen feelings of helplessness."

Most important, turn off the television. Graphic images provoke much more anxiety than conversations, and younger children may believe that every replay is a new disaster. When children have scary images in their heads already, there are several techniques that can help them. Some of the games from chapter four, particularly Remote Control of the Mind and The Projectionist, are particularly useful. You can also suggest that children draw or transform the images, for example by picturing them on a teeny-tiny TV screen far away.

An imaginary fear, such as monsters, might mask a deeper fear. But even real-life dangers can be a way for a child to express something deeper. Imagine a child with a vague but unsettling sense of dread, with no obvious reason for it. This kind of vague free-floating anxiety is confusing, so the anxious mind looks around for a fear that makes more sense, such as burglars, and latches on to that. Fear of burglars makes sense to parents as well, so they don't think to look any further to find a more tender, secret, or nebulous fear. If real-life fears persist or jump from one danger to another, consider what other anxieties might be underneath the surface.

TRAUMATIC FEARS

Traumatic events are by definition scary and often create lingering fears and anxieties. But children are resilient and able to recover from trauma, and we can help them. Isabelle, a girl from Australia who experienced a scary event when she was five years old, illustrates the key elements of recovery from traumatic fear.

Isabelle loved her dance class. She had no trouble with the teacher's rule that parents had to stay out of the studio during class, but she wanted her mother, Martha, to sit right outside the door. Once in a while Martha sneaked out to do a quick errand without telling Isabelle. She later regretted this dishonesty, but it's easy to see why parents of anxious children resort to sneaky behavior. They want to protect their children from unnecessary anxiety, even at the risk of breaching trust.

One day Martha ducked out of the lobby to run an errand and quickly realized she might be late picking up Isabelle. She bought her daughter a lollipop to make up for it, and sure enough she was a little late. It wasn't long, but for those few moments Isabelle thought her mother wasn't coming. She said later that she thought her mother was dead, was never coming to get her, and that she would have to find another family to live with. That's a powerful example of the speed and strength of anxious thoughts and feelings.

Even though it lasted only a short time, this event produced a drastic change in Isabelle. She became fearful whenever she was separated from her mother, had trouble sleeping, and had trouble maintaining her friendships. She became preoccupied with death, especially the fear of losing her mother. She was angry with her mom for lying, and a year after the incident she demanded, "How could you think a lollipop would make it better?"

It took about two years for Isabelle to really be her old self again. She brought the subject up again with her mother one day: "Mum, I thought about that day when you were late picking me up from dancing. I realized that the teacher would have found a way to get in touch with you. She would have made sure I went home to you. And Mum, it's okay that you brought me a lollipop. You were trying to show me that you knew I'd be upset and that you cared about me." That's internalization of safety and security! It took a while, but it happened.

I asked Martha what helped Isabelle get to this point. Martha's first answer was "Listening, listening, listening. I've listened over and over again to her feelings about that incident. I've listened without trying to justify or explain or defend my actions. Just listening, reflecting, understanding, apologizing, and letting her know that I care."

Martha and her husband also overfilled Isabelle's need for security, lying down with her at bedtime for as long as she needed. During the day, Isabelle anxiously checked in with her mother every few minutes. So Martha began checking in with Isabelle first, not waiting for her daughter's anxiety to build up too high. She let Isabelle quit her dance class, recognizing that the extreme stress level wasn't healthy for her (she had panic attacks each week when they tried going back). Some parents become fixated on the idea that they can't let a child quit, or can't let a child give up out of fear. Bravery and perseverance are important values, but they aren't served well if the child is flooded by panic. Better at times to regroup and build up confidence until the time is ripe to try again.

As a religious family, Isabelle and her parents used prayer as a way to gain strength and security. Martha also recommitted herself to honesty, realizing that she had breached Isabelle's trust by telling her she would not run errands during dance class. Martha says, "I don't promise that bad things won't happen, that Mummy will always be here, or that I won't ever die (although I do hope that's not for a long time yet!). I try to be open and honest with her to a level that is appropriate for her understanding. Even though I worry that it might be too much, it always pays to tell her the truth."

Martha asked Isabelle two years later what helped her become braver and more confident. Isabelle listed these factors: Being allowed to stop dancing; saying to herself, "Mum's still here, Mum will be back in a moment"; praying; playing games such as hide-and-seek; and special time with her grandmother and aunt.

Isabelle's story illustrates many of the best strategies for helping children overcome trauma:

• Empathy and understanding (even if the event doesn't seem as though it should be so traumatic).

• Listening (traumatized children may need to tell, draw, or act out the story over and over).

• Filling (and overfilling) the need for security. This may include more physical contact during bedtime or sleep, more cuddling, night-lights, or security blankets.

• Prayer and spirituality.

- Self-talk.
- Respecting children's limits and not forcing them past the point of being flooded with anxiety.
- Games such as hide-and-seek, or games that playfully re-enact the trauma—this time with a happy ending.
- Special time with trusted adults.
- Patience—there is no set timeline for recovery from trauma.
- Dealing with your own feelings and reactions to the event. In Martha's case she had to recognize her feelings of guilt. Other parents might feel horror, fear, or anger when their child survives a trauma.
- Taking time to rebuild trust with a commitment to honesty.

Peter Levine is a psychologist and trauma expert. As I described in chapter five, many of Levine's techniques for overcoming trauma involve finishing the movements that were blocked by the freeze response. We are familiar with fight and flight as basic fear responses, but immobility—freezing—is also part of the extreme fear reaction that follows traumatic events. After a serious accident in which he was struck by a car, Levine noticed that his hand spontaneously rose up to protect his face as he lay in the street. This was a motion he did not have time to complete as the accident occurred. In his therapy technique, Levine has survivors of trauma run in place to finish the unfinished flight response, or hit pillows to finish the frozen fight response. I also urge children to shout "Help!" or "No!" to finish the words that are frozen inside during a scary event.

The feelings of a trauma may be frozen as well as the actions. Children might have been too scared to express their feelings, or they might not have had anyone nearby to listen to them and validate those feelings. For emotional completion, children need adults to listen to the story of what happened, and they need to be held while they cry or tremble, releasing their feelings. If they are too young to tell it in words, we can tell the story for them. With a minor incident it may be perfectly fine to offer a child a lollipop or small toy as recognition of bravery or compensation for the upset. But with big traumas children need to feel their feelings, not have them stuffed away with sweets or bribes. As Isabelle implied to her mother, *How could you think a lollipop would make up for thinking you were dead and gone forever?*

When the trauma is more serious—if a parent does die or abandon a child, for example—all the same principles apply. Healing may take longer and require more patience, but don't forget the importance of play and the healing power of love and affection.

INFLEXIBILITY

Anxiety makes children less flexible in their thinking and their behavior. Some examples of anxious inflexibility are:

- perfectionism
- reluctance to try new things
- indecisiveness
- procrastination
- rigid adherence to routines and expectations

These behaviors are extremely frustrating to parents. Inflexibility isn't any fun for children, either. It is frustrating, painful, and interferes with their lives. Inflexibilities are a kind of self-protection: *If I do everything perfectly, if I stay in my comfort zone, if I never make a wrong decision, if I don't think too much about things that cause me stress, if I stick to the routines, if I keep away from every possible danger—only then will I be safe and secure.*

Children who are inflexible may not look anxious at all—at least not until their inflexibilities are challenged. At that point, they instantly flood with fear or anger because their self-protection is no longer working. This is why so many anxious children fall apart when we tell them: "Your homework is good enough—it's time for bed," "You have to try it," or "We need to change the plans."

When dealing with any type of childhood anxiety we always have to balance a push for change with acceptance of where the child is now. Children who are inflexible need extra acceptance. Some children are just less flexible than others, and that's who they are. They can't just "try harder" or "let it go." They can't be pressured into flexibility. Pressure only increases inflexibility.

Besides increased empathy and acceptance, what can parents do to help children become more flexible? Loosen up! How often do you dance, sing, roll around on the floor, make silly noises, dress up in goofy outfits, start a pillow fight, or prepare peanut butter sandwiches for dinner because you were too busy playing with your children?

I often prescribe playful parent-child roughhousing when parents describe inflexibility in their children. I suggested to one mother that she get off the couch, get down on the floor, and play the Sock Game with her son. (That's where everyone tries to keep their own socks on and take each other's socks off.) She said, "You lost me at get off the couch." I knew then that her son wasn't the only one in the house struggling with inflexibility! So okay, I know it is a stretch. But it pays off tremendously, for parents and children, when parents challenge their own inflexibility.

Inflexible children are easily overwhelmed with emotion: panic, rage, sorrow, or extreme frustration. These floods are painful to experience and horrible to witness as a parent. On a scale from one to ten, their emotions are at eleven. Yet we can't prevent every flood. If we try, we end up desperately rushing around, changing our own plans, neglecting our other children, and giving up everything else in life just to make sure our inflexible children never get that upset. We become exhausted and annoyed—and eventually something will trigger their flood of feelings anyway. Meanwhile they are still inflexible!

The trick is to nudge children into just as much discomfort as they can handle without making them completely fall apart. It's like the edge between flooding and avoidance. It's very hard to stay right in that healing range. That's okay. The important thing is to help children survive the temporary discomfort, with your love and support.

If you have an inflexible child, then you probably know that they can argue with you for hours. Unfortunately, all that talk just increases everyone's frustration and anxiety. For every logical argument you present, they will respond with at least two illogical ones. Who wins? It's hard to step out of that conversation, but it usually helps to talk less and have more nonverbal communication—cuddling, running around the block together, pillow fighting, or falling on the floor in a funny exaggeration of your frustration.

Mistakes on Purpose. My favorite tactic with perfectionist children is to say, "Let's each make three mistakes. I'll go first!" They always think I'm joking—and they don't think it's funny. I explain that I am serious and that it doesn't matter how big or small the mistake is. I might say that two plus two equals five, or mispronounce my own name. The goal is for them to laugh at my mistakes and survive their own. *If* they are willing to try it, then their perfectionism often lightens up.

Most parents of perfectionists insist that they don't pressure their children. Let's get real. We all pressure our children, whether we intend to or not. Anxious children are especially sensitive to that pressure. The pressure might be subtle. What do you praise? What do you brag about to your friends? How do you react to mistakes? When your children look at you do they see a stressed-out overachiever? One final question: What were the subtle (and not so subtle) pressures that you felt as a child?

One piece of information that I like to share with perfectionists is The Upside-Down *U* Curve. Draw a large upside-down *U*. As you move to the right, stress increases from low to medium to high. As you move up, performance improves. Very low stress— at the bottom left corner—leads to low performance: *Why bother—yawn—who cares?* At the top of the hill you can see that peak performance comes from medium stress. This is where people are revved up and ready to go. Very high stress—at the bottom right—again leads to low performance. Even the most capable people can freeze up, choke, or lose their focus when their anxiety is too high.

Bessie, for example, was very proud of her guitar skills after her first few lessons. But when she showed her mother what she had learned, she played very poorly. Her medium level of nervous anticipation during the lesson put her at peak performance. Playing for her (very demanding) mother put her stress over the top as she imagined being criticized or falling short. Her performance plummeted off the downslope of the upside-down *U*.

I have found that children who put a great deal of pressure on themselves benefit the most from understanding this curve. It shows them a good reason to reduce their stress level. Before learning about the curve, Bessie told me relaxing was "a waste of time" because it didn't improve her skills. But now she knows that she will do her best if her stress level is in the middle—which for her usually means taking it down a notch. She laughed at the idea that some people might need to increase their anxiety level a little bit (from zero) in order to perform at their maximum ability.

Indecisiveness is an obvious example of anxious immobilization. Children freeze, afraid to make a wrong decision or to miss out on the right decision. A mother from North Carolina writes, "My children have been known to go into brain freeze. I have found that a 'menu' of options on paper (with drawings instead of words for pre-readers) can often lift us out of these moments. Somehow they process decisions more easily this way when they are under stress (overtired or over-hungry)." This same mom has a great tactic for helping her children when they are unable to decide what to wear. If her daughter can't decide between tights or socks, for example, she puts them on her hands and has each of them beg to be on her daughter's feet. The giggling breaks through the indecisiveness. Modern parents have learned to give children choices instead of choosing everything for them. But some indecisive children need *fewer* choices, so they aren't so overwhelmed.

Some children benefit from learning how to make a pro and con list to aid in decision-making. But others get stuck endlessly listing and weighing those pros and cons. It's important to gather information, but at some point you need to stop thinking and decide. I often use a coin toss to gently push indecisive children to settle for a good-enough decision. I tell them that if they don't make a decision, the coin flip will decide. Usually they realize that either decision is fine, or they suddenly realize their true choice as the coin spins in the air.

Procrastination is not usually considered an anxiety issue.

But procrastination is an avoidance tactic. Gordy's homework makes him anxious, so he puts it off. Falling behind makes him more anxious, but sitting down to work would bring him face-to-face with that anxiety, so he puts it off some more. By avoiding the work he can avoid the anxiety. If he puts it off enough, he doesn't even know he's anxious about it! His mother yells at him for being lazy, but that misses the real story. The solution is to understand the central role of anxiety and avoidance in procrastination. As parents, we often focus on "getting it done," rather than on the child's feelings about sitting down to do something that is unpleasant, uncomfortable, or anxiety-arousing.

No surprises. For many children, the root of anxiety is a strong negative reaction to anything unfamiliar. That's why anxious children often have an urgent need to know exactly what to expect. Then they have an intense emotional reaction when things don't go according to plan. This inflexibility leaves parents in a trap. They can spell out in great detail to the child what to expect, which lowers their immediate anxiety. Unfortunately, that makes the meltdown worse if plans have to change.

Parents feel a similar bind when it comes to deciding when to tell a child about something scary. If they say, "You will get a shot at the doctor's office in three days," the child might spend three miserable days ruminating. If they spring it on the child at the last minute, then there is no anticipatory anxiety, but there is a breach of trust ("You should have warned me!") and an increase in worried thoughts (*What bad thing will happen next— with no warning?*). Routines provide yet another trap for parents of children who are inflexible. Anxious children are soothed by repetition and ritual, but the more ingrained routines become, the more upset children are when they are disrupted.

To break out of these binds, it helps to think about a weekly time frame. Spend most of your time each week accepting children's inflexibility and giving extra comfort and support. Once in a while during the course of the week, push them a little bit out of their comfort zone. Ask children to risk the unpleasant feelings that occur when they challenge their inflexibilities. Make sure to match that push with extra affection and warmth, showing that you have empathy for the discomfort of such a push.

When children are inflexible in their play—"You're doing it all wrong! It has to be my way!"—follow the same basic formula, but think about a time frame of an hour. For most of the hour, enthusiastically play exactly according to their rules. Apologize for playing "wrong," and joyfully let them be in charge of the play. For a few minutes out of the hour, however, push them a little, saying gently, "It's okay for me to do it this way," or "I'm going to choose something now." Comfort the sad or angry feelings that flow as they release the pent-up feelings that were blocked by their inflexibility.

Parents often feel tension about how hard to push their children to try new foods, activities, or friendships. Usually parents feel that their only choices are to force their children or to give in completely. I think we can find a middle ground, where we accept that some children are less flexible, but we gently push them to expand their comfort zone.

Support plus challenge add up to the security and confidence needed for children to venture beyond their inflexibilities. Be sure to challenge your own rigidities at the same time. As an adult, you don't have anyone two feet taller than you making you adapt, so you have to push yourself. But give yourself the same compassion you give your children—it's hard to recover flexibility when we have spent so many years set in our ways.

At its most severe, anxious inflexibility leads to obsessive thinking and compulsive behaviors, such as repeatedly checking locks on the doors, touching things a certain number of times, excessive hand washing, or enormous meltdowns at the tiniest variation in routine. You may want to seek professional help if inflexibility interferes significantly with a child's life. At any degree of severity, however, parents can help with increased love and affection—especially cuddling and playful physical contact—and by avoiding power struggles over inflexibilities.

EXCESSIVE ANXIETY TO PLEASE

The first time I met Loren, a nine-year-old girl, she apologized to me seven or eight times, each time for something that didn't need an apology. She even said she was sorry for saying "sorry" so often! I wasn't surprised, because her parents had said she was very anxious. Over-apologizing, over-niceness, and overeagerness to please are all more common in anxious children. Some parents may yearn for their children to be a little nicer, and to say "sorry" once in a while. But anxious children definitely have too much of a good thing.

James Rapson (a therapist) and Craig English (a writer) co-authored a book about the "chronically nice," children who grow up not sure what they want or how to get it. They apologize too often and are nice "whether it is called for or not." They spend countless hours worrying what other people think of them or what they should have said.

Chronically nice people may not look or feel anxious—as long as they please everyone. Sooner or later, of course, they will fall short. This failure to please everyone is especially painful in children whose parents are divorced or separated and put their eager-to-please child in the middle of their conflict. These chil-

dren are guaranteed to displease at least one of them—probably
both—and then to feel horribly guilty. It is exhausting to focus so
much on other people's feelings and ignore your own.

Girls, as every woman knows, face extra pressure to be nice
as they grow up. When my daughter was in first grade I asked her
and a male friend how a child becomes popular. Her friend said,
"Shoot missiles!" My daughter said, "Be nice." We probably don't
want girls to become preoccupied with weapons, but we can help
them value physical strength, confidence, and honesty at least as
much as they value niceness.

Special Time is an approach to play that can help girls and
boys who are overly anxious to please. Patty Wipfler, director of
Hand in Hand Parenting and a pioneer of Special Time, writes,
"Special Time is when the parent spends a well-defined amount
of time one-on-one with his child, with no interruptions, promis-
ing to do whatever the child wants to do. During Special Time,
the parent tries to remain pleased and fully attentive, and does
not try to teach, advise, or control his child unless safety is an
issue." When children experience regular Special Time, they become more aware of their own needs and desires, and are therefore less focused on overly pleasing others.

Children who are overeager to please will often say, "Whatever you want to do is fine," even during their Special Time. Resist the urge to step in and make suggestions. You might smile
and say, "Nope, I'm going to sit with you, enjoying being together,
while you think about what you want to do." Special Time can
help children find their own voice and their inner source of confidence, but they may need to flounder a little as their over-
pleasing patterns are challenged. With children who are overly
anxious to please, I also like to play games in which they get to
be loud, bold, and even a little wild.

Moral Anxiety. The healthy conscience uses a little stab of moral anxiety to keep us on the straight and narrow path. Young children's consciences remind them that they will get in trouble. Older children's moral anxiety reminds them that they are doing something wrong. There is a sweet spot with just the right amount of pressure from the conscience. If the conscience is too lax, then the child has no boundaries on hurting others. If it's too harsh, then the child suffers from excess shame and guilt.

Children who are too nice often suffer from a conscience that isn't nice to them at all. A harsh conscience is better than no conscience, but it is a problem. Moral anxiety becomes excessive and painful when the conscience is applied to areas where it doesn't belong, such as feelings. I tell anxious children, "There are no shoulds about feelings. We feel what we feel. I hope that your conscience can give you a break on this, because what you are feeling is perfectly normal. It just isn't fair for a conscience to attack someone for a feeling." The same is true for thoughts and impulses, even aggressive impulses. Everyone has them. Morality means not acting on them. Most children laugh when I suggest that they should have less shoulds.

Whenever Leah gets in trouble for teasing her brother she says, "I'm a terrible person. I should die." Well, remorse is a good thing, but the death penalty is a bit extreme for teasing! A harsh conscience can come from being threatened or punished too severely, or from expectations on their behavior that are impossible to meet. If you ask children to describe exactly how their conscience speaks to them—the words and the tone of voice—you may recognize yourself when you are in your scolding mode.

The answer is to educate the conscience. Here's the main lesson: There is no such thing as a bad or wrong feeling, only painful and pleasant feelings. There are no bad thoughts—

everyone has thoughts that just pop into their heads. There are no bad impulses, just impulses that it would be wrong to act on. Consciences need to learn that they are more effective if they are firm and loving than if they are harsh. Harshness may bring immediate obedience but it also brings shame or rebellion.

Finally, I like to teach children that the conscience has two parts. Part A is impulse control: *I shouldn't do that, I mustn't do that, I'll get in trouble if I do that, it's wrong to do that.* If you go ahead and do it anyway, then conscience Part B kicks in: *I shouldn't have done that, I'm bad, I'm in big trouble now, I need to make things right.* Some children have a weak Part A—they act impulsively—then they try to make up for it with an overly harsh Part B. They end up full of guilt and anguish but still impulsive. Some children have an overly strong Part A. They are filled with anxiety that they might have a bad thought or feeling. The goal is a strong Part A and a compassionate but firm Part B, with no harshness in either part.

MATTERS OF LIFE AND DEATH

Most teenagers and adults wonder from time to time about their place in the universe, the meaning of life, the existence of God, and their own mortality. These thoughts can be enjoyable—even transcendent—or they can be a source of anxiety and despair. When such thoughts emerge earlier in childhood, they are more often a source of anxiety. Most children just don't have the experience or the guidance to make sense of such thoughts. Yet certain children seem to arrive early at an awareness of spiritual or existential matters. Childhood existential anxiety can also follow a close experience with death—either grief for a loved one, a serious illness, or a trauma such as child abuse that is so overwhelming that it feels like a life-or-death struggle. These are difficult situations for adults, and even more difficult for children.

To help children who are troubled by such thoughts, we need to reflect on our own core beliefs about life and death, God, and meaning. My colleague David Trimble, a psychologist in Massachusetts, has observed that children with existential anxiety need a guide who can help them make sense of their thoughts and their frightening experiences. Dr. Trimble sometimes teaches children a technique of spiritual self-protection, where they imagine themselves surrounded by a milky white sphere. This allows them to stay engaged with the world while feeling safe from harm. His message to children is: I respect your fear, you are not alone in having these thoughts and feelings, and you deserve to feel whole and self-protected.

As parents, we often try to shield our children from anything to do with death. But that isn't realistic. This urge to protect children from painful realities can go to absurd extremes. I received a call one day from a friend. Her brother had died suddenly, and she was calling to ask me what the family should tell his three-year-old daughter. I was confused. What would they tell her, other than the truth? I learned that no one wanted to upset the child, so each member of the family told her something different. One said her father was on a business trip, one said he was sleeping, and one said he was in a wonderful place called heaven. No one explained to her why everyone was so sad. How could the truth be worse than that? I understand the impulse to protect, but children can handle reality as long as it is offered with love and empathy and they have a chance to ask questions and express their feelings.

We also try to protect children from cruel truths about the world, such as poverty, injustice, or war. When parents avoid scary topics, children may think that their *parents* have to be protected, so they keep their own fears and worries hidden. Far better to acknowledge the existence of social ills—without too much graphic information—and focus on ways children can make a difference—big or small.

Where did I come from? While we are on the subject of the meaning of life, let's look at another subject that makes many parents anxious: sex and reproduction. Children are naturally curious about these topics, until they pick up on their parents' tension. Then they either feel ashamed or become *extremely* curious. As much as we might like to deny it, children are interested in their own bodies, other people's bodies, and where babies come from. That means parents have to overcome their discomfort so they can be expert listeners and good resources for children about sexuality. Don't let your anxiety make you avoid the topic. If children don't learn about sexuality from parents, they will gather a lot of misinformation from peers and the media.

Death. Death is a scary concept. Children develop an understanding of death around the same time they discover that some things are reversible and some things aren't. Death is the ultimate irreversible event. Many children are fascinated with death and want to bury dead pets and look at half-decomposed animals in the woods. They also want to play games where people die and come back to life: "Bang, bang, you're dead." These are healthy impulses to try to make sense of something so confusing.

One common question that parents ask after a death in the family is how much to involve young children in rituals and family gatherings. They want to provide an outlet for their children's grief, but don't want to flood them with anxiety. There is no set answer. The most important thing is to decide together with your child. I have heard so many adults complain that when they were children, they were not given that choice. They might have been forced to go to a funeral, or they might have not been allowed to go. Either way they wish they had more of a say in the matter. Children in a grieving family need a nonmourning friend or relative to be with them, someone who can listen without being overwhelmed by grief herself, and who can take them outside to play when that's what they want to do.

Children use what they know best—play—to make sense of what they understand least—such as death, loss, and grief. Do not try to ban death-related themes from children's play or their stories. It leaves children without their best method of coping. And don't worry when make-believe characters die and come back to life repeatedly. In play, death can be reversible—that is children's way of coping with the painful reality that death is final.

WORRY SOUP

Worry soup is my name for a common variety of childhood anxiety. The exact symptoms are hard to pin down, because they are wide-ranging and always changing. A child with worry soup might be anxious on different days about friendships, parents, health, kidnappers, or upcoming tests or performances. They are easily thrown into anxiety by situations that would not trouble most children, such as a friend not answering a phone call right away, or a friendly tease. They may have compulsive rituals and physical symptoms of anxiety. The sheer volume and pervasiveness of these problems make them very hard to manage. Parents have a hard time reassuring children whose worries multiply faster than they can be soothed. It is especially frustrating when the anxiety is set far into the future, as when a sixth grader worries about which graduate school he will be able to attend.

Children often use the word "paranoid" to describe a state of hyperalertness to every possible danger (though technically that term means something very different—delusions of persecution and unwarranted suspiciousness). As a boy named Ray said, "Things that other people would worry about a little bit, like robbery or failing a test, I am paranoid about. I think about it way too much. My friends tell me I should live in a bubble."

In order to help a child with this type of anxiety, resist the urge to argue with them about each ingredient in the worry soup. You won't win! They will just shift to another worry, even if they believe your reassurance about the first one. Instead, help them recognize that the real problem is anxiety, not a hundred different dangers and threats. Shift to a deeper level where you can work together on the opposite of worry soup: relaxing, building confidence, and doing things that are scary, fun, and safe.

We've explored a wide variety of childhood anxieties in this chapter, from monsters under the bed to worry soup. The list could have been much longer, because there are as many types of anxiety as there are anxious children. Despite this diversity, all anxious children have a few things in common. Childhood anxiety always impacts children's bodies, behaviors, emotions, thoughts, and relationships. All anxious children need comfort, compassion, and empathy from their parents. They need to spend time relaxing, playing, and facing their fears. As parents of anxious children, you play a key role in helping them understand their emotions and challenge their anxious thoughts. These commonalities are the essence of the playful parenting approach.

CHAPTER EIGHT

Finding Joy:
From Anxiety, Worry, and Fear
to Connection and Trust

The cure for anxiety is silly dancing.
—An eleven-year-old girl

I met Zeke when he was five years old and very anxious. Zeke learned some effective strategies for lowering his anxiety and I didn't hear from him for several years. Recently he wrote to tell me that he had been named editor of his fifth-grade newspaper. "I feel very excited and worried at the same time," he said. "I have butterflies in my stomach. I don't know why I feel like that, but I can't wait to get started." Zeke's experience explains why this book is not called *The Anxiety Cure*. Children with high anxiety are always somewhat vulnerable to butterflies or worries as they take on new challenges.

I met Charlie when he was thirty years old. He asked me—anxiously—if he would be completely free of anxiety after therapy. I told him I hoped not. Charlie didn't like that answer. He felt better after I told him about Zeke's letter, and how Zeke's new job as editor of the school newspaper took him right to the edge of his fear—the safe, healthy, growing edge. I expected Charlie would feel anxiety in the future when he left his comfort zone to do meaningful things in his life that he had avoided before. Anxiety isn't an infection to be eliminated and forgotten, but rather a state of mind to be understood and sensitively challenged. Besides, anxiety is always needed as a useful danger signal.

Harriet Lerner, a psychologist and popular author, wrote something similar: "We may believe that anxiety and fear don't concern us because we avoid experiencing them. We may keep the scope of our lives narrow and familiar, opting for sameness and safety. We may not even know that we are scared of success, failure, rejection, criticism, conflict, competition, intimacy, or adventure. . . . Our challenge: To be willing to become *more* anxious, via embracing new situations and stepping more fully into our lives."

In other words, anxiety isn't the only problem caused by anxiety! We also suffer from things we do to avoid feeling anxious. That paradox reminds me of an old joke: A man stands in the aisle of a crowded train, flapping his arms up and down. Most people ignore him, but someone finally asks him what he's doing. "I'm keeping the lions away," he answers. "But there aren't any lions outside of a zoo for thousands of miles from here!" "You see," says the man confidently, "it's working!"

Zeke and Charlie both sought help with anxiety because they were miserable. Ending misery is important, of course, but the ultimate goal is even bigger. After all, the arm-flapper isn't miserable, as long as he can flap to protect himself from being flooded with anxiety. He's probably exhausted, though, and he misses all the scenery. Beyond ending the misery of anxiety, my goal is for all children to live fully, engage with the world, take reasonable risks, embrace the unknown, and break free of limitations. The opposite of high anxiety isn't low anxiety. It's connection, trust, playfulness, and joy.

CONNECTION

Parents contribute to children's anxiety through genetics and their style of child rearing. Of course parents don't intend to make children anxious, but it happens. We express criticism, doubt, overprotectiveness, and impossibly high expectations. Parents can also have a tremendous *positive* impact on anxious children. The essence of antianxiety parenting is when parents provide:

- security so children can internalize a soothing and comforting "inner voice"
- acceptance and welcome of children as they are
- a partnership with children to sensitively challenge them where they are avoidant or frozen in anxiety

The way we talk to our children forms the basis for their inner voices, the way they treat themselves. It's called *internalization* because it is the internal representation of what they originally heard from outside—from you. Which of these thoughts would you want your child to have after making a mistake?

- *I'm so stupid.*
- *Oh no, oh no, oh no.*
- *This is the worst thing that ever happened.*
- *My parents are going to kill me.*
- *Big deal, who cares?*
- *I'll have a cookie so I don't have to feel bad about it.*
- *Oops, that was a mistake. I'll see what I can do to fix it and I'll try something different next time.*

I'd guess that nearly all parents would choose the last one. The other thoughts come from too much criticism or harsh discipline; from being told too often to be careful; or from getting too many bribes to stop feeling sad or upset. If you are anxious yourself, you may have an inner voice that is filled with doubt, insecurity, uncertainty, and dread. Or you may have a drive to avoid those feelings using sweets or other distractions.

That's not the inner voice we want children to have. When there is no danger, we want them to be able to soothe their oversensitive alarm and give themselves an all-clear signal. When there is danger, we want them to act powerfully, not cower in fear. Children develop a confident inner voice from being nurtured, loved, and cherished. As my colleague Stephen Houseworth puts it: "Therapists often recommend to anxious adults that they cultivate *compassionate mind,* a state of acceptance and loving kindness toward themselves. Many adults find this very difficult to achieve. Children can develop compassionate mind an easier way—by being treated with acceptance and love by the adults around them."

Children without excess anxiety have both *roots and wings*—connection and independence, safety and adventure. They can explore the world with the comforting knowledge that they have a secure home base. My favorite example comes from a children's novel, *Ronia, the Robber's Daughter,* by Astrid Lindgren. Ronia is born to a fierce robber chieftain in a broken-down castle in the middle of wild woods. Her father, Matt, is very worried about her safety, but finally lets her go exploring with this advice that conveys both his concern and his confidence:

". . . watch out you don't get lost in the forest," said Matt.

"What shall I do if I get lost in the forest?" Ronia asked.

"Find the right path," Matt said.

"All right," said Ronia.

"And watch out you don't fall in the river," Matt said.

"What shall I do if I fall in the river?" Ronia asked.

"Swim," Matt said.

Matt captures the delicate balance between nurturing love—which builds closeness and inner strength—and a confident push out into the world—which develops courage and competence. Actually, Matt tilts a little too far toward the push, but it is a fantasy novel!

In real life, a warm human connection is the opposite of anxiety and fear. The power of a close connection inspires changes that are deeper and more meaningful than any you can get from medications, reward charts, or punishments. Unfortunately, anxious children often withdraw from connection or lash out at the people closest to them. Our job as parents is to keep reaching out to our children even if they are scared or angry, letting them know they are loved and valued. Play games with your children, or just sit near them if they don't want to play a game with you. Lighten up your own mood—having an anxious child can make a parent overly serious—and be a role model for lighthearted contradictions to anxiety.

A partnership between parents and children is crucial for a successful challenge to childhood anxiety. That doesn't mean we stop being the parents, but it does mean that we aren't in sole control. We can't force them to confront their fears or practice relaxation. We need to listen to what they feel, instead of telling them what they should feel. We need to work together to discover their most effective relaxation and anxiety-reduction strategies. "*Let's* figure out some ways to lower our stress level" is more effective than "*You* need to calm down right now." Anxiety gives children tunnel vision: *Oh, no, get me out of here.* We can provide a broader perspective. We know that facing a fear feels terrible, but we also know that it's worth it. We know that staying at the edge can be incredibly healing, as long as there is a comforting adult to help a child through it.

Partnership is not the same as collusion: "Oh, you don't want to go in the water, that's okay, I will never make you do anything scary." That might briefly protect your child from a difficult feeling, but it doesn't support confidence or inner strength. Your child's avoidance doesn't need any extra help from you!

A more subtle problem is when parents engage in hours of discussions about whether the locks on the door are secure, or about what terrible thing might have happened to Daddy since he is late coming home from work. Anxious children insist on these conversations, but afterward they feel even more anxious. Gently shift the conversation away from those details: "Can you look at me and see that I am not worried? Can you tell the difference between *feeling* unsafe and *being* unsafe? How is anxiety convincing you of danger?"

Partnership means speaking the same language so you and your child can communicate on a deeper level. It doesn't matter if you name the problem anxiety, stress, worry, or My Phunny Phobia, as long as you talk about how to increase safety and security. One purpose of this book is to give you some vocabulary for that shared language, such as the elements of the Security System; the Flame Model; the calm second chicken; and facing feelings instead of flooding, avoiding, or white-knuckling.

PLAYFULNESS AND JOY

If you asked anxious children "What's fun or funny about your worries and fears?," they would probably answer, "Nothing!" Even serious problems, however, can have lighthearted solutions. *Externalization* is a concept from narrative therapy that can bring a playful spirit into any childhood difficulty. Children often see themselves and their problems as one and the same: "*I'm* shy. *I'm* stressed out. *I'm* scared of dogs." This identification leads to shame and makes it hard to find a creative solution. In externalization the problem is separate from the person: "*Shyness* whispers to me to stay in the corner. *Stress* ties my belly into knots."

This externalization allows children to have a new relationship with the problem and provides playful opportunities for change. For example, children can outsmart their shyness or stress, or shout at it to leave them alone. They might pretend that you represent their fear, and then whack you with a pillow. In games of Spy or Detective children match wits with Anxiety, who is trying to stop them from having fun.

Role reversal is another way for children to play with their fears, rather than simply suffer from them. Your child plays the part of someone brave or scary while you pretend to be scared. Your child might chase you around the house pretending to be a bee, pretend to give you a vaccination with a giant imaginary syringe, or rescue you from danger. Roughhousing games also give children a sense of confidence and help them overcome fears. Children build confidence when parents let them win playful wrestling matches and pillow fights. Physical play between parent and child builds closeness as well. Why not make it a daily practice?

The simplest way to transform anxieties through play is to

replay scary events. During the replay there is enough safety that fear releases in laughter. A mother told me how her son used such a game, even before he could talk. He was just under a year old when his older cousin put a blanket over his head. He was trapped very briefly and started to scream and cry. Once he had calmed down, he went straight over to the blanket and picked it up and put it down several times.

His parents realized that he wanted to replay the situation in a safe setting. His mother took the blanket and put it near the baby's head. Right away he started crying, so she ducked her head underneath too. She saw that her son was right near the edge, because he wanted her to repeat this game even though it upset him. She said, "The blanket over our heads reminded him of being trapped, but I was with him this time so he knew he was safe." She switched the game to peekaboo with the blanket, and her son started laughing and laughing. They had found just the right way to use play to recover from the scary incident.

Curiosity is an essential element of childhood play. It is impossible to be curious about something and avoid it at the same time. Anything a parent can do to invite curiosity in an anxious child will lower anxiety—even curiosity about anxiety itself. Children also feel less anxious when they "get out of their own heads," such as when they care for a pet or plant in the garden. Older children often say that they transcend their own worries and fears when they volunteer their time and talents to help others.

Play helps children recover from scary things that happened. But mainly play is fun. Anxiety can take away a child's ability to enjoy simple pleasures. Parents can reactivate joy by setting aside plenty of downtime for play and hanging out. This lets children know that homework, chores, and other serious matters are not the only things that count in life.

THE OPPOSITE OF PARENTAL WORRY

My colleague Michael Thompson told me about a mother who called her pediatrician multiple times a day in extreme anxiety, even though her baby was completely healthy. Finally, the pediatrician called the mother into the office and said, "You have become a mother. That means you have opened yourself up to a lifetime of worry. You have to pace yourself."

Parents worry. Parents of anxious children worry even more. Where can we find calm serenity? As parents, I'm not sure we get much of that. Buddhist monks who meditate all day may be calm and serene, but guess what? They don't have children! I think for parents the opposite of worry is not serenity, but trust. We can let go of worries and fears about our children if we trust in child development, trust in the resilience of children, trust in the power of parent-child closeness, and trust in the natural healing that comes from love and play.

When our children are very anxious and we can't "fix it," we have to trust that comfort and listening are enough. Children may beg us to rescue them, or beg us to promise something we can't deliver—anything to protect them from feeling bad. They may ask us to help them avoid whatever scares them, keeping them away from the edge. It is very tempting to rescue children, because we can't stand to see our children suffer. But we have to trust our knowledge that this isn't helpful. They need to be comforted and soothed, but not by denying reality or supporting avoidance.

Anxious parents have such a hard time with trust. How can we be sure our children are safe when they step out into the world, whether it's to go down a toddler slide at the park or to move in to their first apartment? We can't be sure. We have to accept some risks. Parental worry only increases as children grow up. My friend Ellen was in a panic about her grown son, because he was not answering his phone. She rejected all my well-meaning suggestions to relax. Of course she did! I was insisting that the problem was her anxiety, while she defined the problem as "He might be in trouble and I have to find out where he is." She didn't want to pay attention to her anxious feelings, because her ruminating thoughts were too pressing. Anxious thinking can be very persuasive: *Relaxation won't help him if he's in a hospital bed on life-support and they don't know how to contact me, and besides, if he's injured I shouldn't be relaxing.* I believe, however, that the real problem was her runaway alarm system. We can't demand certainty from an uncertain world. We have to reclaim trust instead. Trust is at the heart of the all-clear signal.

We may not have certainty, but we do have knowledge, and knowledge is power. Parents and children who understand anxiety can lower it. The same goes for knowing how emotions work and why fear creates such uncomfortable bodily sensations.

I met with a mother who was obviously frustrated with her son's anxiety. I counseled her to offer him more comfort and less scolding when he refused to go to baseball practice. She said, "I do comfort him! I tell him he is fine and there isn't anything to be upset about and that he'll have fun once he's there." That isn't comfort. She had a hard time understanding that her hidden message was *You shouldn't be feeling what you feel.* She felt frustrated and angry that he rejected her comfort. He felt frustrated and angry that she didn't understand how overwhelmed and flooded he was. Their relationship became a source of stress and anxiety for both of them, rather than a source of safety and security.

In order to calm children, we need to be able to soothe ourselves, and we need to know what they need for comfort. I learned a technique from the neuroscientist Louis Cozolino that has helped me. He was spending time with two children who were bouncing off the walls, exhausting themselves and him in a frenzy of disorganized activity. This wildness culminated in a game of "burp the baby," in which the two children took turns whacking a baby doll with escalating aggression. Cozolino said he knew a different way to burp the baby, and he took the baby doll on his shoulder and gently patted it, making murmuring noises of nurturing and affection. The children calmed down immediately and wanted to take turns being the baby receiving this same comforting treatment from him. This profound intervention sent all-clear signals to the children (and himself).

I have begun using a variation of this technique—Pat the Baby—whenever I am with children who are overloaded with emotion—whether it is frenzy, sadness, anger, or anxiety. I take a doll, stuffed animal, or pillow and put it on my shoulder and pretend to pat it gently like a baby. Sometimes I just pat myself without a prop. The idea is to evoke the essence of nurturing so that everyone can internalize a feeling of security. Even if children don't notice what I am doing, it seems to change the emotional tone of the situation. If nothing else it slows down my own heart rate and breathing. That's a big improvement over becoming flooded by the overflow of feelings in the room.

We can soothe ourselves or lower our anxiety many other ways. We can talk to a friend, write in a journal, splash cold water on our face, or talk ourselves through it. I sometimes feel anxious when children are being too messy or seem about to break something. When that anxiety arises I replay a special memory I have, which always calms me down. One year on my mother's birthday her grandchildren all gathered to share appreciations of her. Several of them said that she always let them make a mess and leave their toys and blocks out in the living room because "people are more important than things." That memory sends me a powerful all-clear signal to turn off my messiness alarm, which might otherwise blare out of control.

It's so hard not to worry over our children. But when we worry, the message we give our children is that we don't trust them. That's what I was doing to my daughter when I stood underneath the climbing structure shouting, "Be careful, be careful!" The message of trust is very different: "I have confidence in you, I know you can do it." As the second chicken might say, "No hawks around here."

Our worry makes children less likely to share their worries and concerns with us. As a friend of mine put it, "My mother worried about me so much. That conveyed to me that she didn't have confidence and trust in me, and I internalized that. It was hard for me to believe that I was competent. When I got a little older and saw how distressing my mother's worry was to her, I stopped bringing my problems to her. I didn't want to worry her, and also I didn't want to have to take care of her." Parents can't just instantly stop worrying, of course. You can make an effort not to share your worries with your child (as the saying goes, fake it till you make it), but ultimately you have to step back and truly trust.

PLAYFUL PARENTING FOR CHILDHOOD ANXIETIES AND FEARS

Anxiety takes a toll on all aspects of life, especially those that the anxious mind sees as "luxuries," like sleep, eating, digestion, rest, play, friendship, risk-taking, and love. Of course, these aren't luxuries at all. Aesop's fable of *The Town Mouse and the Country Mouse* ends with this moral: "A crust eaten in peace is better than a banquet partaken in anxiety." But best of all is a feast enjoyed in peace. That's why the hard work of overcoming anxiety is worth the effort.

To heal childhood anxiety, we must address every aspect of life affected by anxiety: the body, emotions, thoughts, behaviors, and relationships. You might have noticed that I have stayed away from diagnostic categories and definitions. I have three main reasons for that: *Everybody* is anxious sometimes, diagnosis of childhood anxiety is less accurate than in adults, and overdiagnosis can lead to overprescription of medications. I am quite wary of medications for anxiety, especially in children. Although they can provide short-term symptom relief, they can interfere with deep or long-lasting change. They can also be highly addictive and have other significant side effects. Diagnosis and medication can take away a child's sense of mastery, hope, and accomplishment. Even with a diagnosis of a serious childhood anxiety disorder, however, parents play an important role in providing empathy, playfulness, and sensitive challenges.

The table below is a rough outline of the areas of life affected by anxiety, matched with ways that parents can be most helpful.

	SIGNS OF ANXIETY	HOW PARENTS CAN HELP
Body	Tense muscles Rapid heartbeat Tightness in chest Constricted throat Butterflies in stomach Rapid, shallow breathing Cold hands Clammy skin	Teach relaxation techniques Use the techniques yourself Encourage exercise Roughhouse together Increase affection and comfort Take safe adventures See chapter three for more ideas
Thought	Repetitive thoughts Racing thoughts Obsessive thoughts Scary images Worry "What if?" "If only" Shoulds/shouldn'ts	Respect and validate Encourage challenges Play more than you talk See chapter six for more ideas
Emotion	Alarm Apprehension Panic Dread Nervousness Flooding	Teach how emotions work Welcome all emotions Promote emotional flow Model well-regulated emotions See chapter five for more ideas

	SIGNS OF ANXIETY	HOW PARENTS CAN HELP
Behavior	Nervous habits Avoidance Freeze, hide Compulsions	Patiently accept children as they are Approach fears step-by-step See chapter four for more ideas
Parent-Child Relationship	All of the above	Be the calm second chicken Be empathic Work on your own anxiety See chapter two for more ideas

In this chart, and in this book, I have artificially separated body, thought, emotion, relationship, and behavior in order to keep things simpler. In real life they all blend together. Our thinking changes when we slow our breathing. Our breathing slows when we change our thinking. Our emotions change when we approach something we had previously avoided, or stop ourselves from a nervous habit.

Anxious children tend to be overwhelmed, however, when these areas are all jumbled together. Even though we can't fully separate these different aspects of anxiety, we can focus on them one at a time to slow things down and deepen our understanding. One method is known as *SIBAM,* which stands for sensation, image, behavior, affect, and meaning ("affect" is another word for emotion). Psychologist Peter Levine notes that people who can identify their own SIBAM inner experience have a great tool for combating anxiety. Instead of the vague thought *I'm upset!* or *I don't want to go to school,* for example, a child can learn to unpack their SIBAM into its parts:

- Sensations (a stomachache)
- Images (people staring)
- Behaviors (biting fingernails and clutching a blanket)
- Affects (the emotional state of fear or apprehension)
- Meanings (*Nobody likes me*)

The Antianxiety Notebook

One technique draws together all the areas of life affected by anxiety, and in fact all the ideas presented in this book. It's a notebook (or multimedia computer file) created in partnership between parents and children. I call it the *Antianxiety Notebook,* but some children like to create their own more personal name, such as *My Stress Shatterer* or *Detective Terry's Notes on the Case of the Sneaky Anxiety.*

My inspiration for this idea came from Michael White, the Australian therapist who was a pioneer of narrative therapy. In his lectures and workshops White described his method of asking children what kind of strength they would need to overcome a particular problem, such as bedwetting or nightmares. If a child said, "I'd need the strength of a tiger," he would have the parents and child create a book of stories, pictures, and drawings about tigers. Some parents also sewed tiger costumes for their children. Projects like this use creativity, curiosity, and externalization to give children the chance to be active and creative, instead of just passive victims of a "disorder."

In the Antianxiety Notebook you and your child can write, draw, glue pictures from magazines, and create a tool together for overcoming anxiety. Everyone's notebook is different, so I can only give some general tips and some specific examples of note-book pages. Most notebooks contain some version of a SUDS or Fear-O-Meter scale, as well as different sections for anxiety's impact on a child's body, emotions, thoughts, and behaviors. There could be a SIBAM section, where anxiety is unpacked into sensations, images, behaviors, affects, and meanings. The note-book might contain stories—jointly written and illustrated by you and your child—about your child's heroic success in van-quishing the Anxiety Creature, or *How I Outfoxed the Monsters Under the Bed*. You might have pages called: Secrets I've discov-ered about my anxiety; Ideas that work when stress levels are over ninety out of one hundred; or Techniques that take an hour, five minutes, and five seconds.

The notebook can include explanations and drawings of the Flame Model of Emotions, with real-life examples from your child's emotional life. It may include pages for each element of the Security System: alert, alarm, assessment, and all clear. When your child has a success, you can say, "Let's go write this in the notebook." When you are frustrated and confused, you can say, "Let's go see if there's anything helpful in the notebook."

Robbie's notebook, which he showed me proudly one day in my office, included a page called "Dumb Stuff Larry Said That Actually Worked." It included one idea that I showed him in an exaggerated way just to get him to laugh (The Bounce). I was surprised that he tried it, but not surprised that it worked. Here's how he wrote it: "Stand up and bounce on the balls of my feet. Shake out my hands like I am drying water off them. Make an oooh or aaaah noise (fake-scared). Make the noise really high and squeaky then really low and deep." Robbie told me that the first time he tried it he thought it didn't work, because it just made him laugh. But then he realized that laughing was pretty good when he had been super-anxious before.

I shared with a young girl named Tara and her mother the idea of *emotional projects,* which I learned from Patty Wipfler at Hand in Hand Parenting. Everyone has an area or two where they could make some changes, especially about feelings and getting along with other people. Tara identified one of hers as having a thin skin, since she was easily upset when other children teased her or if things didn't go as she expected. She named her project Growing a Thicker Skin, and that became a section of her notebook. One page had a list of things that bothered her and new ways to think about them, such as "Nancy walked right by me without saying hello: She may have had a lot on her mind and it might not have had anything to do with me." Another page was filled with stories she wrote and illustrated about a really mean fish who insulted all the other fish and made them cry. Even though the stories were filled with tears, when Tara read them out loud she and her family laughed uproariously.

Some other notebook pages that children and their parents have created are: a drawing of a boy jumping off a cliff with a list of examples of jumping to conclusions; a list of scary, fun, and safe adventures—planned and accomplished; and a page titled, "Things I'm NOT worried about."

Ten Principles

A playful parenting approach to anxiety can help children heal from fear and embrace the unknown. First we offer the building blocks of security: love, empathy, and acceptance. Then we lighten up the problem with playfulness. Finally we use our close connection to gently push children to face their fears and avoid avoidance. I have summarized these ideas into ten basic princi-

ples. They are just as relevant to parental anxiety as they are to
childhood anxiety.

Ten Principles of Playful Parenting for Childhood Anxiety

1. Start with warmth, empathy, and understanding.
2. Teach children the basics of the Security System (alert, alarm, assessment, all clear) and the Flame Model of Emotions (spark, flame, fuel, and water).
3. Balance patience and acceptance with sensitive challenges and a gentle push.
4. Do things every day that are scary, fun, and safe.
5. Play! (Play brings laughter and laughter loosens fear.)
6. Welcome every emotion and focus on *what is* instead of *what if.*
7. Help children get out of their anxious thoughts and into their bodies. (Use relaxation, breathing, roughhousing, writing, and drawing.)
8. Be the calm second chicken instead of dismissing or endlessly reassuring.
9. Promote tolerance of uncertainty, risk, and discomfort. (Face-and-feel instead of avoidance, flooding, and white-knuckling.)
10. Address every aspect of life affected by anxiety (bodies, thoughts, emotions, behaviors, and relationships).

Thank you for letting me share my thoughts and feelings about
anxiety with you. Did reading this book bring you face-to-face
with your own worries and fears? If so, I can understand, be-

cause writing it made me more aware of my own anxiety and my own tendencies to avoid. Facing our own fears, worries, and anxieties is definitely the hardest part about helping children cope with theirs. I hope that reading this has brought you and your children the opposite of worry, anxiety, and fear: connection, trust, playfulness, and joy.

Acknowledgments

For inspiration and ideas, thanks to Patty Wipfler, Stephen Houseworth, David Trimble, Louise Omoto Kessel and the Playful Parenting discussion group, and Cathryn Robertson and the staff of Devotion School Extended Day. For encouragement, editing, reading of early drafts, and shepherding this book into existence, thanks to Josh Horwitz, Catherine O'Neill Grace, Barbara Zepp Larson, Liz Wollheim, and Marnie Cochran. For love and support, thanks to my parents, my sisters, my wife, Liz, and my children, Emma and Jake. I am especially grateful to all the parents and children who shared their anxieties—and anxiety remedies—with me.

Notes

INTRODUCTION

xii **My sister's professor, Dr. Gordon Gallup** Gordon G. Gallup, "Tonic Immobility: The Role of Fear and Predation," *Psychological Record* 27 (1977): 41–61.

xvi **In fact, the term "helicopter parent" entered the lexicon** Lawrence Cohen and Anthony DeBenedet, "Are Helicopter Parents Here to Stay?" from *Time* magazine's Ideas website, published November 8, 2011, http://ideas.time.com/2011/11/08/roughhousing-the-answer-to-helicopter-parenting/.

xvii **Connection is the essence of my approach** Lawrence Cohen, *Playful Parenting* (New York: Ballantine Books, 2001).

xix **Roughhousing with children is especially helpful** Anthony DeBenedet and Lawrence Cohen, *The Art of Roughhousing* (Philadelphia: Quirk Press, 2010).

xxi **Teenagers and young adults** One good resource for teens is this Canadian website: http://www.youth.anxietybc.com.

CHAPTER ONE

12 **Hans Selye** Hans Selye, *The Stress of Life* (New York: McGraw-Hill, 1978).

17 **Alerts are almost instantaneous** Daniel Kahneman, *Thinking, Fast and Slow* (New York: Farrar, Straus and Giroux, 2011), 311.

20 **Eventually, however, we need an accurate system** Kahneman, *Thinking, Fast and Slow*.

21   **We take in more information when we're scared** Alexander J. Shackman and others, "Stress Potentiates Early and Attenuates Late Stages of Visual Processing," *Journal of Neuroscience* 31, no. 3, (2011): 1156–1161.

26   **Jerome Kagan, a Harvard psychologist** Jerome Kagan and Nancy Snidman, "Temperamental factors in human development," *American Psychologist* 46, no. 8 (1991): 856–862.

28   **Heather Shumaker's argument** Heather Shumaker, *It's OK Not to Share and Other Renegade Rules for Raising Competent and Compassionate Kids* (New York: Tarcher/Penguin, 2012), 201.

CHAPTER TWO

36   **A father quoted by Mr. Fred Rogers** Fred Rogers, *The Mister Rogers Parenting Resource Book* (Philadelphia: Running Press, 2005), 44.

47   **Parent educator Patty Wipfler** Patty Wipfler, *Listening Partnerships for Parents* (Palo Alto: Hand in Hand Parenting, 2006).

50   *Homesick and Happy* Michael Thompson, *Homesick and Happy* (New York: Ballantine Books, 2012).

51   **As Heather Shumaker writes** Shumaker, *It's OK Not to Share*, 201.

55   *Validate first, reassure second* For more on validation of children see Haim Ginott, *Between Parent and Child* (New York: Macmillan, 1965) and Thomas Gordon, *Parent Effectiveness Training* (New York: Three Rivers Press, 2000).

58   **In *Mom, They're Teasing Me*** Michael Thompson, Lawrence Cohen, and Catherine O'Neill Grace, *Mom, They're Teasing Me* (New York: Ballantine Books, 2002).

CHAPTER THREE

67   **Marsha Linehan** Marsha Linehan, "DBT: Updates to Emotion Regulation and Crisis Survival Skills," lecture, Behavior Tech Training Conference, Needham, Mass., May 10–11, 2010.

71 **Some children aren't interested in stillness** Lisa Flynn, *Yoga for Children* (Avon, Mass.: Adams Media, 2013).

72 **some using imagination (guided visualizations)** I recommend: Lori Lite, *A Boy and a Bear* (Plantation, Fla.: Specialty Press, 1996) and Thich Nhat Hanh, *Planting Seeds* (Berkeley: Parallax Press, 2011).

73 **Progressive Muscle Relaxation** Edmund Jacobson, *You Must Relax!* (London: Whittlesey House, 1934).

75 **Psychologist Margaret Wehrenberg** Margaret Wehrenberg, *The 10 Best-Ever Anxiety Management Techniques* (New York: W. W. Norton, 2008), 51.

78 *Be Here Now* Ram Dass, *Be Here Now, Remember* (San Cristobal, N.M.: Lama Foundation, 1971).

80 **Francine Shapiro, the psychologist who developed EMDR** Francine Shapiro, *Getting Past Your Past* (New York: Rodale, 2012), 57.

81 **The psychologist and trauma expert Peter Levine** Peter Levine, *In an Unspoken Voice* (Berkeley: North Atlantic Books, 2010), 105.

83 **You can get to the heart of that blocked emotion** Patty Wipfler, *No More Thumb, No More Pacifier!* From the Hand in Hand Parenting website, accessed January 5, 2013, http://www.handinhand parenting.org/news/54/64/No-More-Thumb-No-More-Pacifier.

84 **Fidgeting and repetitive movements may also be signs** Mary Lashno, *Mixed Signals* (Bethesda, Md.: Woodbine House, 2009) and Carol Stock Kranowitz, *The Out-of-Sync Child Has Fun* (New York: Perigee Press, 2006).

85 **There are endless variations on roughhousing games** De-Benedet and Cohen, *The Art of Roughhousing*.

87 **Christina Luberto** Dawn Fuller, "University of Cincinnati Research Examines Why Some People Are Afraid to Relax," from the website of the University of Cincinnati, published November 14, 2012, http://www.uc.edu/news/NR.aspx?id=16730.

96 **Stanley Greenspan calls being "playfully obstructive."**

Stanley Greenspan with Robin Simons, *The Child with Special Needs* (Reading, Mass.: Perseus Books, 1998).

CHAPTER FOUR

107 **A neuroscientist might say** Louis Cozolino, *The Neuroscience of Human Relationships* (New York: Norton, 2006).

115 **Patty Wipfler, the founder of Hand in Hand Parenting** Patty Wipfler and Lawrence Cohen, *"Don't Turn out the Light!" Helping Children with Anxiety* (teleseminar, Hand in Hand Parenting, April 19, 2012).

116 **Owen Aldis, who studied animal play** Owen Aldis, *Play Fighting* (New York: Academic Press, 1976).

120 **Louis Cozolino, a neuroscientist and psychotherapist** Louis Cozolino, *The Neuroscience of Psychotherapy* (New York: Norton, 2002), 257–285.

121 **Daniel Siegel is a psychiatrist and a pioneer** Daniel Siegel and Tina Payne Bryson, *The Whole-Brain Child* (New York: Delacorte, 2011), 152.

CHAPTER FIVE

131 **Dr. Spock invited parents** Benjamin Spock, *Common Sense Book of Baby and Child Care* (New York: Duell, Sloan and Pearce, 1945), 266–267.

132 **In one episode** "Plato's Stepchildren," *Star Trek* (NBC, 1968).

132 **The book was *Smile a Lot!*** Nancy Carlson, *Smile a Lot* (Minneapolis: Carolrhoda Books, 2002).

134 **Paul Ekman** Paul Ekman, *Emotions Revealed, Second Edition: Recognizing Faces and Feelings to Improve Communication and Emotional Life* (New York: Holt, 2007).

134 **Other scholars of emotion count them differently** Robert Plutchik, "The nature of emotions," *American Scientist* 89, no. 4 (2001): 344.

134 **The psychologist Marsha Linehan** Marsha Linehan, *Skills Training Manual for Treating Borderline Personality Disorder* (New York: Guilford Press, 1993).

135 **Every emotion has what Marsha Linehan calls** Ibid.

141 **Marsha Linehan describes** Ibid.

141 **Linehan's solution for this escalation** Ibid.

145 **Rumi was a Sufi mystic** Jalal al-Din Rumi, *The Essential Rumi,* trans. Coleman Barks (San Francisco: Harper, 1995), 109.

145 **As psychologist Harriet Lerner says** Harriet Lerner, *Fear and Other Uninvited Guests* (New York: Harper, 2004), 7.

146 **Rumi probably wouldn't be surprised by recent research** Peter Fonagy, et al., *Affect Regulation, Mentalization, and the Development of Self* (New York: Other Press, 2005).

147 **Afterward we "shake off" the fear** Levine, *In an Unspoken Voice,* 8.

147 **The psychologist and trauma expert Peter Levine** Ibid., 116–119.

150 **It's easy for children to feel ashamed** Deborah Roffman, *But How'd I Get in There in the First Place: Talking to Your Young Child About Sex* (Boston: Da Capo Press, 2002).

151 **It's much more effective to be matter-of-fact** Deborah Roffman, *Talk to Me First* (Boston: Da Capo Press, 2012).

152 **A group of therapists coined the term "affect phobia"** Leigh McCullough and others, *Treating Affect Phobia* (New York: Guilford Press, 2003), 179.

155 **The psychologist Mona Barbera** Mona Barbera, *Bring Yourself to Love* (Boston: Dos Monos Press, 2008), 9.

157 **Parent educator Patty Wipfler** Wipfler, *Listening to Children.*

160 **the Isley Brothers song** Rudolph Isley, Ronald Isley, and O'Kelly Isley, Jr., "Shout," from the album *Shout!* by the Isley Brothers (RCA, 1959).

161 **In his discussion of childhood fear** Spock, *Common Sense Book of Baby and Child Care,* 297.

CHAPTER SIX

163 **a Dave Eggers novel** Dave Eggers, *You Shall Know Our Velocity* (New York: Vintage, 2003), 190.

164 **As psychologist Margaret Wehrenberg** Margaret Wehrenberg, *The 10 Best-Ever Anxiety Management Techniques* (New York: W. W. Norton, 2008), 140.

172 *Juggling the Jitters* Deborah Miller, *Juggling the Jitters* (Calgary, Alberta: Frontenac House, 2013).

175 **One of these tricks is WYSIATI** Kahneman, *Thinking, Fast and Slow,* 85–88.

177 **The psychologist Francine Shapiro** Shapiro, *Getting Past Your Past,* 58.

178 **I like to use two questions** Byron Katie and Stephen Mitchell, *Loving What Is: Four Questions That Can Change Your Life* (New York: Three Rivers Press, 2003). And see also the children's book: Byron Katie and Hans Wilhelm, *Tiger-Tiger, Is It True? Four Questions to Make You Smile Again* (New York: Hay House, 2009).

182 **Louis Cozolino, a therapist and neuroscientist** Cozolino, *The Neuroscience of Psychotherapy.*

184 **Most anxious people have discovered** Mihaly Csikszentmihalyi, *Flow: The Psychology of Optimal Experience* (New York: HarperCollins, 1990).

188 **This last question is based on narrative therapy** Michael White and David Epston, *Narrative Means to Therapeutic Ends* (New York: Norton, 1990).

188 **Psychiatrist Daniel Siegel** Siegel and Bryson, *The Whole-Brain Child,* 107.

CHAPTER SEVEN

197 **Psychologist Michele Borba asks parents** Michele Borba, *The Big Book of Parenting Solutions* (San Francisco: Jossey-Bass, 2009), 243.

198 **Excessive social anxiety is painful** For more information on helping children with friendships and belonging, see Michael Thompson, Catherine O'Neill Grace, and Lawrence Cohen, *Best Friends, Worst Enemies* (New York: Ballantine Books, 2001).

199 **If you are resistant to working on your own social anxiety** Meghan Budinger, Tess Drazdowski, and Golda Ginsburg, "Anxiety-Promoting Parenting Behaviors: A Comparison of Anxious Parents with and without Social Anxiety Disorder," *Child Psychiatry and Human Development* (September, 2012).

199 **Psychologist Tamar Chansky recommends** Chansky, *Freeing Your Child from Anxiety,* 157.

200 **Michele Borba suggests** Borba, *The Big Book of Parenting Solutions,* 297.

201 **Michele Borba breaks down social confidence** Ibid.

205 **In a tribute on *Time* magazine's website** James Poniewozik, "He Was Not Afraid of the Dark," from the *Time* magazine website, published March 2, 2003, http://www.time.com/time/magazine/article/0,9171,428052,00.html.

209 **Peg Flandreau West was a pioneer in safety education** Peg Flandreau West, *The Basic Essentials: Protective Behaviours Anti-victimization and Empowerment Process* (Madison, Wi.: Protective Behaviors, Inc., 1989).

213 **Psychologist Aureen Wagner** Aureen Wagner, *Worried No More* (Rochester, N.Y.: Lighthouse Press, 2005), 201.

217 **Peter Levine is a psychologist and trauma expert** Levine, *In an Unspoken Voice.*

225 **James Rapson (a therapist) and Craig English (a writer)** James Rapson and Craig English, *Anxious to Please: 7 Revolutionary Practices for the Chronically Nice* (Chicago: Sourcebooks, 2006), 3.

226 **Special Time is an approach to play** Patty Wipfler, *How Special Time Works with Teens,* On the Hand in Hand Parenting website, accessed January 5, 2013, http://www.handinhandparenting.org/news/17/64/How-Special-TimeWorks-with-Teens.

230 **Far better to acknowledge the existence of social ills** See

the organization Me to We (http://www.metowe.com) for ideas and inspiration about children taking significant social action.

230 *Where did I come from?* For an excellent guide to parent-child discussions about sexuality, see Roffman, *Talk to Me First.*

CHAPTER EIGHT

234 **Harriet Lerner, a psychologist** Lerner, *Fear and Other Uninvited Guests,* 6–7 (italics in original).

236 **My favorite example comes from a children's novel** Astrid Lindgren, *Ronia, The Robber's Daughter* (New York: Puffin, 1985), 11–12.

239 **Externalization is a concept from narrative therapy** Jennifer Freeman, David Epston, and Dean Lobovits, *Playful Approaches to Serious Problems* (New York: Norton, 1997).

243 **the neuroscientist Louis Cozolino** Cozolino, *The Neuroscience of Psychotherapy,* 41–44.

247 **Psychologist Peter Levine** Levine, *In an Unspoken Voice,* 133–154.

250 **I shared with a young girl named Tara** Patty Wipfler, *Emotional Projects—Rebuilding Closeness Step by Step,* from the Hand in Hand Parenting website, accessed January 5, 2013, http://www .handinhandparenting.org/news/205/64/Emotional-Projects -Rebuilding-Closeness-Step-by-Step.

Bibliography

Aldis, Owen. *Play Fighting.* New York: Academic Press, 1976.

Barbera, Mona. *Bring Yourself to Love.* Boston: Dos Monos Press, 2008.

Borba, Michele. *The Big Book of Parenting Solutions.* San Francisco: Jossey-Bass, 2009.

Budinger, Meghan, Tess Drazdowski, and Golda Ginsburg. "Anxiety-Promoting Parenting Behaviors: A Comparison of Anxious Parents with and without Social Anxiety Disorder," *Child Psychiatry and Human Development* (September, 2012). doi: 10.1007/s10578-012-0335-9.

Carlson, Nancy. *Smile a Lot!.* Minneapolis: Carolrhoda Books, 2002.

Chansky, Tamar. *Freeing Your Child from Anxiety.* New York: Broadway Books, 2004.

Cohen, Lawrence. *Playful Parenting.* New York: Ballantine Books, 2001.

Cohen, Lawrence, and Anthony DeBenedet. "Are Helicopter Parents Here to Stay?" From *Time* magazine's website, published November 8, 2011, http://ideas.time.com/2011/11/08/roughhousing-the-answer-to-helicopter-parenting/.

Cozolino, Louis. *The Neuroscience of Human Relationships.* New York: Norton, 2006.

Cozolino, Louis. *The Neuroscience of Psychotherapy.* New York: Norton, 2002.

Csikszentmihalyi, Mihaly. *Flow: The Psychology of Optimal Experience.* New York: HarperCollins, 1990.

DeBenedet, Anthony, and Lawrence Cohen. *The Art of Roughhousing*. Philadelphia: Quirk Press, 2010.

Eggers, Dave. *You Shall Know Our Velocity*. New York: Vintage, 2003.

Ekman, Paul. *Emotions Revealed: Recognizing Faces and Feelings to Improve Communication and Emotional Life, Second Edition*. New York: Holt, 2007.

Flynn, Lisa. *Yoga for Children*. Avon, Mass.: Adams Media, 2013.

Fonagy, Peter, Gyorgy Gergely, Elliot Jurist, and Mary Target. *Affect Regulation, Mentalization, and the Development of Self*. New York: Other Press, 2005.

Freeman, Jennifer, David Epston, and Dean Lobovits. *Playful Approaches to Serious Problems*. New York: Norton, 1997.

Fuller, Dawn. "University of Cincinnati Research Examines Why Some People Are Afraid to Relax." From the website of the University of Cincinnati, published November 14, 2012, http://www.uc.edu/news/NR.aspx?id=16730.

Gallup, Gordon. "Tonic Immobility: The Role of Fear and Predation." *Psychological Record* 27 (1977): 41–61.

Ginott, Haim. *Between Parent and Child*. New York: Macmillan, 1965.

Gordon, Thomas. *Parent Effectiveness Training*. New York: Three Rivers Press, 2000.

Greenspan, Stanley, Serena Wieder, and Robin Simons. *The Child with Special Needs*. Reading, Mass.: Perseus Books, 1998.

Isley, Rudolph, Ronald Isley, and O'Kelly Isley, Jr. "Shout," from the Album *Shout!* by the Isley Brothers (RCA), 1959.

Jacobson, Edmund. *You Must Relax!* London: Whittlesey House, 1934.

Kagan, Jerome, and Nancy Snidman. "Temperamental factors in human development." *American Psychologist* 46, no. 8 (1991): 856-862.

Kahneman, Daniel. *Thinking, Fast and Slow*. New York: Farrar, Straus and Giroux, 2011.

Katie, Byron, and Stephen Mitchell. *Loving What Is: Four Questions That Can Change Your Life*. New York: Three Rivers Press, 2003.

Katie, Byron, and Hans Wilhelm. *Tiger-Tiger, Is It True: Four Questions to Make You Smile Again*. New York: Hay House, 2009.

Kranowitz, Carol Stock. *The Out-of-Sync Child Has Fun*. New York: Perigee Press, 2006.

Lashno, Mary. *Mixed Signals*. Bethesda, Md.: Woodbine House, 2009.

Lerner, Harriet. *Fear and Other Uninvited Guests*. New York: Harper, 2004.

Levine, Peter. *In an Unspoken Voice*. Berkeley: North Atlantic Books, 2010.

Lindgren, Astrid. *Ronia, the Robber's Daughter*. New York: Puffin, 1985.

Linehan, Marsha. *DBT: Updates to Emotion Regulation and Crisis Survival Skills*. Lecture presented at the Behavior Tech Training Conference, Needham, Mass., May 2010.

Linehan, Marsha. *Skills Training Manual for Treating Borderline Personality Disorder*. New York: Guilford Press, 1993.

Lite, Lori. *A Boy and a Bear*. Plantation, Fla.: Specialty Press, 1996.

McCullough, Leigh, Nat Kuhn, Stuart Andrews, Amelia Kaplan, Jonathan Wolf, and Cara Lanza Hurley. *Treating Affect Phobia*. New York: Guilford Press, 2003.

Miller, Deborah. *Juggling the Jitters*. Calgary, Alberta: Frontenac House, 2013.

Nhat Hanh, Thich. *Planting Seeds*. Berkeley: Parallax Press, 2011.

"Plato's Stepchildren," *Star Trek*. NBC, 1968.

Plutchik, Robert. "The nature of emotions," *American Scientist* 89, no. 4 (2001): 344.

Poniewozik, James. "He Was Not Afraid of the Dark." From *Time* magazine's website, published March 2, 2003, http://www.time.com/time/magazine/article/0,9171,428052,00.html.

Ram Dass. *Be Here Now, Remember*. San Cristobal, N.M.: Lama Foundation, 1971.

Rapson, James, and Craig English. *Anxious to Please: 7 Revolutionary Practices for the Chronically Nice*. Chicago: Sourcebooks, 2006.

Roffman, Deborah. *But How'd I Get in There in the First Place?: Talking to Your Young Child About Sex.* Boston: Da Capo Press, 2002.

Roffman, Deborah. *Talk to Me First.* Boston: Da Capo Press, 2012.

Rogers, Fred. *The Mister Rogers Parenting Resource Book.* Philadelphia: Running Press, 2005.

Rumi, Jalal al-Din. *The Essential Rumi.* Translated by Coleman Barks. San Francisco: Harper, 1995.

Selye, Hans. *The Stress of Life.* New York: McGraw-Hill, 1978.

Shackman, Alexander, Jeffrey Maxwell, Brenton McMenamin, Lawrence Greischar, and Richard Davidson. "Stress Potentiates Early and Attenuates Late Stages of Visual Processing." *Journal of Neuroscience* 31, no. 3 (2011): 1156-1161.

Shapiro, Francine. *Getting Past Your Past.* New York: Rodale, 2012.

Shumaker, Heather. *It's OK Not to Share and Other Renegade Rules for Raising Competent and Compassionate Kids.* New York: Tarcher/Penguin, 2012.

Siegel, Daniel, and Tina Payne Bryson. *The Whole-Brain Child.* New York: Delacorte, 2011.

Spock, Benjamin. *Common Sense Book of Baby and Child Care.* New York: Duell, Sloan and Pearce, 1945.

Thompson, Michael. *Homesick and Happy.* New York: Ballantine Books, 2012.

Thompson, Michael, Lawrence Cohen, and Catherine O'Neill Grace. *Mom, They're Teasing Me.* New York: Ballantine Books, 2002.

Thompson, Michael, Catherine O'Neill Grace, and Lawrence Cohen. *Best Friends, Worst Enemies.* New York: Ballantine Books, 2001.

Wagner, Aureen. *Worried No More.* Rochester, N.Y.: Lighthouse Press, 2005.

Wehrenberg, Margaret. *The 10 Best-Ever Anxiety Management Techniques.* New York: W. W. Norton, 2008.

West, Peg Flandreau. *The Basic Essentials: Protective Behaviours Anti-victimization and Empowerment Process.* Madison, Wi.: Protective Behaviors, 1989.

White, Michael, and David Epston. *Narrative Means to Therapeutic Ends*. New York: Norton, 1990.

Wipfler, Patty. *Emotional Projects—Rebuilding Closeness Step by Step*. From the Hand in Hand Parenting website, accessed January 5, 2013, http://www.handinhandparenting.org/news/205/64/Emotional-Projects-Rebuilding-Closeness-Step-by-Step.

Wipfler, Patty. *How Special Time Works With Teens*. From the Hand in Hand Parenting website, accessed January 5, 2013, http://www.handinhandparenting.org/news/17/64/How-Special-TimeWorks-with-Teens.

Wipfler, Patty. *Listening Partnerships for Parents*. Palo Alto: Hand in Hand Parenting, 2006.

Wipfler, Patty. *No More Thumb, No More Pacifier*. From the Hand in Hand Parenting website, accessed January 5, 2013, http://www.handinhandparenting.org/news/54/64/No-More-Thumb-No-More-Pacifier.

Wipfler, Patty, and Lawrence Cohen. *"Don't Turn out the Light!" Helping Children with Anxiety*. Teleseminar presented by Hand in Hand Parenting, April 19, 2012.

Index

276 Index

PHOTO CREDIT: © Matt Stone

About the Author

Lawrence J. Cohen, Ph.D., is a clinical psychologist specializing in children's play, play therapy, and parenting. He is the author of *Playful Parenting* and co-author, with Michael Thompson, Ph.D., and Catherine O'Neill Grace, of *Best Friends, Worst Enemies* and *Mom, They're Teasing Me*. Dr. Cohen leads Playful Parenting workshops for parents, teachers, and child-care professionals. He lives in Boston, Massachusetts, with his wife, Liz. They have two grown children.